Error Patterns in Computation

A Semi-programmed Approach

Fifth Edition

Robert B. Ashlock

Covenant College
Lookout Mountain, Georgia

MERRILL PUBLISHING COMPANY
A Bell & Howell Information Company
Columbus   Toronto   London   Melbourne

Published by Merrill Publishing Company
A Bell & Howell Information Company
Columbus, Ohio 43216

This book was set in Times Roman.

Administrative Editor: Jeff Johnston
Production Coordinator: Linda Kauffman Peterson
Art Coordinator: Gilda Edwards
Cover Designer: Brian Deep

Library of Congress Catalog Card Number: 89–60934
International Standard Book Number: 0–675–21069–0
Printed in the United States of America
1 2 3 4 5 6 7 8 9—93 92 91 90

to Julia, Joli, Joe,
Joshua, Joanna, Joseph, John,

Alan, Kathy, April,
Justin, Benjamin

Foreword

Carelessness is responsible for some student errors in computation. Estimating the result will often reveal an error, and repeating the steps will usually result in a correct answer on the second try. However, many students' mistakes are systematic. These students have faulty computational rules which they consistently follow. They may have learned their rules from noticing a pattern, but they did not abstract the same rule as others. They may have learned rules from listening to explanations, but they did not get all the steps intended by the teacher. This book is about detecting and correcting systematic errors that children make while doing computation.

With the increasing availability of technology, some experts in mathematics education suggest that the amount of time spent on computational skills should be decreased. But this does not mean that computational skills are no longer important. Use of calculators for computation increases the importance of estimation skills.

These beliefs are consistent with the philosophy and purpose of this volume. It is inappropriate to leave individuals with incorrect or incomplete procedures just because calculators are available. Time can be saved by more efficient teaching of these procedures and correcting faulty ones. This updated edition suggests taking full advantage of estimation skills to aid students in monitoring their own errors.

Research indicates that students benefit more from having their mistakes pointed out than from having only the correct answers noted. Moreover, students benefit more from having diagnostic feedback, comments, and precise suggestions than from having errors marked only "wrong." Other research indicates that only a small minority of novice or experienced teachers give diagnostic/prescriptive feedback. This book is designed to sensitize teachers to the need for diagnostic feedback and, more importantly, to enable teachers to give specific diagnostic feedback. Beyond this, strategies are suggested for teaching children who have had difficulties under previous instruction. This fifth edition reflects the latest relevant research and literature.

In previous editions, this book has helped thousands of teachers of mathematics teach more effectively. Indeed, *Error Patterns in Computation* has become a classic in the diagnostic teaching of arithmetic and in mathematics education.

Douglas T. Owens
University of British Columbia

Concerning This Book

Once you have studied and begun to apply what Professor Ashlock so effectively teaches in this book, I am convinced you will agree it is among the most practical books you have ever encountered. It is practical for the immediate classroom as well as for long-term use.

One reason this book is immediately practical for classroom teachers is that it deals with real problems in a realistic manner. The types of errors in computation illustrated in this book are those of real children, and the suggested corrective procedures are those that have succeeded with real children. Moreover, both the procedures for diagnosis and those for correction require neither esoteric procedures nor specialized settings. The procedures are now successfully in use in the classroom.

Another reason this book is immediately practical is its clever organization. Chapter 1 sets the stage for the reader with a comprehensive, yet concise and thoroughly understandable, review of the research on children's computational errors. A discussion of how children learn these errors and a set of guidelines for diagnosing and treating difficulties in elementary school mathematics is provided in Chapters 1 and 2. Beginning in Chapter 3, and throughout the remainder of the book, the reader is cleverly led into participating directly in diagnosing and prescribing each of the error patterns illustrated. At each step, readers can "test" their diagnoses and prescriptions by comparing them with those Professor Ashlock and his students have found successful. The appendices in this edition have additional suggestions for improving our diagnostic-prescriptive teaching of mathematics. It has been my experience using this book with both pre- and inservice teachers that this direct involvement not only helps them become proficient in diagnosing the specific errors illustrated, but also in becoming more adept at using the diagnostic-prescriptive process in all areas of the elementary school mathematics curriculum.

These immediately practical characteristics by themselves make this book well worth the reader's study. However, although not directly stated as a goal, I believe this book also contributes effectively to the clarification of two major issues which are of more long-term significance than just the identification and correlation of specific errors in computation.

All of us are aware of the considerable changes that have occurred in elementary school mathematics programs during the past three decades. Some have called these changes a "revolution." Two major interrelated issues have emerged during this revolution. One issue relates to the goals of elementary school mathematics education, the other relates to methods of instruction.

Among the most notable changes in the goals has been a greatly increased emphasis on the acquisition of mathematical concepts and principles, i.e., the learning of the structures of mathematics. In our eagerness to achieve this goal, some programs have significantly deemphasized the achievement of computational proficiency. Some even took these two goals to be mutually exclusive.

In the late sixties and early seventies, as reports began to come in of children's falling scores on tests of computational skills, we began to hear from many quarters the demand to "return to the basics." This generally meant more work on adding, subtracting, multiplying, and dividing with skill. For many, this "return to the basics" also meant a return to instructional methods thought appropriate to basic skills, i.e., lots and lots of practice or drill.

For many, these issues have become dichotomies: mathematical concepts vs. computational skill; teaching for understanding vs. drill. Professor Ashlock's book, I believe, clearly demonstrates that to separate mathematical concepts from computational skill as goals and to separate the teaching for meaning from the administration of drill as methods are both false dichotomies.

The computational procedures in which we want children to be skillful only work because they are based on mathematical concepts and principles. The children's errors illustrated in this book clearly show this in reverse. All of the errors are based on *faulty* or incompletely learned mathematical concepts. Hence, all the corrective procedures involve developing or redeveloping these mathematical concepts.

Furthermore, Professor Ashlock clearly demonstrates that the patterns of error children display are not due to carelessness alone nor to insufficient drill. These error patterns are conceptual and are learned. Concepts, correct or incorrect, are not learned by drill. Once correct concepts are acquired, drill does help fix or consolidate that learning. Therefore, drill is a desirable and important component of instructional method—but only *after* the concepts have been acquired. It follows, then, that "just more practice" is not going to help the child identify his/her errors, nor is it going to help the child learn to correct them. Indeed, just more drill without meaningful, corrective instruction first is very likely to consolidate any error pattern a child has learned, thereby making it more difficult to correct.

This book helps put these two false dichotomies to rest. We can then get on with the task of helping children acquire skill in computation by teaching the mathematical concepts upon which computational procedures are based. Professor Ashlock's book, with its immediately practical features, helps us in this task as few others do.

*John W. Wilson**

*Dr. Wilson was Director of the Arithmetic Clinic at the University of Maryland at the time of his death in 1979. This statement appeared as the foreword to the second edition.

Preface

This book is designed for those who want to help children learn to compute. The reader learns to identify error patterns in computation, and he also learns about possible causes of such errors. He learns specific ways to help children who need to compute successfully.

The patterns of error in computation that are included in this book are not figments of my imagination; they are observed patterns used by real boys and girls—children in regular classrooms. The problems in diagnosis posed for the reader are typical of difficulties encountered among those children everywhere who have difficulty with arithmetic.

The errors of many students follow a pattern because, although they have learned something, what they have actually learned is incorrect. Looking for such patterns can be a very worthwhile diagnostic activity for two reasons: by observing such patterns a teacher is able to refrain from assigning drill activities that reinforce incorrect concepts and procedures, and it provides the teacher with more specific knowledge of the child's strengths and weaknesses upon which to base corrective instruction.

The format of Chapters 3, 4, and 5 has the advantage of simulation. The reader has opportunities to respond overtly, and feedback is provided relating to those responses. Skill is gained by actually looking for patterns, making decisions, and planning instruction.

The introductory chapter contains specific suggestioins as well as helpful guidelines for anyone who would help children learn to compute. Most readers will use Chapters 3, 4, and 5 by topic, beginning in Chapter 3 and turning to later parts of the book as instructed. It is important that the reader "play the game" and actually take time to respond. This semi-programmed format was used in earlier editions, and it proved to be quite effective.

Additional children's papers are included in Appendix A where the reader can find more than forty error patterns. In Appendix B, error patterns are illustrated for other areas of mathematics: geometry, measurement, problem solving, and algebra. Also, specific instructional aids are described in Appendix E.

I wish to acknowledge the encouragement of the many classroom teachers who have shown great interest in the material in this book, and the help of teachers, former students, and even their students, for they have identified many of the error patterns presented. I also wish to acknowledge the contributions of the following reviewers:

Susan Chapin
Boston University

Jon Engelhardt
Arizona State University

Gerald Cierpilowski
Lock Haven State College

Dan Farris
State University of New York–Cortland

Robert B. Ashlock

Contents

ONE Diagnosing Error Patterns in Computation   **1**

Research on Errors in Computation   3
Why Children Learn Error Patterns   6
Levels of Diagnosis   9
Diagnostic Tests   9
Interviews and Other Diagnostic Techniques   11
Metacognition   13
Guidelines for Diagnosis   14

TWO Providing Needed Instruction in Computation   **17**

Teaching Children to Compute   17
Estimation   19
Using Manipulatives   21
Using Calculators and Computers   22
Understanding Numeration   23
Mastery of Basic Facts   24
Alternative Algorithms   27
Guidelines for Instruction   33

THREE Identifying Error Patterns in Computation   **37**

FOUR Analyzing Error Patterns in Computation   **79**

FIVE Helping Children Correct Error Patterns in Computation   **115**

Selected References   **165**
   References Focusing on Diagnosis and Remediation   165
   References Focusing on Instruction in Computation   177
   References Available from RCDPM   182

**Appendix A: Additional Children's Papers and
     Key to Error Patterns**   **185**

**Appendix B: Error Patterns in Other Areas
     of Mathematics**   **199**

Appendix C: The Nature of Wrong Answers   **205**
   Whole Numbers   205
   Fractions   208

**Appendix D: Sample Learning Hierarchy for
     Addition of Unlike Fractions**   **211**

Appendix E: Selected Materials   **213**

Error Patterns in Computation

A Semi-programmed Approach

Chapter 1

Diagnosing Error Patterns in Computation

Arithmetic is where the answer is right and everything is nice and you can look out of the window and see the blue sky—or the answer is wrong and you have to start all over and try again and see how it comes out this time.[1]

Carl Sandburg

The child into whose mind Sandburg leads us seems to view arithmetic as an *either-or* sort of thing. Either he gets the right answers and he enjoys arithmetic and life is rosy, or he does not get the right answers and arithmetic and life are frustrating. You may think this child has a very limited view of arithmetic, and you may wonder why he is so answer-oriented. Yet, you *do* need to face the question of why *some* children are not able to get correct answers.

Consider Fred's paper (Figure 1). If you merely determine how many are correct and how many are incorrect, you will not learn *why* his answers are not correct. Examine Fred's paper and note that when multiplication involves renaming, his answer is often incorrect. Look for a pattern among the incorrect responses; observe that he seems to be adding his "crutch" and then multiplying. This can be verified by studying other examples and briefly interviewing Fred.

You need to examine each child's paper diagnostically; look for patterns, hypothesize possible causes, and verify your ideas. Written work should be approached as if each paper is itself a problem to be solved.

The diagnosis of errors in arithmetic is an essential part of evaluation in the mathematics program, but any such diagnosis must be followed by appropriate

---

[1] Excerpt from "Arithmetic" in *The Complete Poems of Carl Sandburg*, copyright 1950 by Carl Sandburg; renewed 1978 by Margaret Sandburg, Helga Sandburg Crile and Janet Sandburg. Reprinted by permission of Harcourt Brace Jovanovich, Inc.

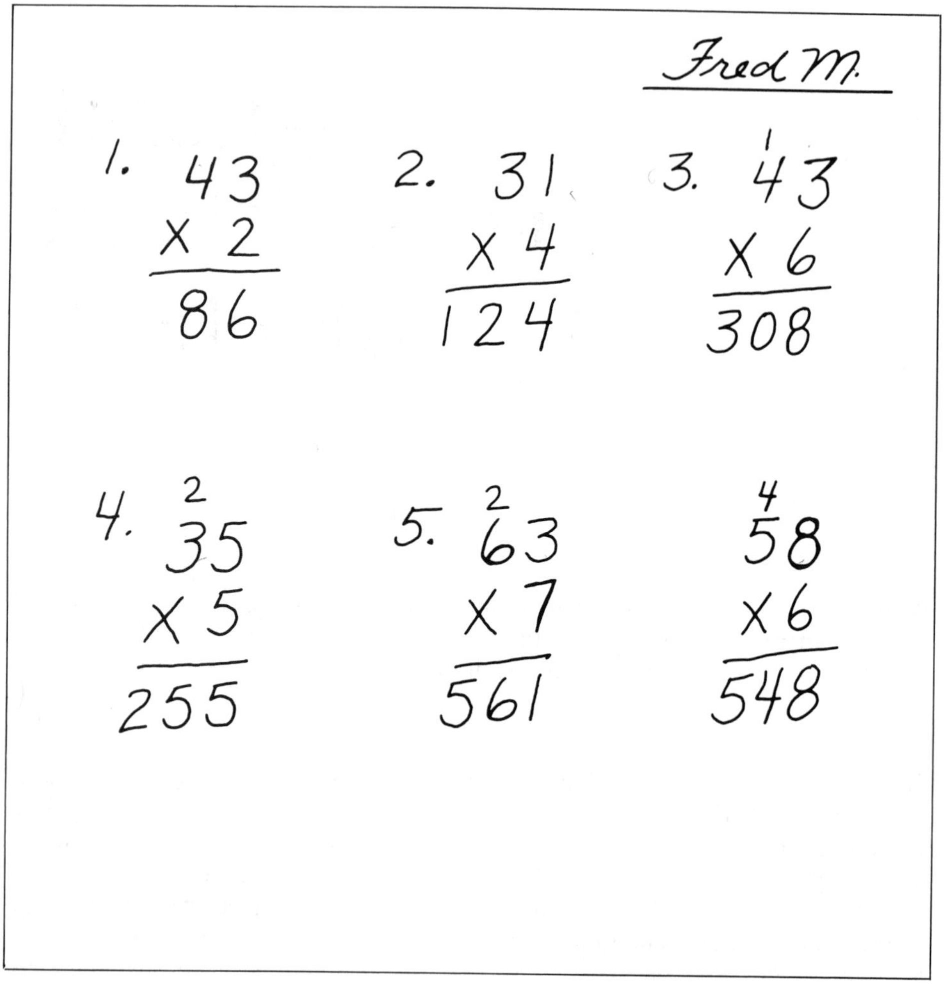

Fred M.

1.
$$\begin{array}{r} 43 \\ \times\ 2 \\ \hline 86 \end{array}$$

2.
$$\begin{array}{r} 31 \\ \times\ 4 \\ \hline 124 \end{array}$$

3.
$$\begin{array}{r} \overset{1}{4}3 \\ \times\ 6 \\ \hline 308 \end{array}$$

4.
$$\begin{array}{r} \overset{2}{3}5 \\ \times\ 5 \\ \hline 255 \end{array}$$

5.
$$\begin{array}{r} \overset{2}{6}3 \\ \times\ 7 \\ \hline 561 \end{array}$$

$$\begin{array}{r} \overset{4}{5}8 \\ \times\ 6 \\ \hline 548 \end{array}$$

FIGURE 1

instruction. It is hoped that reading this book and responding to the puzzle-like situations presented will help you develop skills needed in order to effectively diagnose errors in computation and provide the instruction required by each child.

Researchers have known for a long time that we can learn much by carefully observing erroneous procedures. As Hart comments: "We can find out a considerable amount about a child's stage of understanding if we study his or her reasoning process when . . . using an erroneous strategy."[2]

---

[2] Kathleen M. Hart, "I Know What I Believe; Do I Believe What I Know?" *Journal for Research in Mathematics Education* 14, no. 2 (March 1983): 120.

Research on Errors in Computation

Errors in computation are not necessarily just the result of carelessness or not knowing how to proceed. In a study of written computation, Roberts identified four error categories or "failure strategies."[3]

1. *Wrong operation.* The pupil attempts to respond by performing an operation other than the one that is required to solve the problem.
2. *Obvious computational error.* The pupil applies the correct operation, but the response is based on error in recalling basic number facts.
3. *Defective algorithm.*[4] The pupil attempts to apply the correct operation but makes errors other than number fact errors in carrying through the necessary steps.
4. *Random response.* The response shows no discernible relationship to the given problem.

Roberts noted that careless numerical errors and lack of familiarity with the addition and multiplication tables occurred with near-equal frequency at all ability levels. However, using the wrong operation and making random responses were observed more frequently with students of low ability and progressively less frequently with students of higher and higher ability. *The largest number of errors was due to erroneous or incorrect algorithm techniques* in all groups except the lowest quartile, which had more random responses. Incorrect algorithms were used by even the most able achievers (39 percent of the errors made by the upper quartile of pupils studied). Other researchers have made similar observations. Schacht concluded that "differences in performance appear to be of degree and not of kind, with the less able making errors more frequently than the more able."[5] Clearly, the practice papers of *all* pupils must be considered carefully.

In his extension of Roberts' study, Engelhardt classified errors into eight types: basic fact error, defective algorithm, grouping error, inappropriate inversion, incorrect operation, incomplete algorithm, identity error, and zero error.[6] The categories called defective algorithm, grouping error, and inappropriate inversion (all of which involve erroneous procedures) accounted for *61 percent* of the 2279 errors made by third and sixth grade children in the study. Again, it is obvious that teachers dare not assume that errors in computation are caused by carelessness or by a child not knowing the basic facts. The actual procedures used are likely to be wrong.

---

[3] Gerhard H. Roberts, "The Failure Strategies of Third Grade Arithmetic Pupils," *The Arithmetic Teacher* 15 (May 1968):442–46.

[4] An algorithm is a step-by-step written procedure for determining the result of an arithmetic operation (*i.e.,* a sum, a difference, a product, or a quotient). A variety of algorithms or computational procedures can be used to determine any one missing number; and indeed, at different times and in different parts of the world, many differing but useful algorithms are taught. However, the algorithm used by a child is said to be "incorrect" or "defective" if the procedure does not always produce the correct result.

[5] Elmer J. Schacht, "A Study of the Mathematical Errors of Low Achievers in Elementary School Mathematics," *Dissertation Abstracts* 28A (September 1967): 920–21.

[6] Jon M. Engelhardt, "Analysis of Children's Computational Errors: A Qualitative Approach," *British Journal of Educational Psychology* 47 (1977): 149–54.

Brueckner did extensive work identifying types of errors in computation as early as the 1920s. These studies were reported in journals, in his classic 1930 text,[7] and in yearbook articles.[8] He stressed the importance of analyzing written work but also emphasized the need to supplement such activity with interviews. His study of difficulties children have when computing with decimals is characteristic of his research. This report, published in 1928, includes the tabulation of 8785 errors into 114 different kinds.[9] However, many of his categories are ambiguous, and some we would question today, for he listed the annexation of unnecessary zeros as an error and considered the vocalization of procedures a faulty habit.

Others have described categories of errors in computation. Guiler noted that in the addition and subtraction of decimals, seven times as many children had trouble with the computation per se than had trouble with the decimal phases of the process. Further, in division of decimals, more than 40 percent of the children placed the decimal point three or more places too far to the right.[10] Such studies remind us of the value of a thorough understanding of numeration and the ability to estimate. Arthur, in a study of difficulties with arithmetic found among high school students, included types of errors such as adding denominators when adding fractions and failing to invert the divisor when dividing fractions.[11] He concluded that the reteaching of arithmetic skills should be based upon short diagnostic tests and given attention in all high school math classes. Cox concluded from her research that not only did children make systematic errors but, without instructional intervention, they continued with the error patterns for long periods of time.[12] In his study of students in grades 5–8, MacKay reported that many children actually had a high degree of confidence in their erroneous procedures.[13]

Sadowski and McIlveen studied error patterns in sentence-solving.[14] They found that some procedures children use (although inadequate) produce a correct solution quite frequently, thereby reinforcing continued use of the error pattern. Error studies have also been conducted in algebra. Davis and Cooney studied the work of algebra students and described categories of errors.[15] Carry, Lewis, and

---

[7] Leo J. Brueckner, *Diagnostic and Remedial Teaching in Arithmetic* (Philadelphia: John C. Winston Co., 1930).

[8] For example, his "Diagnosis in Arithmetic," in *Educational Diagnosis*, 34th Yearbook, National Society for the Study of Education (Bloomington, Ill.: Public School Publishing Co., 1935): 269–302.

[9] Leo J. Brueckner, "Analysis of Difficulties in Decimals," *Elementary School Journal* 29 (September 1928): 32–41.

[10] Walter S. Guiler, "Difficulties in Decimals Encountered in Ninth-Grade Pupils," *Elementary School Journal* 46 (March 1946): 384–93.

[11] Lee E. Arthur, "Diagnosis of Disabilities in Arithmetic Essentials," *The Mathematics Teacher* 43 (May 1950): 197–202.

[12] L. S. Cox, "Diagnosing and Remediating Systematic Errors in Addition and Subtraction Computations," *The Arithmetic Teacher* 22 (February 1975): 151–57.

[13] I. D. MacKay, *A Comparison of Students' Achievement in Arithmetic with Their Algorithmic Confidence* (Vancouver, B.C.: Mathematics Education Diagnostic and Instructional Centre, University of British Columbia, 1975.) (ERIC Document Reproduction Service No. ED 128 228)

[14] Barbara R. Sadowski and Delayne Houston McIlveen, "Diagnosis and Remediation of Sentence-solving Error Patterns," *The Arithmetic Teacher* 31 (January 1984): 42–45.

[15] Edward J. Davis and Thomas J. Cooney, "Identifying Errors in Solving Certain Linear Equations," *The MATYC Journal* 11 (1977): 170–78.

Bernard studied errors in solving linear equations and listed types of errors they found.[16] In both studies, patterns of errors were observed.

Noting the similarity of errors across studies, Bright suggested the following categories for future studies of errors in solving linear equations: arithmetic errors, combination errors, transposition errors, operation errors, incomplete solutions, and execution errors.[17]

Several researchers have studied the frequency with which different error patterns occur. One example is Lankford's study of seventh graders.[18] He conducted "diagnostic interviews" of 176 pupils in six schools located in different parts of the United States. The detailed report of the research includes many examples of the use of erroneous algorithms and the frequency of their occurrence among pupils in the study. Lankford's general observations concerning how wrong answers were derived for whole numbers and fractions are included in this text as Appendix C. In his conclusions he notes that "Unorthodox strategies were frequently observed—some yielding correct answers and some incorrect ones."[19] Cox's study also gives us insight into the frequency with which erroneous procedures are used.[20] Her study focused on whole number algorithms and compared the work of children in "regular" classrooms with computation done by children placed in special education classrooms. A third study was conducted by Research for Better Schools, Inc., and reported by Graeber and Wallace.[21] This study examined addition, subtraction, and multiplication of whole numbers on individually prescribed instruction (IPI) mathematics pretests. In both the Cox study and the IPI study, an erroneous procedure was not classified as "systematic" unless it occurred at least three times.

Researchers are also giving attention to construction of computer systems for diagnosing systematic student errors. The name of one diagnostic system, DEBUGGY, reflects the fact that patterns of error are often called "bugs" in the computer world. Although its potential for use by regular classroom teachers is unclear, DEBUGGY has been found to be an excellent research tool. Even so, some error patterns were not diagnosed by DEBUGGY, and Repair Theory has been developed to explain many of the remaining error patterns.[22] VanLehn reports that the bugs or error patterns of some students are unstable from one test to the next. It appears that error patterns are sometimes used as problem-solving strat-

---

[16] L. Ray Carry et al., *Psychology of Equation Solving: An Information Processing Study, Final Technical Report* (Austin, Texas: Department of Curriculum and Instruction, University of Texas, 1979). (ERIC Document Reproduction Service No. ED 186 243)

[17] George W. Bright, "Student Errors in Solving Linear Equations," *RCDPM Newsletter* 6, no. 2 (Fall 1981): 3–4.

[18] Francis G. Lankford, Jr., *Some Computational Strategies of Seventh Grade Pupils*, U.S. Department of Health, Education, and Welfare, Office of Education, National Center for Educational Research and Development (Regional Research Program) and The Center for Advanced Study, The University of Virginia, October 1972. (Project number 2-C-013, Grant number OEG-3,72-0035)

[19] *Ibid.*, p. 40.

[20] L. S. Cox, "Systematic Errors in the Four Vertical Algorithms in Normal and Handicapped Populations," *Journal for Research in Mathematics Education* 6, no. 4 (November 1975): 202–20.

[21] Anna O. Graeber and Lisa Wallace, *Identification of Systematic Errors: Final Report* (Philadelphia: Research for Better Schools, Inc., 1977). (ERIC Document Reproduction Service No. ED 139 662)

[22] John S. Brown and Kurt VanLehn, "Repair Theory: A Generative Theory of Bugs in Procedural Skills," *Cognitive Science* 4 (1980): 379–426.

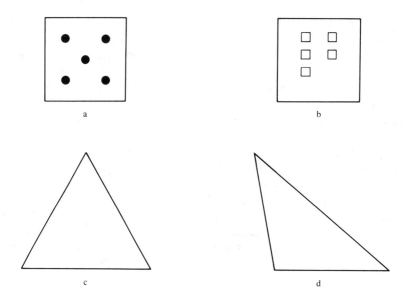

FIGURE 2

egies, and used by a student only long enough to get the student through the test.[23] Of course, other error patterns are used tenaciously, even during instruction.

Why Children Learn Error Patterns

How do children learn concepts and procedures? Children's mathematical ideas and computational procedures may be correct or erroneous, but the *process* of abstracting those ideas and procedures is basically the same. From a set of experiences with a concept or a process, a child pulls out or abstracts those things which the experiences have in common. The intersection of the experiences defines the idea or process for the child.

If a child's only experiences with the idea *five* are with manila cards having black dots in the familiar domino pattern (see Figure 2a), he may abstract from these experiences a notion of five which includes many or all of the characteristics his experiences have had in common. The ideas of black on manila paper, round dots, or a specific configuration may become part of the child's idea of five. One of the author's students, when presenting to children the configuration associated with Stern pattern boards (see Figure 2b) was told, "That's not five. Five doesn't look like that."

More children will name as a triangle the shape in Figure 2c than the shape in Figure 2d; yet both are triangles. Again, configuration (or even the orientation of the figure) may be a common characteristic of the child's limited range of experiences with triangles.

[23] Kurt VanLehn, *Bugs Are Not Enough: Empirical Studies of Bugs, Impasses and Repairs in Procedural Skills* (Palo Alto, California: Cognitive and Instructional Sciences Group, Xerox, Palo Alto Research Center, March 1981).

Dr. Geoffrey Matthews, organizer of the Nuffield Mathematics Teaching Project in England, tells of a child who computed correctly one year but missed about half of the problems the next year. As the child learned to compute, he adopted the rule, "Begin on the side by the piano." The next school year the child was in a room with the piano on the other side, and he was understandably confused about where to start computing.

When multiplication of fractions (or rational numbers) is introduced, children frequently have difficulty believing their correct answers make sense because throughout their previous experiences with factors and products the product was always at least as large as the smaller factor. (Actually, the product is noticeably larger than either factor in most cases.) In the mind of the child, the concept of product had come to include the idea of larger number because this was common throughout most of his experiences with products. This may be one reason many children have difficulty with the zero property for multiplication of whole numbers. The product zero is usually smaller than one of the factors.

Creature Cards also illustrate this view of concept formation (see Figure 3). The child confronted with a Creature Card is given a name or label such as Gruffle

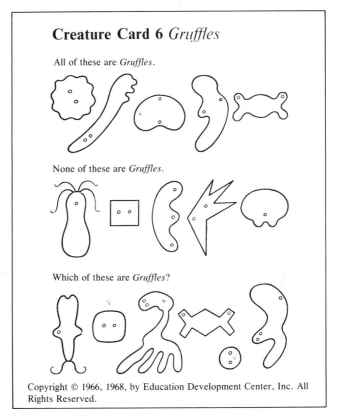

Creature Card 6 *Gruffles*

All of these are *Gruffles*.

None of these are *Gruffles*.

Which of these are *Gruffles*?

Source: Reproduced from the Elementary Science Study unit, *Attribute Games and Problems*, by permission of Education Development Center, Inc.

FIGURE 3

and told to decide what a Gruffle is. He looks for common characteristics among a set of Gruffles. Then, experiences with non-Gruffles help him eliminate from consideration those characteristics which happen to be common in the set of Gruffles but are not essential to "Gruffleness" (i.e., the definition of a Gruffle would not include such attributes). Finally, the cards provide an opportunity for the child to test out his newly derived definition.

Children often learn erroneous concepts and processes similarly. They look for commonalities among their initial contacts with the idea or procedure. They pull out or abstract certain common characteristics, and their concept of algorithm is formed. The common attributes may be very specific, such as crossing out a digit, placing a digit in front of another, or finding the difference between two one-digit numbers (regardless of order). From time to time such inadequate procedures even produce correct answers. When this happens, use of the erroneous procedure is reinforced for the child who is anxious to succeed. The child who decides that rounding whole numbers to the nearest ten means erasing the units digit and writing a zero is correct about half of the time! After observing similar "discoveries" by children, the psychologist Friedlander noted that as teachers "seek to capitalize on the students' reasoning, errors of fact, of perception, or of association can lead to hopelessly chaotic chains of mistaken inferences and deductions."[24]

There are many reasons why children are prone to overgeneralize and learn patterns of error. It most certainly is not the intentional result of instruction. Yet all too often, especially when taught in groups, children do not have prerequisite understandings and skills they need when introduced to new ideas and procedures. When this happens, they want to please the teacher (or at least survive in the situation), so they tend to "grab at straws." Furthermore, teachers who introduce paper-and-pencil procedures while a child still needs to work problems out with concrete aids are encouraging the child to try to memorize a complex sequence of mechanical acts. This, again, prompts the child to adopt simplistic procedures he can remember. Because incorrect algorithms do not usually result in correct answers, it would appear that a child receives limited positive reinforcement for continued use of erroneous procedures. However, children sometimes hold tenaciously to incorrect procedures even during remedial instruction. Each incorrect algorithm is an interesting study in itself, and in succeeding sections of this book you will have opportunities to identify several erroneous computational procedures and consider possible reasons for adoption of such procedures by children.

Keep in mind the fact that children who learn patterns of error *are* capable of learning. They generally have what we might call a learn*ed* disability, not a learn*ing* disability.[25] In his *Children's Arithmetic: The Learning Process,* Ginsburg points out that the rules young children adopt are meaningful to them.[26] Their

[24] Bernard Z. Friedlander, "A Psychologist's Second Thoughts on Concepts, Curiosity, and Discovery in Teaching and Learning," *Harvard Educational Review* 35 (Winter 1965): 29.

[25] These terms were used frequently by John Wilson, director of the Arithmetic Clinic at the University of Maryland before his death.

[26] Herbert Ginsburg, *Children's Arithmetic: The Learning Process* (New York: D. Van Nostrand Company, 1977). See especially Chapter 6.

rules are derived from a search for meaning, and a sensible learning process is involved. This is true even for the erroneous rules they invent, though such rules may involve a distortion or a poor application. More than computational procedure is in view here. For example, Ginsburg describes the invention of erroneous rules as children learn to count.[27] Children can also be observed inventing similar rules when introduced to the equals sign, rules like "The equals sign means 'the answer turns out to be.' "[28]

Levels of Diagnosis

Diagnosis is not something reserved for special times and places nor is it an activity reserved for specialists. Effective teachers make diagnoses many times every day as they teach children. We even speak of *teaching diagnostically*.

But there are times you seek enough information to decide which children need special help. You may be forming instructional groups or you may be deciding which children need the help of a resource room teacher. Additional diagnosis is required before you can plan lessons.

At an even deeper level you try to find a child's areas of strength and weakness. It is helpful to know which concept and skill categories are well developed and which require special attention. For example, a child may be doing well with addition of whole numbers but not with subtraction. Often, paper-and-pencil tests can be used to help identify areas of strength and weakness. You may decide to set up a special instructional group for those children needing help in one area.

But an even deeper level of diagnosis is often required. Within an area, such as subtraction of whole numbers, there exists concept and skill categories which involve numeration concepts, zero facts, regrouping, and the like. For each child having difficulty, you really need to know which of these categories are strengths and which are weaknesses. Some tests are too broad to provide this information, though others will be helpful. Individual interviews can be invaluable, especially when they involve a child's responses to tasks with manipulative materials.

Diagnostic Tests

As you diagnose a child's concepts and skills in computation, much of what you learn comes from paper-and-pencil tests or other written work. In a sense, this entire book is designed to help you learn as much as possible from the written work of children.

For diagnostic purposes, standardized achievement tests have some value but it is limited. They usually sample such a broad range of content that you do not learn what you need to know about specific concept and skill categories. Diagnostic tests sample a narrower range of content, often in a way that permits you to identify areas of strength and weakness. The following diagnostic tests are examples of

---

[27] Ginsburg, *op. cit.,* Chapter 1.

[28] See Merlyn Behr, Stanley Erlwanger, and Eugene Nichols, "How Children View the Equals Sign," *Mathematics Teaching* 92 (September 1980): 13–15, or a paper with the same title available from ERIC Document Reproduction Service No. ED 144 802.

those commercially available. An extensive listing of mathematics tests available in the United States and Canada can be obtained from the National Council of Teachers of Mathematics.[29]

KeyMath-R.[30] This test is intended for use with children in kindergarten through grade 9. It is administered to children individually and its exceptionally attractive format maintains the child's interest during administration. The thirteen untimed subtests cover basic concepts, operations, and applications. Two forms of the test are available for pre- and posttesting.

KeyMath-R subtest scores can be used for identifying categories of strength and weakness, such as numeration (numbers 0–99), and fraction concepts. Accordingly, it is often used for screening purposes. Though the KeyMath-R is an individual test, more in-depth diagnosis may be necessary before instruction can be planned for children who are having difficulty learning mathematics. The *KeyMath Teach and Practice* is designed to provide further identification and remediation of special skills.

Stanford Diagnostic Mathematics Tests, Third Edition.[31] Different levels of tests are available for use with children in grades 1.5 to 12. They are paper-and-pencil tests and can be administered to groups of children.

Each test includes three subtests: number systems and numeration, computing, and applications. Each subtest is then divided further into more specific concept-skill categories. Therefore, the information gained points to specific categories of strength and weakness. Even so, additional data about children having difficulty is needed in order to plan truly effective instruction. Carefully designed individual interviews of selected children can provide an excellent followup for the Stanford tests.

Diagnostic Test of Arithmetic Strategies.[32] This is an individually administered test intended for children who have difficulty computing with whole numbers. Separate scoring sheets are available for addition, subtraction, multiplication, and division. Each scoring sheet examines (1) ability to set up the problem; (2) number fact knowledge; (3) use of algorithms, invented procedures, bugs, and slips; and (4) use of informal procedures. The scoring sheets actually list specific error patterns that may be observed and recorded.

Most teachers do not have time to interview *each* child. From time to time you probably need to prepare your own diagnostic test for a specific concept or skill category. You may need a test to administer to children who have difficulty subtracting when regrouping is involved. The error patterns presented in Chapter 3 and discussed in Chapter 4 suggest distractors you can use for test items. Dis-

---

[29] James S. Braswell and Alicia A. Dodd, *Mathematics Tests Available in the United States and Canada* (Reston, Virginia: NCTM, 1988).

[30] American Guidance Service, Inc., 1988.

[31] The Psychological Corporation, 1984.

[32] Pro-Ed, 1984.

tractors drawn from error patterns may give you clues to the child's thought process. The following multiple-choice item was built from error patterns; each distractor is an answer a child might choose if he or she has learned an erroneous procedure.

The answer is:

4372
− 2858
_____

a. 2526   *big to list*
b. 1514
c. 524
d. 2524

Computers have great potential as tools to assist with diagnosis of computational skills. Much of the software that is currently available is not greatly advanced beyond a set of paper-and-pencil tests, so make sure that use of the computer program is preferable to a paper-and-pencil procedure. Examples of currently available programs include the following:

1. *APPLE-Based Elementary Mathematics Classroom Learning System: Set 1 Whole Numbers; Set 2 Fractions/Decimals,* Sterling Swift Publishing Company, 1981. Reviewed in *The Arithmetic Teacher* (October 1982).
2. *Mastering Math: Diagnostic System* for the Apple II family, Minnesota Educational Computing Corp., 1985. Reviewed in *The Arithmetic Teacher* (April 1988).
3. *Math Assistant I and II: Error Analysis in Addition and Subtraction; Multiplication and Division* for Apple II family, Scholastic Inc., 1985. Reviewed in *The Arithmetic Teacher* (December 1986).

Researchers are developing more sophisticated programs for diagnosis in which selection of the next test item for a child is based on analysis of the child's response.

Interviews and Other Diagnostic Techniques

Written tests are helpful in diagnosis, but they are limited. Interviews have long been recognized as an effective way to collect additional information about a child's mathematical concepts, to gain both quantitative and qualitative data. Interviewing is not just "oral testing" to determine whether a child can do a task. In an interview you can focus on the child's thinking and determine if he or she is learning in a meaningful way. You can determine what strategies are used to solve problems.

An interview is not a time for expressing your opinion or asking questions that are merely prompted by your own curiosity. Rather, it is a time to observe the child carefully, a time to *listen.* Adapt the pace of the interview so the child can respond comfortably. Be careful not to give clues or ask leading questions.

Record the child's responses as you proceed with the interview. Make written notes or tape record the interview and write down only those things which will not appear on tape, say, an expression of delight or disgust. You may also want to record your judgments as to the child's level of understanding. Do not rely on your memory to make a true record.

Interviews can vary widely in their structure. You may ask a child to choose among the alternatives you present, but generally you will want the child to respond freely. To get at a child's thinking, you will want the child to comment on his or her own thought processes. This can be accomplished either through introspection or through retrospection. To elicit introspection, ask the child to comment on thoughts as the task is being done; have the child "think out loud." Of course, the very process of commenting aloud can influence the thinking a child does.[33] To elicit retrospection, ask the child to comment on thoughts after a task is completed. Remember that, when commenting in retrospect, a child may forget wrong turns that were taken, etc. It is probably best to elicit introspection part of the time and retrospection part of the time.

Stimulus situations should be given in varied modes. Consider the following:

Mode	Examples
Verbal	Words, oral and written
Written symbols	Numerals
Two-dimensional representations	Paper-and-pencil diagrams, photographs
Three-dimensional representations	Base ten blocks, math balance, place value chart

A stimulus situation can be given in any of the above modes. Each stimulus situation will call for a response, and responses for a given stimulus can be similarly varied. If a child's responses are ambiguous, you may vary the questions in order to draw out the child.

Consider the following techniques; they may help you obtain information you will not get any other way.

1. Say, "This time I'll hold the pencil and you tell me what to do."
2. Have students describe to other students how they solved a problem, or have them write their descriptions on paper.
3. Provide a slightly different context, and ask students to use the idea.
4. Ask students to rate mathematical examples on a scale of 1–4. For example, ask students to "Show how you see each example as multiplication."

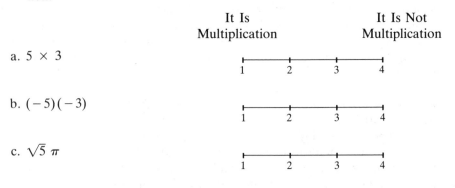

[33] See Alan H. Schoenfeld, "Making Sense of 'Out Loud' Problem-Solving Protocols," *The Journal of Mathematical Behavior* 4 (October 1985): 171–191.

5. Discuss the responses with the child. Children who interpret multiplication only as repeated addition usually consider example *a* to be more truly an example of multiplication than *b* or *c*.

During the interview carefully observe students' behavior in response to their own errors. Be sure to diagnose each student's ability to estimate; instruction may well need to focus on this important skill and the concepts involved. Remember that students with learning disabilities often communicate information that is incorrect, yet it is what they actually see.

While a student is solving a verbal problem, determine how the student represents the problem mentally. Does the student conceive the problem in terms of a whole and its parts? Can the situation be shown with a diagram or manipulatives? It is often helpful to have students retell a problem in their own words.

Watch students as they play mathematical games. Note how they get the information they need. Intervene with diagnostic questions from time to time.

Metacognition

In recent years researchers have become increasingly interested in metacognition, that is, in what a child knows about his or her own cognitive performance and the child's ability to regulate that performance. Garofalo maintains that "mathematics educators are convinced that what one knows or believes about oneself as a learner and doer of mathematics and how one controls and regulates one's behaviors while working through mathematical tasks can have powerful effects on one's performance."[34]

Many of the questions you ask while interviewing a child will help the child become more aware of his own cognitive processes. Garofalo lists the following sample questions.[35]

Think of everything you do when you practice solving mathematics problems. Why do you do these things?

What kinds of errors do you usually make? Why do you think you make these errors? What can you do about them?

Tell why taking one's time might be important. Is it always important?

What do you do when you see an unfamiliar problem? Why?

Name some things that you can do when you are stuck on a problem. Do these things always help?

Name several things that you can do to keep track of what you're doing.

Tell when it's useful to check your work. Why? Is that the only time?

What kinds of things do you forget to do when solving mathematics problems?

What kinds of problems are you best at? Why?

What kinds of problems are you worst at? Why? What can you do to get better at these?

---

[34] Joe Garofalo, "Metacognition and School Mathematics," *The Arithmetic Teacher* 34 (May 1987): 22.

[35] *Ibid.*, pp. 22–23.

Some instructional activities help students monitor their own cognitive activity and at the same time provide diagnostic information for the teacher. Have students keep a math journal in which they not only record story problems, but also write out their thinking as they solve them. You may find students who read for key words or read only the parts with numbers.

You may also want to have students make concept maps by writing concepts on paper, then showing relationships with lines. Linking words can also be added. Emphasize the importance of putting *their* thoughts on paper.[36] Figure 4 illustrates how differently two fourth grade boys in the same classroom drew maps for the word "subtraction."

Guidelines for Diagnosis

A child's work must not only be scored, it must be analyzed as well if it is to provide useful information for diagnosis. Many times it is possible for students to mark which examples are correct or incorrect, and you can spend more of your professional time analyzing the written work of children and planning needed instruction.

Observe what the child does and does not do; note the computation that has a correct answer and the computation that does not; and look for those procedures used by the child which might be called mature and those which are less mature. Distinguish between situations in which the child uses an incorrect procedure and situations in which the child does not know how to proceed at all.

The following statements provide a brief summary of principles to keep in mind as you diagnose the work of children having difficulty with computation.

1. *Be accepting.* Diagnosis is a highly personal process. Before a child will cooperate with you as his teacher in a manner which may lead to lessening or elimination of his problems with computation, he must perceive that you are interested in and respect him as a person, that you are genuinely interested in helping him, and that you are quite willing to accept a response even when the response is not correct. In short, if sufficient data are to be collected for an adequate diagnosis, the child must understand that you are willing to accept his failures. You must exhibit something of the attitude of a good physician toward his patient, and, as Tournier, a Swiss physician, has noted, "What antagonizes a patient is not the truth, but the tone of scorn, pity, criticism, or reproof which so often colors the statement of the truth by those around him."[37]

2. *Collect data—do not instruct.* In making a diagnosis, you must differentiate between the role of collecting data (testing) and the role of teaching. Diagnosing involves gathering as much useful data as possible and making judgments on the

---

[36] For suggestions on introducing concept maps to children, see Joseph D. Novak and D. Bob Gowin, "How to Introduce Students to Concept Mapping," *Learning How to Learn* (New York: Cambridge University Press, 1984): 24–39.

[37] Paul Tournier, *The Healing of Persons* (New York: Harper and Row, 1965): 243.

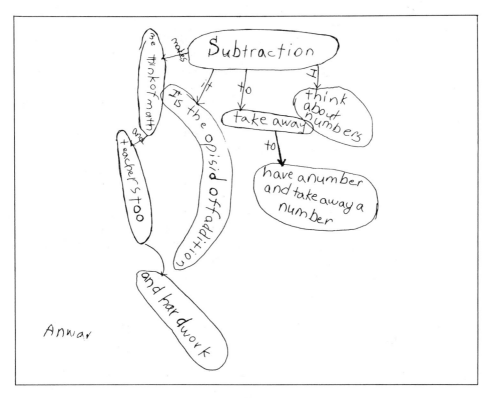

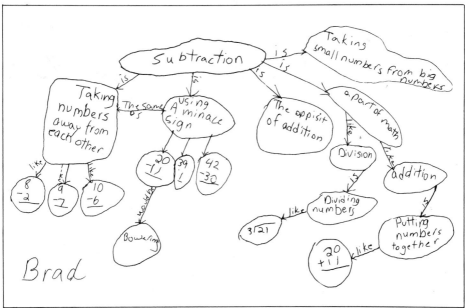

Cognitive Maps by Fourth Grade Boys

FIGURE 4

basis of the data collected; in general, the more data, the more adequate the judgments which follow. The child is apt to provide many samples of incorrect and immature procedures if he sees that you are merely collecting information which will be used to help him overcome his difficulties. However, if you point out errors, label responses as "wrong," and offer instruction, the child is far less likely to expose his own inadequate performance. When a teacher who usually offers help as soon as he sees incorrect or immature performance begins to distinguish between collecting data and instruction, he is often delighted with the way children begin to open up and lay bare their thinking.

3. *Be thorough.* A given diagnosis is rarely thorough enough to provide direction for continuing instruction. From time to time it is necessary to have short periods of diagnosis even during remedial instruction. In fact, if you are alert during the instruction which follows a diagnosis, you may pick up cues that suggest additional diagnostic activities apt to provide helpful data about the child and his problem. Whenever possible say: "Can you read it another way?" or "Can you do it another way?" Carefully observe the child's behavior in novel situations.

4. *Look for Patterns.* Data should be evaluated in terms of patterns, not isolated events. A decision about remedial instruction can hardly be based upon collected bits of unrelated information. As you look for patterns you engage in a kind of problem-solving activity, for you yourself look for elements common to several examples of a child's work. Look for repeated applications of erroneous definitions and try to find consistent use of incorrect or immature procedures. The importance of looking for patterns can hardly be overstressed, for many erroneous procedures are practiced by children while their teachers assume the children are merely careless or "don't know their facts."

For further study of diagnosis, specialists in school mathematics and serious students of diagnosis will want to examine many of the references listed after Chapter 5.

Chapter 2

Providing Needed Instruction

You know that when Fred multiplies he usually adds the "crutch" before multiplying, so you need to plan instruction for him. This chapter is designed to help you provide effective instruction; later, in Chapter 5, specific suggestions are listed for different error patterns.

When teaching computational procedures, interweave instruction with diagnosis. Be alert to what each child is actually doing and eager to probe deeper. Be willing to change your plans as soon as what you see or hear suggests that an alternative would be more fruitful in the long run. Diagnostic teaching is, first of all, an attitude that cares very much about each child's learning.

If you think about it for a moment you will realize that diagnostic teaching is cyclical. After your initial diagnosis, you plan and conduct the lesson, but what you see and hear during the lesson prompts you to modify your previous judgment and possibly seek more information before planning the next lesson. Sometimes you move through the cycle very rapidly several times in the course of a single lesson. At other times, it occurs over a span of several lessons.

Teaching Children to Compute

While planning remedial instruction, keep in mind the teaching sequences normally followed when algorithms are introduced. An overview follows but you may want to consult a methods text for a more complete discussion.

It is usually wise to introduce an algorithm by presenting children with interesting verbal problems and letting them use what they already know to work out solutions. If you let them use their own informal techniques initially, you will be surprised to learn that some children know more than you thought. Other children will be very creative in using what they know. By beginning in this way, you help children relate the algorithm you are teaching to the informal knowledge of arithmetic they already possess. As the procedure is taught, mathematical mean-

ings should be emphasized: ideas such as place value concepts and properties of the operations.

In the normal developmental sequence for teaching an algorithm for whole numbers, children solve problems with the aid of manipulatives. Eventually, a step-by-step record of manipulations and thinking is written with numerals. If you keep in mind the algorithm you are working toward as you guide this activity, the written record will be the algorithm itself or, more likely, a variation of the algorithm. After children are comfortable going from manipulatives to a written record, they begin to use the written procedure while only referring to the manipulatives, not actually handling them. In many cases, the standard algorithm itself is derived by gradually shortening the written record because, "Mathematicians are a bit lazy and they try not to write everything out; they like to write fewer symbols if they can."

Those algorithms which are not easily developed as a record of observations are sometimes introduced as a shortcut. For example, the standard procedure for dividing fractions can be developed by reasoning through a rather elaborate but meaningful procedure involving complex fractions, application of the multiplicative identity, and the like, then observing a pattern which suggests that most of the steps can be eliminated by merely inverting the divisor and multiplying.

In the experience of the author, when manipulatives are used to teach an algorithm the critical step is progressing from the manipulatives to written symbols. This is why a *step-by-step* record is helpful. The record or algorithm must make sense to the child if he or she is going to do more than push symbols around on paper. Use of varied materials may facilitate transfer; children who have already worked out solutions with different manipulatives often find it easy to progress to written symbols.

Some children will make mistakes while learning to compute, but mistakes can be an important and positive part of the initial learning process. Emphasize estimating needed answers continually, for this will help children discover many of their errors. When a child who is learning to compute produces an unreasonable answer, the child faces a personal problem-solving situation which can lead to creative thinking and a greater understanding of the algorithm itself. Whenever children discover that their ideas do not produce correct or reasonable answers, they should be motivated to resolve the dilemma rather than penalized for the mistake. Use errors as springboards for the learning of mathematics. Thereby, mistakes can be the occasion for positive experiences that are an important part of the learning process. Remember that students build up mathematical concepts and knowledge of procedures in their own minds. Help them make wise choices and develop good habits as they learn.

Be alert to any perceptual difficulties a child may have. In order to respond to instruction children need to be able to perceive and imagine the physical properties of digits: vertical vs. horizontal elongation, straightness vs. curvature, degree of closure. If instruction emphasizes understanding, children also need to be able to perceive properties of multi-digit numerals, such as position of a digit to the left or right of another digit. Poor spatial ability may affect a child's capacity to respond to instruction emphasizing place value concepts.

Other children may find it difficult to respond to instruction because of language patterns. The syntax of English language expressions is often different from the structure of mathematical statements, and we complicate the situation by using different but equivalent language expressions for the same situation. (For example, *twelve minus four* and *four from twelve* express the same mathematical concept.) Researchers are studying the implications for instruction. While conducting research with both Hispanics and Anglos, Mestre and Gerace found, for example, that we need to focus careful attention on helping students discern the differences between labels and variables.[1] In her book *Twice As Less,*[2] Orr raises questions about the effects of nonstandard English on students' learning of mathematics. She concludes that nonstandard language is often associated with erroneous concepts, and she urges teachers to replace rote memorization of procedures with an emphasis on understanding and verbalization of mathematical concepts, relationships, and processes.

After a child gains some competence with an algorithm, less stress should be placed on mathematical understanding. As Wheatley notes, "The advantage of algorithms lies in the routine established and the minimum amount of decision making or problem analysis required."[3] It is primarily while a computational procedure is being learned that understanding plays a role. After it is learned the greater concern is with the meaning of the arithmetic operation itself, so that children will know when it is appropriate to *use* the algorithm. For example, What is given in a problem situation? What is wanted? If a sum and an addend are given and the other addend is wanted, then a subtraction algorithm can be used to find that missing addend.

If you find error patterns in a child's computation, ask yourself why children adopt such procedures. Ask, "What can I do to make sure my pupils learn *correct* computational procedures and not these erroneous procedures?" You will want to teach in a way which makes the use of erroneous procedures a very unlikely event!

What is needed is thorough, developmental instruction in which it is possible for each child to move through a carefully planned sequence of different types of learning activities. The amount of time needed for each type of activity will vary from child to child, and, for any one individual, the pace will likely vary from day to day. If you are to lessen the likelihood that children learn patterns of error, you will have to resist the temptation to cover the text or the curriculum guide by completing two pages a day or some similar plan. Careful attention will have to be given to ideas and skills needed by each child in order to learn the concept or algorithm under study.

Estimation

A proper emphasis on estimation during instruction will eliminate much of the need for future remediation, so try to establish an estimation mind-set among your students.

---

[1] Jose Mestre and William Gerace, "The Interplay of Linguistic Factors in Mathematical Translation Tasks," *Focus on Learning Problems in Mathematics* 8 (Winter 1986): 59–72.

[2] Eleanor W. Orr, *Twice As Less: Black English and the Performance of Black Students in Mathematics and Science* (New York: W. W. Norton and Co., 1987).

[3] Grayson H. Wheatley, "A Comparison of Two Methods of Column Addition," *Journal for Research in Mathematics Education* 7, no. 3 (May 1976): 145–54.

One of the recommendations of the Lankford study cited in the previous chapter was that teachers "give more attention to teaching pupils to check the reasonableness of answers."[4] Those who caution that the widespread availability of calculators will not eliminate the need for computational skills also stress the need for skill in estimation. "The calculator is designed to do only the keypuncher's bidding. Nor will the calculator tell whether or not an answer is reasonable. Estimation to judge the reasonableness of an answer will still require computational skill."[5]

Estimation can be emphasized by allowing children time to guess, test their guesses, and revise their guesses as needed. Flexible thinking is required, and children can be encouraged to develop their own ways of deciding when an answer is reasonable. It may also be desirable to show them more standard procedures. Thankfully, current elementary school texts present specific procecures for estimating answers even before computational procedures are taught.

Estimation is itself a complex of skills, any one of which may require instruction and practice apart from the more general question "Is your answer reasonable?" Included among such skills for whole numbers are:

1. Adding a little bit more than one number to a little bit more than another; a little bit less than one number to a little bit less than another; and, in general, adding, subtracting, etc., with a little bit more than or a little bit less than.
2. Rounding a whole number to the nearest ten, hundred, etc.
3. Multiplying by ten and powers of ten in one step.
4. Multiplying two numbers each of which is a multiple of a power of ten (e.g., 20×300). This should be done as one step, without the use of a written algorithm.

With fractions, estimation often involves identifying a particular fraction as close to zero, one-half, or one.

To practice estimating, children can be presented with a problem and several answers. They can then choose the answer which is most reasonable. If appropriate, their choice can be verified by computation. The practice of recording an estimated answer before computation should be encouraged. In general, children become more and more able to determine when an answer is reasonable as they gain the habit of asking if the answer makes sense, and as they progress from guessing to educated guessing to more specific estimating procedures. Children who have the habit of considering the reasonableness of their answers are not as prone to adopt incorrect computational procedures.

Computational Estimation, developed by Reys and others, provides helpful instructional materials for teaching estimation in grades 6, 7, and 8. Copies of actual worksheets are included for whole numbers, fractions, decimals, and percents.[6]

---

[4] Lankford, 1972, p. 42.

[5] Eugene P. Smith, "A Look at Mathematics Education Today," *The Arithmetic Teacher* 20 (October 1973): 505

[6] Available from ERIC, Clearinghouse for Science, Mathematics, and Environmental Education, The Ohio State University, 1200 Chambers Road, Columbus, Ohio 43212. (Document Reproduction Service No. ED 242 526 for sixth grade, ED 242 527 for seventh grade, and ED 242 528 for eighth grade)

Using Manipulatives

When an error in computation is observed, it is not sufficient to tell the child how to do it correctly. On the other hand, manipulatives are not always needed. Sometimes help with the mechanics of notation is sufficient. For example, a digit can be written larger or smaller, or in a different location, so as to be less confusing. Much of the time, however, an error pattern suggests an incorrect learning that is going unchallenged by the child. Manipulatives may help the child understand the steps in the procedure and why they make sense.

In general, well-chosen manipulatives can create an environment of what Kerslake calls "natural activity" upon which a child can base an understanding of concepts and operations. Because whole numbers are a normal part of a child's environment, young children typically create their own informal procedures while working with them. But Kerslake concludes that it is because fractions are not a normal part of a child's environment (with few exceptions) that children were not observed creating their own informal methods; instead, children relied on rote memory of what were often half-remembered rules.[7] Materials available to create such environments include Chip Trading Activities for whole numbers and Fraction Bars for fractions. Extensive use of materials like these during the early phases of instruction usually helps children develop meanings they can apply flexibly.

As you teach mathematics you, of necessity, use language. Each child must understand the words you speak (whether ordinary speech or mathematical terms) in order to comprehend what you say, and manipulatives can help children understand concepts, relationships, and sequences. It is often wise to redevelop the algorithm as a step-by-step record of observations while using manipulatives. Hopefully, this procedure will help the child who has just been pushing symbols around in a rote manner to make sense of his record.

When choosing manipulative materials, you need to keep in mind the need for varied exemplars. It has already been noted that children look for commonalities among their contacts with an idea or an algorithm, and as they come to understand, they pull out or abstract the common characteristics among their experiences. Therefore, children need experiences in which all perceptual stimuli are varied except those which are essential to the mathematical idea or procedure. A cardboard place-value chart may be of great value, but it should not be the only exemplar you use for abstracting and schematizing activities concerned with numeration. Other exemplars made with juice cans or wooden boxes should also be used. Similarly, at the symbolic level you need to take care to vary the examples. In a subtraction example like $42 - 17 = ?$, a child may conclude that the five units in the answer is simply the result of finding the difference between the two and the seven. Examples must be varied so that such characteristics are not common among the examples under study.

Whenever possible choose an activity for which a procedure with manipulatives *can* be recorded step-by-step as the desired computational procedure. Sometimes even the manipulatives can be arranged in relation to one another just

---

[7] Daphne Kerslake, *Fractions: Children's Strategies and Errors* (Windsor, Berkshire: The NFER-NELSON Publishing Company Ltd., 1986), p. 87.

as digits are placed when computing. This is true for some of the activities suggested in Chapter 5 for whole number algorithms. For such procedures sticks (singles and bundles), base ten blocks and place value charts are usually used. For algorithms with fractions, especially unlike fractions, it is not always possible to demonstrate each step with manipulatives. The procedure must often be developed by reasoning with mathematical ideas. Manipulatives are then used to verify the result itself.

It is important that the use of manipulatives be natural for the child. They are not helpful when the mathematical tasks are artificial or require a child to perceive and process spatial data beyond his ability.[8]

Using Calculators and Computers

Those who expect to see calculators used increasingly for routine calculations believe students should be encouraged "to perform computation without the calculator if the problem is more efficiently completed that way."[9] If children are to be able to judge the most efficient procedure in a given situation, they will need to know how to use a calculator and also how to do paper-and-pencil calculations. The National Council of Teachers of Mathematics, while recommending that mathematics programs "take full advantage of the power of calculators," also recognizes that "a significant portion of instruction in the early grades must be devoted to the direct acquisition of number concepts and skills without the use of calculators."[10] However, a calculator is not simply an alternative to paper-and-pencil procedures; it can help children *learn* those procedures.

A calculator can be used to reinforce underlying concepts and procedures—especially numeration concepts.[11] It can also be used to focus on one step in an algorithm: for example, placement of partial products in multiplication or estimating quotients in division.[12] Calculators can be used to provide immediate feedback when children practice the basic facts of arithmetic. They can be used to check answers when children compute with paper and pencil. A calculator has many uses but its limitations must also be demonstrated. For example, it takes more time to multiply by a power of ten on a calculator than to perform the multiplication mentally.

Quality computer software for instruction in mathematics is becoming increasingly available. As far as computation is concerned, computer programs should be carefully selected whenever the computer is the best medium available for a particular phase of instruction. When a paper-and-pencil skill is being taught,

---

[8] See Hendrik Radatz, "Error Analysis in Mathematics Education," *Journal for Research in Mathematics Education* 10, no. 3 (May 1979): 165.

[9] Thomas P. Carpenter et al., "Calculators in Testing Situations: Results and Implications from National Assessment," *The Arithmetic Teacher* 28, no. 5 (January 1981): 37.

[10] *An Agenda for Action: Recommendations for School Mathematics of the 1980s* (Reston, Virginia: National Council of Teachers of Mathematics, 1980), p. 8.

[11] See the game "Wipe Out" in Wallace Judd, "Instructional Games with Calculators," *The Arithmetic Teacher* 23, no. 7 (November 1976): 516.

[12] See the game "Check It" in Earl Ockenga, "Calculator Ideas for the Junior High Classroom," *The Arithmetic Teacher* 23, no. 7 (November 1976): 519.

students will need to use paper-and-pencil during much of the instructional process. However, computer programs may assist with mastery of basic facts, skill in estimating, and use of learned computational procedures in problem-solving settings. From time to time, talk to children while they work at the computer; have them explain what they are doing and why specific choices are made.

Understanding Numeration

Probably the chief reason children have difficulty with algorithms for whole number operations is that they do not have an adequate understanding of multi-digit numerals at the time they are introduced to the algorithms. Frequently, remediation of difficulties with computation is best accomplished by focusing upon the meaning of multi-digit numerals rather than upon the processes of computation.

Understanding our Hindu-Arabic numerals is *not* just "knowing place value." The concept of place value is important, but it is but one of many ideas children need to know if they are to understand multi-digit numerals and learn computational procedures readily. Consider this content objective: "A multi-digit numeral names a number which is the *sum* of the products of each digit's face value and place value."[13] The terms used in this definition alert us to a number of ideas which are chained together in a functional understanding of multi-digit numerals.

In order to understand multi-digit numerals, a child must first have some understanding of the operations of addition and multiplication. A child must also be able to distinguish between a digit and the complete numeral. An understanding of a digit's face value involves the cardinality of the numbers zero through nine. The idea of place value involves the assignment of a value to each position within a multi-digit numeral; that is, each place within the numeral is assigned a power of ten. We, therefore, identify and name the tens place and the thousands place. This rather specific association of value with place is independent of whatever digit may happen to occupy the position within a given numeral.

Usually, children having difficulty can identify and name place values, but they cannot get the next step. They have not learned to combine the concepts of face value and place value. It is the *product* of a digit's face value and its place value, sometimes called "total value of the digit" or "product value," which must be used. The sum of such products is the value of the numeral, and, in renaming a number, these products of face value and place value must continually be considered.

Ginsburg observes that "It takes several years for children to master the place value system for writing numbers."[14] In fact, in the very first of the three stages he proposes with reference to a child's understanding of numerals, the child can already write the numeral correctly. However, the child cannot explain why it is written that way.[15]

---

[13] Robert B. Ashlock, et. al., *Guiding Each Child's Learning of Mathematics* (Columbus, Ohio: Merrill Publishing Company, 1983), p. 482.

[14] Herbert Ginsberg, *Children's Arithmetic: The Learning Process* (New York: D. Van Nostrand Company, 1977), p. 81.

[15] *Ibid.*, pp. 85–89.

When teaching children our numeration system, we should introduce numerals as a written record of observations made while looking at or manipulating objects. For multi-digit numerals, these observations frequently follow manipulating the materials according to accepted rules in order to obtain the fewest pieces of wood (or the like), and, thereby, representations for the standard or simplest name for a number are obtained.

In all activities where children associate a numeral with materials, it is important that they have opportunities to go both ways. Children may be given materials to sort, regroup, trade, etc., and then they record the numeral that shows how much is observed. At the same time, children need to be given multi-digit numerals to interpret by constructing a set of materials which shows how much the numeral means. The ability of a child to go from objects to symbol and also from symbol to objects is an important indicator that the child is coming to understand the meaning of multi-digit numerals.

There are many aids available for numeration instruction, most of which are also used for demonstrating computational procedures. If teachers consider these aids carefully, they will recognize that it is possible for some aids to be used with little or no understanding of concepts such as face value, place value, and product value. Frequently, children merely learn complex mechanical procedures for getting answers.

Involve children with materials that make clear the equivalence of one object with many objects of a different value: e.g., bundling sticks or base blocks. Later, use aids in which many objects are traded for a single object that is identical except for placement: e.g., sticks in place value cans, or trading activities with chips of one color. These aids are necessary because they more accurately picture the way digits are used in multi-digit numerals.

Mastery of Basic Facts

A problem encountered frequently when helping a child learn to compute is the child's inability to recall the basic facts of arithmetic without resorting to an inefficient procedure. The *basic facts* of arithmetic are the simple, closed number sentences we use when we compute. These number sentences involve two one-digit addends if they are basic addition or subtraction facts, or two one-digit factors if they are basic multiplication or division facts. They are sometimes called the "primary facts." Examples of the basic facts of arithmetic include the following:

$$6 + 7 = 13 \qquad 12 - 8 = 4 \qquad 3 \times 5 = 15 \qquad 27 \div 9 = 3$$

Mastery of the basic facts of arithmetic is the ability to supply missing sums, addends, products, and factors for basic facts promptly and without hesitation. The child who has mastered the basic fact "6 + 8 = 14" will, when presented with "6 + 8 = ? ," simply recall "14" without counting or figuring it out. When a child is learning how to find the product of any two whole number factors (such as "36 × 457") by using one of the appropriate computation procedures, any lack of mastery of the basic multiplication facts results in the child using time-consuming and distracting ways of finding needed basic products. As a result, the child's attention is drawn from the larger task of thinking through the compu- tational procedure for multiplication. The child is often uncertain about where she is in the process and frequently proceeds at random, having lost her way. If a child is to use arithmetic to solve quantitative problems, it is important that the basic facts of arithmetic be mastered.

To say that mastery is important should not imply that it is necessarily easy. Consider the child who is in need of remedial instruction. In all probability this child has already met considerable failure in learning to compute and regards the whole matter with notable anxiety. Biggs has observed that "In arithmetic and mathematics, the inhibition produced by anxiety appears to swamp any motivating effect, particularly where the children concerned are already anxious; or to put it another way, anxiety appears to be more easily aroused in learning mathematics than it is in other subjects."[16]

If the child has not mastered the basic facts of arithmetic, the child probably persists in using counting or elaborate procedures for finding the needed numbers. The child may seem to understand the operations on whole numbers in terms of joining disjoint sets, repeated additions, etc., yet continues to require the security of counting or other time-consuming procedures. Baroody recommends that di- agnosis *begin* with a careful look at such informal procedures.[17]

A child using counting probably does not feel confident simply to recall the number. If the child practices computing, he will only reinforce his use of less- than-adequate procedures. The danger of extensive practice has been noted when the processes being practiced are developmental ones rather than the efficient practices desired. What is needed is practice *recalling* the number.

How then can you provide instructional activities that create an environment in which a child feels secure enough to try recalling missing numbers? Games provide the safest environment for simple recall, for when playing games, some- one has to lose. Where the teacher always seems to want "the right answer," in a game it is acceptable to lose at least part of the time. The competition in a game encourages a child to use the least time-consuming procedure and to try simply recalling needed numbers. Further, games often make possible greater attending behavior by a child because of the materials involved in the game itself. For example, a child who rejects a paper-and-pencil problem such as "6 + 5 = ?" because it is a reminder of failure and unpleasantness may attend with interest when the same problem is presented with numerals painted on brightly colored cubes which can be moved about.

Obviously, what is intended is *not* the kind of arithmetic game modeled after an old-fashioned spelling bee designed to eliminate the less able children. Nor is it a game designed to put a child under pressure in front of a large group of peers. The best games will be games involving only a few children, preferably children of rather comparable ability. (If children are not of comparable ability,

---

[16] John Biggs, "The Psychopathology of Arithmetic," in *New Approaches to Mathematics Teach- ing,* F. W. Land, ed. (London: Macmillan & Co., 1963). p. 59.

[17] Arthur J. Baroody, "Children's Difficulties in Subtraction: Some Causes and Cures," *The Arithmetic Teacher* 32 (November 1984): 14–19.

FIGURE 5

some may need to be given handicap points.) In such games a child can feel
secure enough to try simple recall. Games which provide immediate or early
verification should be chosen. The child should learn as soon as possible if he
did indeed recall correctly. Many commercial games are available, but games can
be made up using materials already in the classroom or simple homemade materials.[18] Children are quite capable of making up games and altering the rules
of games to suit their own fancy when they are encouraged to do so. For example,
a homemade game using mathematical balances would provide immediate verification for each child's response (see Figure 5).

When working privately with a child who is very insecure and insists on
continuing to use elaborate procedures for "figuring out" basic facts, it may help
to change the ground rules and dismiss "getting the correct answers." Try letting
the child say the first number thought of after hearing or seeing the problem.
Chances are the answer will be correct many times and you can show considerable
surprise that the child "pulled the correct answer right out of her head." In such
a setting, some children have been helped to practice recalling where they did
not feel able to recall before.

Games are also useful for skill retention once the basic facts are mastered.
Research using the games MULTIG and DIVTIG suggests that relatively infre-
quent use of games can maintain skill with basic facts.[19]

[18] For guidelines see Robert B. Ashlock and Carolynn A. Washbon, "Games: Practice Activities for the Basic Facts," in Marilyn N. Suydam and Robert E. Reys, eds., *Developing Computational Skills: 1978 Yearbook* (Reston, Virginia: National Council of Teachers of Mathematics, 1978),
pp. 39–50.

[19] George W. Bright, John G. Harvey and Margariete M. Wheeler, "Using Games to Maintain
Multiplication Basic Facts," *Journal for Research in Mathematics Education* 11, no. 5 (November 1980):
379–85.

Do not infer from what has been said about mastery as a goal and the use of games that children should merely be given number sentences with missing numbers and expected to "memorize their facts." Games provide reinforcement which must *follow* developmental instruction. Children who have not mastered the basic facts may not have actually received the instruction that is needed. Before mastery activities are provided, children need to be taught efficient thinking strategies, and more mature ways to determine the missing number. In a very useful yearbook chapter, Rathmell describes strategies at several different levels of maturity.[20] For addition he lists: counting on, one more or one less than a known fact, and compensation to make a known fact. For multiplication he includes: skip counting, repeated addition, one more set, twice as much as a known fact, facts of five, and patterns. It is also true that teaching distribution of multiplication over addition (multiplying "in parts") can help children proceed independently when solving untaught or forgotten multiplication combinations. By teaching such thinking strategies we help a child see relationships. Thereby, the child is able to use what he already knows as he tries to recall the missing number.

Alternative Algorithms

One remedial approach involves the use of a *variety* of computational procedures. If you are really willing to accept the idea that there are many legitimate ways to subtract, divide, and so on, you may choose to introduce a child having difficulty to an algorithm which is fresh and new. By so doing, you may circumvent the mind set of failure which beleaguers the child. But if you are convinced that there is really only one "right" way to subtract or divide, you will have no heart for introducing alternative computational procedures. When the immediate need of the child is for successful experience in mathmatics, the use of alternative algorithms holds promise, but you should first face yourself squarely and make sure you can heartily endorse such computational procedures as having value in themselves apart from any "right" way of computing. If you believe you are leading the child to an inferior technique, the child will sense your feeling.

An important question arises when you decide to show a child an alternate computational procedure, for many of the algorithms which have been employed through the centuries have been used much as you would use a machine—without knowledge of why the procedure produces the correct result. Indeed, many of the algorithms of historical interest are quite difficult to explain mathematically. As you will see, some of the alternatives available can be shown to make sense, but, in your work with an unsuccessful child, many of the alternatives will be learned only as a machine to use when a result is needed. The difficult question remains, Do you present only algorithms which are likely to make sense to a child, or do you sometimes try to teach a child how to use a machine.

---

[20] Edward C. Rathmell, "Using Thinking Strategies to Teach the Basic Facts" in Marilyn N. Suydam and Robert E. Reys, eds., *Developing Computational Skills: 1978 Yearbook* (Reston, Virginia: National Council of Teachers of Mathematics, 1978), pp. 13–38.

I am convinced of the need to teach computation procedures which make sense to a child. In view of the evidence reported in our research literature, any other conviction would hardly be warranted. Meaningful instruction is needed not just for the able child, but also for the slow-learning child. At the same time, remember that when planning remedial instruction you are sometimes dealing with a child who has known much failure and who will not really attend to instruction similar to past unhappy experiences. In order to secure the interest and attention of such a child, very different instructional procedures are needed. Further, it may be that the *most* important need for the child is to get a *correct* answer, to experience success. In view of these considerations, there are times when a computational procedure *which is fresh and new to the child* can be taught as a machine to use whenever a result is needed. If the child learns and remembers the procedure, the needed success experience has been provided. If the child does not, then the procedure can be set aside much as you would set aside anything else you try and do not like. Interestingly, alternative algorithms have always been explored unhesitatingly as enrichment or recreational activity.

What are some of the algorithms which can be used as alternatives when working remedially with a child? A few examples are described below, and others will be found in the literature of mathematics education and recreation. For example, see Pearson's article on pre-1900 algorithms.[21]

Some of the algorithms below are low-stress algorithms. When working with children who are having difficulty learning to compute you may find that low-stress algorithms are learned more readily than other alternatives. Like other algorithms, they can often be taught as sensible records of manipulations with sticks, blocks, or number rods. The advantage of low-stress algorithms is that they separate fact recall from regrouping and thereby place fewer memory demands on the child who is computing.

Addition of Whole Numbers: The Tens Method.[22]

In this low-stress algorithm the columns can be added downward or upward. Beginning at the top right in the example shown, 8 plus 5 equals 13, which can be renamed as 1 ten and 3 ones. A line is drawn through the 5 to show that it was the last digit used in obtaining ten. The ten does not need to be held in mind because the line represents it for us. Now, with the 3 which was left over, add

---

[21] Eleanor S. Pearson, "Summing It All Up: Pre-1900 Algorithms," *The Arithmetic Teacher* 33 (March 1986): 38–41.

[22] Elbert Fulkerson, "Adding by Tens," *The Arithmetic Teacher* 10 (March 1963): 139–40.

until another ten is obtained. In this case 3 plus 9 equals 12, which can be renamed as 1 ten plus 2. Another line is drawn (through the 9) to indicate another ten. The sum of the 2 left over and 6 is 8, which is recorded as the unit's digit at the bottom of the column.

The two lines which are drawn in the units column represent 2 tens, and addition begins in the tens column by adding these 2 tens to the 6 tens and continuing until there is a sum greater than 10 tens; 2 tens plus 6 tens plus 9 tens equals 17 tens. A line is drawn through the 9 to represent 10 tens, and 7 tens remain. As we proceed, 7 plus 0 plus 8 equals 15; a line is drawn through the 8, and the 5 is recorded as the tens digit at the bottom.

In the tens column, each line represents 10 tens or 1 hundred. It is noted that there are two such lines, so 2 hundreds are added to the 4 hundreds in the next column; and addition proceeds similarly.

Addition of Whole Numbers: Hutchings's Low-Stress Method.[23] This procedure is similar to the first method illustrated, except the written record is more complete in this procedure and even less remembering is required.

As illustrated in examples A and B, sums for basic facts are written with small digits to the left and to the right instead of in the usual manner.

When a column is added, the 1 ten is ignored and the one's digit is added to the next number. In example C, $5 + 9 = 14$, $4 + 8 = 12$, $2 + 4 = 6$, and $6 + 7 = 13$. The remaining 3 ones are recorded in the answer. The 3 tens are counted and also recorded. Multi-column addition proceeds similarly, except the number of tens counted is recorded at the top of the next column.

Many of the children for whom regrouping in addition is difficult find this alternative algorithm rather easy to learn. It often brings success quickly, even with large examples. Other children, especially those with perceptual problems,

---

[23] Barton Hutchings, "Low-Stress Algorithms," *Measurement in School Mathematics*, 1976 Yearbook of the National Council of Teachers of Mathematics (Washington, D.C.: NCTM, 1976), pp. 218–39.

may be confused by the abundance of crutches. This is especially true when it is not possible to write examples with large digits, which is the case with most published achievement tests.

Subtraction of Whole Numbers: Hutchings's Low-Stress Method.[24]

A.
$$\begin{array}{r} 4352 \\ -\ 1826 \\ \hline \end{array}$$

B.
$$\begin{array}{r} 4352 \\ 4'2 \\ -1826 \\ \hline \end{array}$$

C.
$$\begin{array}{r} 4352 \\ 3'3\ 4'2 \\ -1826 \\ \hline \end{array}$$

D.
$$\begin{array}{r} 4352 \\ 3'3\ 4'2 \\ -1826 \\ \hline 2526 \end{array}$$

This algorithm has been shown to be an especially effective procedure for remedial use. Note that the minuend (sum) is renamed and written between the minuend and the subtrahend. In the renamed minuend, 1 ten of ones (or tens or hundreds) is written with a half-space unit's digit. All renaming is completed before subtraction facts are recalled. When zeroes occur in the minuend, they are "skipped over." Then a nine is written in each empty place.

E.
$$\begin{array}{r} 5\ 0\ 0\ 4 \\ 4\qquad\ '4 \\ -3\ 1\ 2\ 8 \\ \hline \end{array}$$

F.
$$\begin{array}{r} 5\ 0\ 0\ 4 \\ 4\ 9\ 9\ '4 \\ -3\ 1\ 2\ 8 \\ \hline 1\ 8\ 7\ 6 \end{array}$$

Subtraction of Whole Numbers: The Equal Additions Method.

A.
$$\begin{array}{r} 45\overset{\downarrow}{\overset{\prime}{3}} \\ -1_{\,8}\cancel{8} \\ \hline 5 \end{array}$$

B.
$$\begin{array}{r} \overset{\downarrow}{\ }\ \overset{\downarrow}{\ } \\ 4\overset{\prime}{5}\overset{\prime}{3} \\ {}_{2}\cancel{1}_{8}\cancel{8} \\ \hline 275 \end{array}$$

---

[24] Barton Hutchings, "Low-Stress Subtraction," *The Arithmetic Teacher* 22 (March 1975): 226–32.

The principle of compensation is applied: when equal quantities are added to both the minuend and the subtrahend, the difference remains the same. In this computation, ten is added to the sum, i.e., to the three in the ones place. To compensate for this addition, ten is also added to the known addend; the seven in the tens place is replaced with an eight. Similarly, 1 hundred is added to the sum, i.e., the five in the tens place becomes a fifteen. To compensate, one hundred is added to the known addend; the one in the hundreds place is replaced with a two.

Multiplication of Whole Numbers: The Lattice Method.

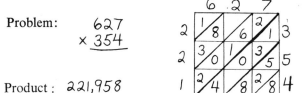

Problem: 627
        × 354

Product: 221,958

The two factors are written above and to the right of a grid. The products of basic multiplication facts are recorded within the grid, and addition proceeds from lower right to upper left within the diagonal lines. The final product is read at the left and at the bottom of the grid.

Multiplication of Whole Numbers: Hutchings's Low-Stress Method.[25]

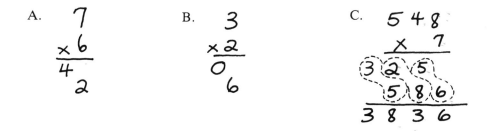

This method is related to the lattice method. However, place value columns in the partial products are vertical instead of diagonal because a special notation is used. As illustrated in examples A and B, the unit's digit is dropped one row. If there are no tens, as in example B, a zero is written.

As Hutchings notes, there are advantages to proceeding from left-to-right with this algorithm. But the computation may be easier for you to follow if performed from right-to-left, at least with a one-digit multiplier. In example C,

[25] Barton Hutchings, "Low-Stress Algorithms," *Measurement in School Mathematics*, 1976 Yearbook of the National Council of Teachers of Mathematics (Washington, D.C.: NCTM, 1976), pp. 218–39.

$7 \times 8 = 56$ and 7×4 tens $= 28$ tens. When writing the 28 tens, the 8 tens is recorded below the 5 tens

As with Hutchings's other algorithms, neat work must be stressed. Some teachers find it helpful to use squared paper at first, or at least lined paper turned 90°.

Division of Whole Numbers: The Doubling Method.[26]

Problem: $290 \div 8 = ?$

Quotient: $36\,r2$

$$8 \times 1 = 8$$
$$8 \times 2 = 16$$
$$8 \times 4 = 32$$
$$8 \times 8 = 64$$
$$8 \times 16 = 128$$
$$8 \times 32 = 256$$

$$
\begin{array}{r}
290 \\
-256 \leftarrow 32 \\
\hline
34 \\
-32 \leftarrow 4 \\
\hline
2 \qquad 36
\end{array}
$$

The divisor is doubled until the next double would be larger than the dividend, thereby determing the largest partial quotient. Smaller partial quotients are determined for the part of the dividend remaining. Finally, the partial quotients are added to determine the quotient.

Subtraction of Rational Numbers: The Equal Additions Method.[27]

Problem:

$$
\begin{array}{r}
7\frac{1}{4} \\
-3\frac{3}{4} \\
\hline
\end{array}
\quad
\begin{array}{l}
\text{add one } \left(\frac{4}{4}\right) \longrightarrow \\
\text{add one } (1) \longrightarrow
\end{array}
\quad
\begin{array}{r}
7\frac{5}{4} \\
-4\frac{3}{4} \\
\hline
3\frac{2}{4}
\end{array}
$$

Difference: $3\frac{1}{2}$

The principle of compensation is applied. One is added to both the minuend and the subtrahend in order to subtract easily.

---

[26] C. Alan Riedesel, *Guiding Discovery in Elementary School Mathematics* (New York: Appleton-Century-Crofts, 1967), pp. 199–200.

[27] Barbara Signer, "The Method of Equal Addition . . . It's Rational!!" *Dimensions in Mathematics* 5 (Winter 1985): 15–17.

Guidelines for Instruction

Teachers have found the following guidelines to be helpful. They provide a summary of principles to keep in mind when instructing children who are having difficulty learning to compute.

Focus on the Child.

1. *Personalize instruction.* Even when children meet in groups for instruction, individuals must be assessed and corrective programs must be planned for *individuals.* Some individual tutoring may be required.

2. *Protect and strengthen the child's self-image.* A child who has met repeated failure needs to believe that he is a valued person and is capable of eventually acquiring the needed skill. This does not mean that instruction should be avoided. On the contrary, as Ginsburg notes, "In some cases, helping children to improve their schoolwork may do more for their emotional health than well-meaning attempts to analyze and treat their emotional disturbances directly."[28] But remember that if children are to learn, they need a safe environment in which they are perceived as capable of learning.

3. *Make sure the child has the goals of instruction clearly in mind.* Take care to ensure that the behavior that is needed on the child's part is known, for the child needs to know the direction instruction is heading. He needs to know where it will head eventually ("I'll be able to subtract and get the right answers"), but also, where it is headed immediately ("I'll soon be able to rename a number many different ways").

4. *Encourage self-appraisal by the child.* From the beginning, involve him in the evaluation process. Let the child help set the goals of instruction.

5. *Assure consistent expectations.* Make sure that you and the child's parents have the same expectations in regard to what the child will accomplish. People in the United States tend to assume that difficulties with learning result from a lack of ability; in many other countries, they are more likely to assume that difficulties are a result of insufficient effort. Be sure that you and the child's parents are together in regard to such expectations.

6. *Provide the child with a means to observe any progress.* Charts and graphs kept by the child often serve this function.

---

[28] Herbert Ginsberg, *Children's Arithmetic: The Learning Process.* (New York: D. Van Nostrand Company, 1977), p. 197.

Teach Concepts and Skills.

7. *Build on underlying concepts and procedures the child knows.* Corrective instruction should build on a child's strengths; it should consider what the child is ready to learn. Typically, children need a thorough understanding of subordinate mathematical concepts before they can be expected to integrate them into more complex ideas.

8. *Emphasize ideas that help the child organize what he learns.* Children often assume that the concept or procedure they learn applies only to the specific task they are involved in at the time. Tie new learnings in with what a child already knows. When so organized, new learnings can be more easily retrieved from a child's memory as the need arises; also, they can be more readily applied in new contexts. Stress ideas such as multiple names for a number, commutativity, identity elements, and inverse relations.

9. *Stress the ability to estimate.* A child who makes errors in computation will become more accurate with the ability to determine the reasonableness of answers.

10. *Emphasize careful penmanship and proper alignment of digits.* A child must be able to read the work and tell the value assigned to each place where a digit is written. Columns can also be labeled if appropriate.

Provide Instruction.

11. *Base instruction on your diagnosis.* Take into account the patterns you observed while collecting data. What strengths can you build upon?

12. *Choose instructional procedures that differ from the way the child was previously taught.* The old procedures are often associated with fear and failure by the child; something new is needed.

13. *Use a great variety of instructional procedures and activities.* Variety is necessary for adequate concept development. A child forms an idea or concept from many experiences embodying that idea; the child perceives the concept as that which is common to all of the varied experiences.

14. *Encourage the child to "think outloud" while working through a problem situation.* Have the child show how and explain why certain materials and procedures are being used. Speaking outloud often enables a child to focus more completely on the task at hand.[29]

---

[29] Brenda H. Manning, "A Self-Communication Structure for Learning Mathematics," *School Science and Mathematics* 84 (January 1984): 43–51.

15. *Let the child state his understanding of a concept in his own language.* Do not always require the terminology of textbooks. It may be appropriate to say, for example, "Mathematicians have a special name for that idea, but I rather like your name for it!"

16. *Structure instruction in a sequence of small steps for children having difficulty learning.* A large task may overwhelm a child. However, when instruction is based upon a carefully determined sequence of smaller steps that lead to the larger task, the child can focus on more immediately attainable goals. A child can also be helped to see that the immediate goals lead along a path going in the desired direction.

17. *Move toward symbols gradually.* Move from manipulatives to two-dimensional representations and visualizations to the use of symbols. Carefully raise the level of the child's thinking.

Use Concrete Materials.

18. *Let the child choose from materials available.* Whenever possible, the child should be permitted to select a game or activity from materials which are available and which lead toward the goals of instruction. Identify activities for which the child has needed prerequisite skills and which lead to the goals of instruction; then let the child have some choice in deciding what he will do.

19. *Encourage a child to use aids as long as they are of value.* Peer group pressure often keeps a child from using an aid even when the teacher places such aids on a table. The use of aids needs to be encouraged actively. At times a child needs to be encouraged to try thinking a process through with just paper and pencil, but by and large children give up aids when they feel safe without them. After all, the use of aids is time-consuming.

Provide Practice.

20. *Make sure the child understands the process before assigning practice.* We have known for some time that, in general, drill reinforces and makes more efficient that which a child *actually* practices.[30] In other words, if a child counts on his fingers to find a sum, drill will only tend to help him count on his fingers more efficiently. The child may find sums more quickly, but he is apt to continue any immature procedure he is using. You stand forewarned against the use of extensive practice activities at a time when they merely reinforce processes which are

---

[30] See William A. Brownell and Charlotte B. Chazel, "The Effects of Premature Drill in Third Grade Arithmetic," *The Journal of Educational Research* 29 (September 1935): 17–28ff: also in Robert B. Ashlock and Wayne L. Herman, Jr., *Current Research in Elementary School Mathematics* (New York: The Macmillan Co., 1970), pp. 170–88.

developmental. Drill for mastery should come when the actual process being practiced is an efficient process. Admittedly, it is not always easy to determine what process is actually being practiced. By looking for patterns of error and by conducting data-gathering interviews in an atmosphere in which a child's failures are accepted, you can usually learn enough to decide if a child is ready for more extensive practice.

21. *Select practice activities which provide immediate confirmation.* When looking for games and drill activities to strengthen skills, choose those activities which let the child know immediately if the answer is correct. Many games, manipulative devices, programmed materials, and teacher-made devices provide such reinforcement.

22. *Spread practice time over several short periods.* A given amount of time spent in drill activities is usually more fruitful if distributed over short periods. A short series of examples (perhaps five to eight) is usually adequate to observe any error pattern. Longer series tend to reinforce erroneous procedures. If a correct procedure *is* being used, then frequent practice with a limited number of examples is more fruitful than occasional practice with a large number of examples.

Later, in Chapter 5, you will read about many specific ideas for remedial instruction. For additional ideas, examine the lists of references after Chapter 5.

Chapter 3

Identifying
Error Patterns
in Computation

Remedial or corrective instruction should be based upon sufficient data to suggest patterns of incorrect and immature procedures. As a teacher of elementary school mathematics, you need to be alert to error patterns in computation. On the following pages you will find examples of the written work of boys and girls who are having difficulty with some phase of computation. With these simulated children's papers you have the opportunity to develop your own skill in identifying error patterns. However, these are more than simulated papers, for these papers contain the error patterns of real boys and girls, error patterns observed by my colleagues and me among children in regular elementary school classrooms. These are the children who may be in your own classroom.

As you examine each paper, look for a pattern of error; then check your findings by using the error pattern yourself with the examples provided. In other parts of this book you will learn if your observations are accurate and you will get feedback on your own suggestions for corrective instruction.

Be careful not to decide on the error pattern too quickly. (Children often make hasty decisions and, as a result, adopt the kind of erroneous procedures presented in this book.) When you think you see the pattern, verify your hypothesis by looking at the other examples on the child's paper.

If this book is to help you with your teaching of elementary school mathematics, you will need to "play the game." Take time to try out the error pattern before turning on to another part of the book. Write out brief descriptions of instructional activities before moving ahead to see what suggestions are recorded later. Do not be content just to read about patterns of error; as a teacher you also learn by *doing*. Take time to respond in writing in the designated places.

Additional children's papers and a key are provided in Appendix A, where you can test your ability to identify error patterns. As the tendency for children to adopt such patterns applies to more than arithmetical computation, you may also want to study Appendix B where error patterns from other areas of mathematics are presented.

Error Pattern A-W-1

Examine Mike's work carefully. Can you find the error pattern he has followed?

Name _Mike_

A.   74   B.   35   C.   67   D.   56
   + 56   + 92   + 18   + 97
   ─────   ─────   ─────   ─────
   1210   127   715   1413

Have you found the error pattern? Check yourself by using the error pattern to compute these examples.

E.   43   F.   88
   + 65   + 39
   ─────   ─────

Next, turn to pattern A-W-1 on page 80 to see if you were able to identify the error pattern. Why might Mike or any student use such an erroneous computational procedure?

Error Pattern A-W-2

What error pattern is Mary following in her written work?

Name _Mary_

A.
$$\begin{array}{r} 43\overset{1}{2} \\ +265 \\ \hline 697 \end{array}$$

B.
$$\begin{array}{r} 7\overset{1}{4} \\ +43 \\ \hline 18 \end{array}$$

C.
$$\begin{array}{r} 38\overset{4}{5} \\ +667 \\ \hline 9116 \end{array}$$

D.
$$\begin{array}{r} 5\overset{\circ}{6}\overset{\circ}{3} \\ +545 \\ \hline 118 \end{array}$$

Check to see if you found Mary's pattern by using her erroneous procedure to compute these examples.

E.
$$\begin{array}{r} 254 \\ +535 \\ \hline \end{array}$$

F.
$$\begin{array}{r} 618 \\ +782 \\ \hline \end{array}$$

Next, turn to page 81 to see if you were able to identify Mary's error pattern. Why might Mary or any child use such a procedure?

Error Pattern A-W-3

Carol gets some correct answers, but she seems to miss many of the easiest examples. See if you can find her error pattern.

Name _Carol_

A.
$$\begin{array}{r} 46 \\ +\ 3 \\ \hline 13 \end{array}$$

B.
$$\begin{array}{r} 18 \\ +30 \\ \hline 48 \end{array}$$

C.
$$\begin{array}{r} 8 \\ +16 \\ \hline 15 \end{array}$$

D.
$$\begin{array}{r} 42 \\ +56 \\ \hline 98 \end{array}$$

E.
$$\begin{array}{r} 85 \\ +\ 6 \\ \hline 19 \end{array}$$

Use Carol's procedure for these examples to make sure you have found her error pattern.

F.
$$\begin{array}{r} 26 \\ +\ 3 \\ \hline \end{array}$$

G.
$$\begin{array}{r} 60 \\ +24 \\ \hline \end{array}$$

H.
$$\begin{array}{r} 74 \\ +\ 5 \\ \hline \end{array}$$

When you have completed examples F, G, and H, turn to page 82. Why might Carol be using such a procedure?

Error Pattern A-W-4

Can you find Dorothy's pattern of errors?

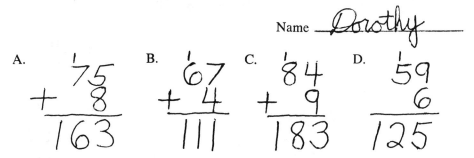

Name Dorothy

A.
$$\begin{array}{r} \overset{1}{75} \\ +8 \\ \hline 163 \end{array}$$

B.
$$\begin{array}{r} \overset{1}{67} \\ +4 \\ \hline 111 \end{array}$$

C.
$$\begin{array}{r} \overset{1}{84} \\ +9 \\ \hline 183 \end{array}$$

D.
$$\begin{array}{r} \overset{1}{59} \\ 6 \\ \hline 125 \end{array}$$

Did you find the pattern? Make sure by using the error pattern to compute these examples.

E.
$$\begin{array}{r} 46 \\ +8 \\ \hline \end{array}$$

F.
$$\begin{array}{r} 98 \\ +3 \\ \hline \end{array}$$

When you have completed examples E and F, turn to page 82 and see if you identified the pattern correctly. Why might Dorothy be using such a procedure?

Children can be observed using other error patterns while adding whole numbers. Practice your own diagnostic skills by identifying the patterns shown in Appendix A.

Error Pattern S-W-1

Look carefully at Cheryl's written work. What error pattern has she followed? (Note: Cheryl used a different procedure for one of the examples.)

Name *Cheryl*

A.
$$\begin{array}{r} 32 \\ -16 \\ \hline 16 \end{array}$$

B.
$$\begin{array}{r} 245 \\ -137 \\ \hline 112 \end{array}$$

C.
$$\begin{array}{r} 524 \\ -298 \\ \hline 374 \end{array}$$

D.
$$\begin{array}{r} 135 \\ -67 \\ \hline 132 \end{array}$$

If you have found the error pattern, check yourself by using the error pattern to compute these examples.

E.
$$\begin{array}{r} 458 \\ -372 \\ \hline \end{array}$$

F.
$$\begin{array}{r} 241 \\ -96 \\ \hline \end{array}$$

Now turn to pattern S-W-1 on page 83 to see if you were able to identify the error pattern. Why might a child use such a computational procedure?

Error Pattern S-W-2

Look over George's paper carefully. Can you find the error pattern he is using?

Name _George_

A.
$$\begin{array}{r} \overset{8}{1}\overset{1}{9}7 \\ -\ 43 \\ \hline 1414 \end{array}$$

B.
$$\begin{array}{r} \overset{6}{1}\overset{1}{7}6 \\ -\ 23 \\ \hline 1413 \end{array}$$

$$\begin{array}{r} \overset{7}{3}\overset{1}{8}4 \\ -\ 59 \\ \hline 325 \end{array}$$

Did you find the error pattern? Check yourself by using George's error pattern to compute examples D and E.

D.
$$\begin{array}{r} 273 \\ -\ 38 \\ \hline \end{array}$$

E.
$$\begin{array}{r} 285 \\ -\ 63 \\ \hline \end{array}$$

If you have completed examples D and E, turn to page 85 to learn if you have identified George's error pattern correctly. What instructional procedures might you use to help George or any other student with this problem?

Error Pattern S-W-3

Donna gets many incorrect answers when she subtracts. Can you find a pattern of errors?

Name _Donna_

A.
$$\begin{array}{r} 147 \\ -\ 20 \\ \hline 120 \end{array}$$

B.
$$\begin{array}{r} 624 \\ -\ 323 \\ \hline 301 \end{array}$$

C.
$$\begin{array}{r} 527 \\ -\ 304 \\ \hline 203 \end{array}$$

D.
$$\begin{array}{r} 805 \\ -\ 201 \\ \hline 604 \end{array}$$

Use Donna's error pattern to complete these examples.

E.
$$\begin{array}{r} 446 \\ -\ 302 \\ \hline \end{array}$$

F.
$$\begin{array}{r} 760 \\ -\ 230 \\ \hline \end{array}$$

After examples E and F are completed, turn to page 86 and see if you have actually found Donna's pattern of errors. What might have caused Donna to begin such a procedure?

Error Pattern S-W-4

Barbara seemed to be doing well with subtraction until recently. Can you find a pattern of errors in her work?

Name _Barbara_

A.
$$\begin{array}{r} \overset{8}{6}\overset{1}{9}3 \\ -\ 248 \\ \hline 445 \end{array}$$

B.
$$\begin{array}{r} \overset{2}{3}\overset{1}{2}5 \\ -\ 151 \\ \hline 174 \end{array}$$

C.
$$\begin{array}{r} \overset{5}{7}2\overset{1}{6} \\ -\ 349 \\ \hline 287 \end{array}$$

D.
$$\begin{array}{r} \overset{2}{4}3\overset{1}{4} \\ -\ 276 \\ \hline 68 \end{array}$$

To make sure you have found the pattern, use Barbara's procedure to complete these examples.

E.
$$\begin{array}{r} 436 \\ -\ 172 \\ \hline \end{array}$$

F.
$$\begin{array}{r} 625 \\ -348 \\ \hline \end{array}$$

After you complete examples E and F, turn to page 86 to see if you found Barbara's error pattern. What might have caused Barbara to begin using such a procedure?

Error Pattern S-W-5

Sam is having difficulty subtracting whole numbers. Do you find erroneous patterns in his work? He may be making more than one.

Name _Sam_

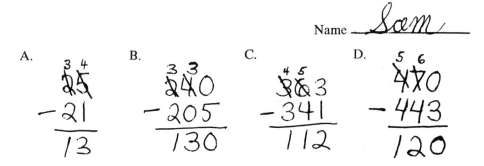

A.
$$\begin{array}{r} \overset{3}{\cancel{2}}\overset{4}{\cancel{5}} \\ -\ 21 \\ \hline 13 \end{array}$$

B.
$$\begin{array}{r} \overset{3}{\cancel{2}}\overset{3}{\cancel{4}}0 \\ -\ 205 \\ \hline 130 \end{array}$$

C.
$$\begin{array}{r} \overset{4}{\cancel{5}}\overset{5}{\cancel{6}}3 \\ -\ 341 \\ \hline 112 \end{array}$$

D.
$$\begin{array}{r} \overset{5}{\cancel{4}}\overset{6}{\cancel{7}}0 \\ -\ 443 \\ \hline 120 \end{array}$$

In order to check your findings, use Sam's error patterns to compute examples E and F.

E.
$$\begin{array}{r} 385 \\ -\ 322 \\ \hline \end{array}$$

F.
$$\begin{array}{r} 640 \\ -\ 626 \\ \hline \end{array}$$

After you complete examples E and F, turn to page 87 to see if you found Sam's procedures. How would you help Sam or any child using procedures such as these?

Children can be observed using other error patterns while subtracting whole numbers. Practice your own diagnostic skills by identifying the patterns shown in Appendix A.

Error Pattern M-W-1

Examine Bob's written work carefully. What error pattern has he adopted?

Name *Bob*

A.
$$\begin{array}{r} \overset{2}{46} \\ \times\ 24 \\ \hline 184 \\ 102 \\ \hline 1204 \end{array}$$

B.
$$\begin{array}{r} \overset{1}{76} \\ \times\ 32 \\ \hline 152 \\ 228 \\ \hline 2432 \end{array}$$

C.
$$\begin{array}{r} \overset{5}{48} \\ \times\ 57 \\ \hline 336 \\ 250 \\ \hline 2836 \end{array}$$

Were you able to identify Bob's error pattern? Check yourself by using the error pattern to compute examples D and E.

D.
$$\begin{array}{r} 98 \\ \times\ 56 \\ \hline \end{array}$$

E.
$$\begin{array}{r} 86 \\ \times\ 45 \\ \hline \end{array}$$

When you have completed examples D and E, turn to page 88 to see if you identified Bob's error pattern correctly. What instructional procedures might you use to help Bob or another student with this problem?

Error Pattern M-W-2

Many of Bill's answers are not correct. Can you find an error pattern?

Name _Bill_

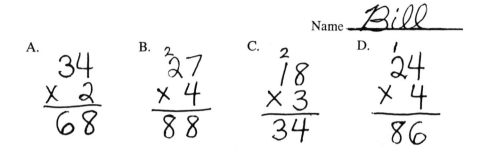

A.
$$\begin{array}{r} 34 \\ \times\ 2 \\ \hline 68 \end{array}$$

B.
$$\begin{array}{r} \overset{2}{2}7 \\ \times\ 4 \\ \hline 88 \end{array}$$

C.
$$\begin{array}{r} \overset{2}{1}8 \\ \times\ 3 \\ \hline 34 \end{array}$$

D.
$$\begin{array}{r} \overset{1}{2}4 \\ \times\ 4 \\ \hline 86 \end{array}$$

Check yourself by using the error pattern your have observed to complete examples E and F.

E.
$$\begin{array}{r} 35 \\ \times\ 3 \\ \hline \end{array}$$

F.
$$\begin{array}{r} 28 \\ \times\ 4 \\ \hline \end{array}$$

Turn to page 89 and see if you have correctly identified Bill's error pattern. How might you help Bill or other children who have adopted this procedure?

Error Pattern M-W-3

Joe's paper illustrates a common error pattern. Can you find it?

Name ___Joe___

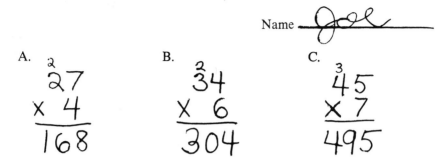

A.
$$\overset{2}{2}7$$
$$\times\ 4$$
$$\overline{168}$$

B.
$$\overset{2}{3}4$$
$$\times\ 6$$
$$\overline{304}$$

C.
$$\overset{3}{4}5$$
$$\times\ 7$$
$$\overline{495}$$

When you think you have found Joe's error pattern, use his pattern to complete these examples.

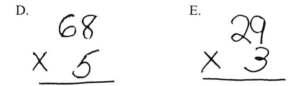

D.
$$68$$
$$\times\ 5$$
$$\overline{}$$

E.
$$\overset{}{2}9$$
$$\times\ 3$$
$$\overline{}$$

After you have finished examples D and E, turn to page 89 to see if you have correctly identified Joe's error pattern. What could possibly have caused Joe to learn such a procedure?

Error Pattern M-W-4

Doug seems to multiply correctly by a one-digit multiplier, but he is having trouble with two- and three-digit multipliers. Can you find this error pattern?

Name ___Doug___

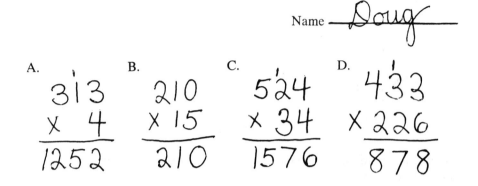

A.
$$3\overset{1}{1}3$$
$$\times\ \ 4$$
$$\overline{1252}$$

B.
$$210$$
$$\times 15$$
$$\overline{210}$$

C.
$$5\overset{1}{2}4$$
$$\times 34$$
$$\overline{1576}$$

D.
$$4\overset{1}{3}3$$
$$\times 226$$
$$\overline{878}$$

Did you find his pattern? Check yourself you using Doug's error pattern to complete examples E and F.

E.
$$621$$
$$\times 23$$

F.
$$517$$
$$\times 463$$

After examples E and F are completed, turn to page 90 to learn if you have correctly identified Doug's procedure. What remedial instruction might you initiate with Doug or any child using such a procedure?

You may observe children using other error patterns while multiplying whole numbers. Practice your own diagnostic skills by identifying the patterns shown in Appendix A.

Error Pattern D-W-1

Look very carefully at Jim's written work. What erroneous procedure has he used?

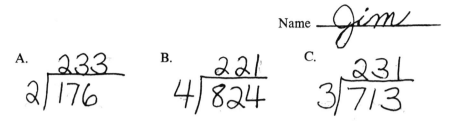

Name *Jim*

A.
$$2\overline{)176}^{\ 233}$$

B.
$$4\overline{)824}^{\ 221}$$

C.
$$3\overline{)713}^{\ 231}$$

Did you find the erroneous procedure? Check yourself by using Jim's procedure to compute examples D and E.

D.
$$3\overline{)639}$$

E.
$$4\overline{)518}$$

After completing examples D and E, turn to pattern D-W-1 on page 91 and learn if you correctly identified Jim's error pattern. What instructional procedures might you use to help Jim or any other student using this procedure?

Error Pattern D-W-2

Look carefully at Gail's written work. Can you find the error pattern she has
followed?

Name *Gail*

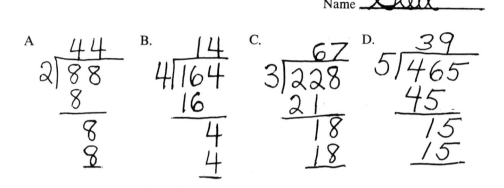

Did you find the incorrect procedure? Check yourself by using the error
pattern to compute these examples.

E.

3⟌75

F.

6⟌516

Next turn to page 92 to see if you identified the error pattern correctly. Why
might Gail or any child have adopted such an incorrect procedure?

Error Pattern D-W-3

John has been doing well with much of his work in division, but he is having difficulty now. Can you find his error pattern?

Name _John_

A.

$$7\overline{)456} \quad 65r1$$
42
36
35
1

B.

$$6\overline{)5426} \quad 94r2$$
54
26
24
2

C.

$$8\overline{)4860} \quad 67r4$$
48
60
56
4

D.

$$8\overline{)4035} \quad 54r3$$
40
35
32
3

Try John's procedure with these examples.

E.

$$9\overline{)2721}$$

F.

$$6\overline{)4250}$$

After you have completed examples E and F, turn to page 93 to learn if you have correctly identified John's error pattern. Why might John be using such a procedure?

Error Pattern D-W-4

Anita seems to have difficulty with some division problems but she solves other problems correctly. Can you find her pattern of error?

Name *Anita*

A.
$$
\begin{array}{r}
50\text{R}4 \\
5\overline{)254} \\
250 \\
\hline
4
\end{array}
$$

B.
$$
\begin{array}{r}
560\text{R}6 \\
9\overline{)4560} \\
4500 \\
\hline
60 \\
54 \\
\hline
6
\end{array}
$$

C.
$$
\begin{array}{r}
730 \\
8\overline{)5840} \\
5600 \\
\hline
240 \\
240
\end{array}
$$

D.
$$
\begin{array}{r}
370 \\
7\overline{)2149} \\
2100 \\
\hline
49 \\
49
\end{array}
$$

Did you find Anita's procedure? Check yourself by using her pattern to complete these examples.

E.

$$6\overline{)4818}$$

F.

$$7\overline{)3525}$$

When examples E and F are completed, turn to page 94 and learn if you found Anita's error pattern. How might you help Anita or any other child using such a procedure?

You may observe children using other error patterns while dividing whole numbers. Practice your own diagnostic skills by identifying the pattern shown in Appendix A.

Error Pattern E-F-1

Greg frequently makes errors when attempting to change a fraction to lower terms. What procedure is he using?

Name *Greg*

A. $\frac{19}{95} = \frac{1}{5}$

B. $\frac{13}{39} = \frac{1}{9}$

C. $\frac{18}{81} = \frac{1}{1}$

D. $\frac{12}{24} = \frac{1}{4}$

Determine if you have correctly identified Greg's error pattern by using his procedure to change examples E and F to lower terms.

E. $\frac{16}{64} =$

F. $\frac{14}{42}$

Now, turn to page 95 and see if you have identified the error pattern correctly. Why might Greg be using such an incorrect procedure?

Error Pattern E-F-2

Jill determined the simplest terms for each given fraction, some already in simplest terms and some not. What procedure did she use?

Name _Jill_

A. $\dfrac{4}{9} = \dfrac{2}{3}$ B. $\dfrac{3}{9} = \dfrac{1}{3}$ C. $\dfrac{3}{8} = \dfrac{1}{4}$ D. $\dfrac{4}{8} = \dfrac{2}{4}$

Find out if you have correctly identified Jill's procedure by using her error pattern to complete examples E and F.

E. $\dfrac{3}{4} =$ F. $\dfrac{2}{8} =$

Next, turn to page 96 where Jill's pattern is described. How might you help Jill or others using such a pattern?

Error Pattern E-F-3

Sue tried to change each fraction to lowest or simplest terms, but her results are quite unreasonable. Can you find her error pattern?

Name _Sue_

A. $\dfrac{4}{8} = \dfrac{2}{8}$ B. $\dfrac{6}{8} = \dfrac{1}{8}$ C. $\dfrac{2}{4} = \dfrac{2}{4}$

D. $\dfrac{7}{7} = \dfrac{1}{7}$ E. $\dfrac{4}{6} = \dfrac{1}{6}$ F. $\dfrac{9}{3} = \dfrac{3}{9}$

Use Sue's procedures with these fractions to learn if you have found her pattern.

G. $\dfrac{3}{6} =$ H. $\dfrac{6}{4} =$

After examples G and H are completed, turn to page 97 to see if you found Sue's error pattern. How would you help Sue or any child using such a procedure?

Error Pattern A-F-1

Can you find Robbie's pattern of error?

Name *Robbie*

A. $\dfrac{4}{5} + \dfrac{2}{3} = \dfrac{6}{8}$

B. $\dfrac{1}{4} + \dfrac{2}{3} = \dfrac{3}{7}$

C. $\dfrac{7}{8} + \dfrac{5}{6} = \dfrac{12}{14}$

D. $\dfrac{3}{7} + \dfrac{1}{2} = \dfrac{4}{9}$

Did you find the pattern? Make sure by using the pattern to compute these examples.

E. $\dfrac{3}{4} + \dfrac{1}{5} =$

F. $\dfrac{2}{3} + \dfrac{5}{6} =$

When you have completed examples E and F, turn to page 97 and see if you identified the pattern correctly. Why might Robbie be using such a procedure?

Error Pattern A-F-2

What error pattern has Dave adopted?

Name _Dave_

A.
$$6\tfrac{1}{2} = \tfrac{2}{4}$$
$$+ 7\tfrac{1}{4} = \tfrac{1}{4}$$
$$\overline{\tfrac{3}{4}}$$

B.
$$10\tfrac{5}{6} = \tfrac{5}{6}$$
$$+25\tfrac{2}{3} = \tfrac{4}{6}$$
$$\overline{\tfrac{9}{6}} = 1\tfrac{1}{2}$$

C.
$$24\tfrac{1}{2} = \tfrac{4}{8}$$
$$+ 17\tfrac{5}{8} = \tfrac{5}{8}$$
$$\overline{\tfrac{9}{8}} = 1\tfrac{1}{8}$$

Did you find Dave's error pattern? Check yourself by using the error pattern to compute examples D and E.

D.
$$9\tfrac{1}{3}$$
$$+ 5\tfrac{5}{9}$$

E.
$$16\tfrac{3}{4}$$
$$+ 23\tfrac{1}{2}$$

When you complete examples D and E, turn to page 98 and see if you have identified Dave's error pattern correctly. What instructional procedures could you use to help Dave or another student using this error pattern?

Error Pattern A-F-3

Allen is having difficulty with addition of unlike fractions. Is there a pattern of errors in his work?

Name _Allen_

A.
$$\frac{1}{4} + \frac{2}{3} = \frac{6}{7} + \frac{4}{7} = \frac{10}{7}$$

B.
$$\frac{1}{3} + \frac{3}{5} = \frac{15}{8} + \frac{3}{8} = \frac{18}{8}$$

C.
$$\frac{2}{3} + \frac{1}{2} = \frac{2}{5} + \frac{6}{5} = \frac{8}{5}$$

To find out if you have identified Allen's error pattern, use his erroneous procedure to complete these examples.

D.
$$\frac{1}{4} + \frac{1}{5} =$$

E.
$$\frac{2}{5} + \frac{1}{2} =$$

When you have completed examples D and E, turn to page 99 and see if you have actually found Allen's pattern of errors. What might have caused Allen to begin using such a senseless procedure?

Error Pattern A-F-4

Robin is also having difficulty. What is she doing?

Name _Robin_

A.
$$\frac{1}{2} = \frac{1}{4}$$
$$+\frac{1}{4} = \frac{1}{4}$$
$$\overline{\quad\quad} \;\; \frac{2}{4}$$

B.
$$\frac{2}{5} = \frac{2}{10}$$
$$+\frac{1}{2} = \frac{1}{10}$$
$$\overline{\quad\quad} \;\; \frac{3}{10}$$

C.
$$\frac{3}{5} = \frac{3}{15}$$
$$+\frac{1}{3} = \frac{1}{15}$$
$$\overline{\quad\quad} \;\; \frac{4}{15}$$

Did you determine what Robin is doing? Make sure by using her procedure to compute examples D and E.

D.
$$\frac{3}{4}$$
$$+\frac{1}{2}$$
$$\overline{\quad\quad}$$

E.
$$\frac{4}{5}$$
$$+\frac{1}{4}$$
$$\overline{\quad\quad}$$

When you have completed examples D and E, turn to page 100 and see if you identified the procedure correctly. Why might Robin have learned to compute in this way?

You may observe children using other error patterns while adding with fractions. Practice your own diagnostic skills by identifying the patterns shown in Appendix A.

Error Pattern S-F-1

Andrew did fairly well with addition of fractions and mixed numbers, but he seems to be having trouble with subtraction. Can you find a pattern or patterns in his work?

Name *Andrew*

A.
$$7\tfrac{1}{2}$$
$$-3$$
$$\overline{4\tfrac{1}{2}}$$

B.
$$8\tfrac{1}{3}$$
$$-\tfrac{2}{3}$$
$$\overline{8\tfrac{1}{3}}$$

C.
$$6$$
$$-1\tfrac{1}{4}$$
$$\overline{5\tfrac{1}{4}}$$

D.
$$3\tfrac{1}{4}$$
$$-2\tfrac{3}{4}$$
$$\overline{1\tfrac{2}{4}}$$

Make sure you have found Andrew's pattern or patterns by using his procedures to complete these examples.

E.
$$5\tfrac{1}{5}$$
$$-3\tfrac{3}{5}$$

F.
$$1$$
$$-\tfrac{1}{3}$$

When you have completed examples E and F, turn to page 101 to see if you found Andrew's procedures. Why might Andrew be using such procedures?

Error Pattern S-F-2

Don is having difficulty with subtracting mixed numbers. Can you find his pattern of errors?

Name _Don_

A.
$$5\tfrac{3}{4} = 5\tfrac{3}{4}$$
$$-2\tfrac{1}{2} = 2\tfrac{2}{4}$$
$$\overline{3\tfrac{1}{4}}$$

B.
$$7\tfrac{1}{6} = 7\tfrac{6}{6}$$
$$-6\tfrac{2}{3} = 6\tfrac{4}{6}$$
$$\overline{\tfrac{2}{6} = \tfrac{1}{3}}$$

C.
$$8\tfrac{1}{3} = 8\tfrac{2}{6}$$
$$-2\tfrac{1}{2} = 2\tfrac{3}{6}$$
$$\overline{5\tfrac{3}{6} = 5\tfrac{1}{2}}$$

Did you find Don's procedure? Check yourself by using his procedure to complete these examples.

D.
$$6\tfrac{5}{8}$$
$$-3\tfrac{1}{4}$$

E.
$$4\tfrac{3}{8}$$
$$-1\tfrac{1}{2}$$

After you have completed examples E and F, turn to page 102 to see if you have found Don's error pattern. How might you help Don or any student using such a procedure?

Error Pattern S-F-3

Look carefully at Chuck's written work. What error pattern has he followed?

Name _Chuck_

A. $8\frac{3}{4} - 6\frac{1}{8} = 2\frac{2}{4}$ B. $5\frac{3}{8} - 2\frac{2}{3} = 3\frac{1}{5}$

C. $9\frac{1}{5} - 1\frac{3}{8} = 8\frac{2}{3}$ D. $7\frac{2}{5} - 4\frac{7}{10} = 3\frac{5}{5}$

If you found Chuck's error pattern, check yourself by using his procedure to compute these examples.

E. $6\frac{2}{3} - 3\frac{1}{6} =$ F. $4\frac{5}{8} - 1\frac{3}{4} =$

Now turn to page 102 to see if you identified the error pattern correctly. Why might a child use such a computational procedure?

Error Pattern S-F-4

Ann is having difficulty. Can you determine the faulty procedure she is using?

Name ___Ann___

A.
$$2 \tfrac{3}{4} = 2 \tfrac{11}{4}$$
$$-1 \tfrac{1}{2} = 1 \tfrac{3}{4}$$
$$\overline{}$$
$$1 \tfrac{8}{4}$$

B.
$$11 \tfrac{1}{6} = 11 \tfrac{67}{48}$$
$$-3 \tfrac{7}{8} = 3 \tfrac{31}{48}$$
$$\overline{}$$
$$8 \tfrac{36}{48}$$

C.
$$9 \tfrac{1}{3} = 9 \tfrac{28}{3}$$
$$-\tfrac{2}{3} = \tfrac{2}{3}$$
$$\overline{}$$
$$9 \tfrac{26}{3}$$

When you have found Ann's procedure, check yourself by using her procedure to compute these examples.

D.
$$5 \tfrac{3}{8}$$
$$-2 \tfrac{1}{2}$$
$$\overline{}$$

E.
$$4 \tfrac{1}{3}$$
$$-1 \tfrac{4}{5}$$
$$\overline{}$$

Turn to page 103 and see if you found the pattern of error. Why might a child use a procedure like this?

> You may observe children using other error patterns while subtracting with fractions. Practice your own diagnostic skills by identifying the patterns shown in Appendix A.

Error Pattern M-F-1

Dan is having considerable difficulty. What error pattern is he following in his written work?

Name _Dan_

A. $\frac{4}{5} \times \frac{3}{4} = 166$ B. $\frac{1}{2} \times \frac{3}{8} = 68$

C. $\frac{2}{9} \times \frac{1}{5} = 100$ D. $\frac{2}{3} \times \frac{4}{6} = 132$

Use Dan's procedure for these examples to make sure you have found his error pattern.

E. $\frac{3}{4} \times \frac{2}{3} =$ F. $\frac{4}{9} \times \frac{2}{5} =$

When you have completed examples E and F, turn to page 104. Why might Dan be using such a procedure?

Error Pattern M-F-2

Grace gets many answers correct when computing with fractions, but she is having difficulty with multiplication examples. See if you can find her error pattern.

A.
$$\frac{3}{8} \times \frac{5}{6} = \frac{3}{8} \times \frac{6}{5} = \frac{18}{40}$$

Name _Grace_

B.
$$\frac{2}{5} \times \frac{3}{4} = \frac{2}{5} \times \frac{4}{3} = \frac{8}{15}$$

C.
$$\frac{4}{5} \times \frac{2}{3} = \frac{4}{5} \times \frac{3}{2} = \frac{12}{10}$$

Use Grace's procedure for the following examples to make sure you have found her error pattern.

D.
$$\frac{2}{3} \times \frac{3}{4} =$$

E.
$$\frac{5}{7} \times \frac{3}{8} =$$

When you have completed examples D and E, turn to page 105. Why might Grace be using such a procedure?

Error Pattern M-F-3

Look carefully at Lynn's paper. Can you find the procedure she is following?

Name — *Lynn*

A. $\frac{1}{8} \times 1 = \frac{1}{8}$

B. $\frac{2}{3} \times 3 = \frac{6}{9}$

C. $\frac{1}{4} \times 6 = \frac{6}{24}$

D. $\frac{4}{5} \times 2 = \frac{8}{10}$

Did you find the procedure? Check yourself by using her error pattern to compute these examples.

E. $\frac{3}{8} \times 4 =$

F. $\frac{5}{6} \times 2 =$

Now that you have completed examples E and F, turn to page 105 and verify your responses. Why would someone like Lynn learn to compute in this way?

You can observe children using other error patterns while multiplying with fractions. Practice your own diagnostic skills by identifying the patterns shown in Appendix A.

Error Pattern D-F-1

Linda has difficulty when she tries to divide with fractions. What procedure is she using?

Name *Linda*

A. $$\frac{4}{6} \div \frac{2}{2} = \frac{2}{3}$$
B. $$\frac{6}{8} \div \frac{2}{8} = \frac{3}{1}$$

C. $$\frac{6}{10} \div \frac{2}{4} = \frac{3}{2}$$
D. $$\frac{7}{5} \div \frac{3}{2} = \frac{2}{2}$$

Find out if you correctly identified Linda's procedure by using her error pattern to complete examples E and F.

E. $$\frac{4}{12} \div \frac{4}{4} =$$
F. $$\frac{13}{20} \div \frac{5}{6} =$$

Next, turn to page 106 where Linda's pattern is described. How might you help Linda and others using such a procedure?

Error Pattern D-F-2

Consider Joyce's work. Can you determine what procedure she is using?

Name ___Joyce___

A. $\dfrac{2}{3} \div \dfrac{3}{8} = \dfrac{3}{2} \times \dfrac{3}{8} = \dfrac{9}{16}$

B. $\dfrac{2}{5} \div \dfrac{1}{3} = \dfrac{5}{2} \times \dfrac{1}{3} = \dfrac{5}{6}$

C. $\dfrac{3}{4} \div \dfrac{1}{5} = \dfrac{4}{3} \times \dfrac{1}{5} = \dfrac{4}{15}$

Were you able to determine her procedure? Use Joyce's error pattern for these examples to make sure.

D. $\dfrac{5}{8} \div \dfrac{2}{3} =$

E. $\dfrac{1}{2} \div \dfrac{1}{4} =$

When you have completed examples D and E, turn to page 107. Why might Joyce be using such a procedure?

You can observe children using other error patterns while dividing with fractions. Practice your own diagnostic skills by identifying the patterns shown in Appendix A.

Error Pattern A-D-1

Examine Harold's work carefully. Can you find the error pattern he is following?

Name ___Harold___

A.
$$
\begin{array}{r}
.8 \\
+.4 \\
\hline
.12
\end{array}
$$

B.
$$
\begin{array}{r}
.6 \\
+.9 \\
\hline
.15
\end{array}
$$

C.
$$
\begin{array}{r}
.4 \\
+.3 \\
\hline
.7
\end{array}
$$

D.
$$
\begin{array}{r}
.5 \\
+.8 \\
\hline
.13
\end{array}
$$

Did you find the pattern? Check yourself by using his error pattern to compute these examples.

E.
$$
\begin{array}{r}
.3 \\
+.5 \\
\hline
\end{array}
$$

F.
$$
\begin{array}{r}
.7 \\
+.7 \\
\hline
\end{array}
$$

After you have completed examples E and F, turn to page 107 and verify your responses. What might have caused Harold to begin using such a procedure?

You can observe children using other error patterns while adding with decimals. Practice your own diagnostic skills by identifying the other patterns shown in Appendix A.

Error Pattern S-D-1

Les sometimes has difficulty when subtracting decimals. Can you determine his procedure?

Name ___Les___

A.

$87 - .31 = ?$

$$\begin{array}{r} 87 \\ -\ .31 \\ \hline 87.31 \end{array}$$

B.

$99.4 - 27.86 = ?$

$$\begin{array}{r} 99.4 \\ -27.86 \\ \hline 71.66 \end{array}$$

C.

$200 - .65 = ?$

$$\begin{array}{r} 200 \\ -\ \ .65 \\ \hline 200.65 \end{array}$$

Find out if you correctly determined Les's error pattern by using his procedure to complete examples D and E.

D.

$60 - 1.35 = ?$

E.

$24.8 - 2.26 = ?$

If you completed examples D and E, turn to page 108 and check your responses. How might you help Les or others using such a procedure?

Error Pattern M-D-1

Marsha seems to have difficulty with some multiplication problems involving decimals but she solves other examples correctly. Can you find her pattern of error?

Name *Marsha*

A.
$$
\begin{array}{r}
6.45 \\
\times\ \ 3 \\
\hline
19.35
\end{array}
$$

B.
$$
\begin{array}{r}
32.7 \\
\times\ \ \ .5 \\
\hline
16.35
\end{array}
$$
this in

C.
$$
\begin{array}{r}
21.8 \\
\times\ \ .4 \\
\hline
87.2
\end{array}
$$

D.
$$
\begin{array}{r}
4.35 \\
\times\ \ 2.3 \\
\hline
13\ 05 \\
87\ 0\ \ \\
\hline
100.05
\end{array}
$$

Did you find Marsha's procedure? Check yourself by using her pattern to complete these examples.

E.
$$
\begin{array}{r}
40.5 \\
\times\ .6 \\
\hline
\end{array}
$$

F.
$$
\begin{array}{r}
6.7 \\
\times\ 3 \\
\hline
\end{array}
$$

When examples E and F are completed, turn to page 109 and learn if you found Marsha's error pattern. How might you help Marsha or any other child using such a procedure?

Error Pattern D-D-1

Ted frequently makes errors when dividing decimals. Can you find his procedure?

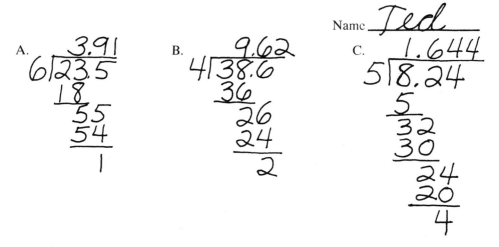

Name _Ted_

Use Ted's procedure with these examples to see if you have found his error pattern.

D. 3⟌2.57   E. 7⟌9.35

Now, turn to page 109 and see if you have identified the error pattern correctly. Why might Ted be using such an incorrect procedure?

Error Pattern P-P-1

Sara correctly solves some percent problems, but many answers are incorrect. Can you find an error pattern?

Name ___*Sara*___

A. On a test with 30 items, Mary worked 24 items correctly. What percent did she have correct?

$$\frac{24}{30} = \frac{X}{100}$$

Answer: ___80%___

B. Twelve students had perfect scores on a quiz. This is 40% of the class. How many students are in the class?

$$\frac{12}{40} = \frac{X}{100}$$

Answer: ___*30 students*___

C. Jim correctly solved 88% of 50 test items. How many items did he have correct?

$$\frac{50}{88} = \frac{X}{100}$$

Answer: ___*57 items*___

When you think you have found Sara's error pattern, use it to solve these problems.

D. Brad earned $400 during the summer and saved $240 from his earnings. What percent of his earnings did he save?

Answer:_____

E. Barbara received a gift of money on her birthday. She spent 80% of the money on a watch. The watch cost her $20. How much money did she receive as a birthday gift?

Answer:_____

F. The taffy sale brought in a total of $750, but 78% of this was used for expenses. How much money was used for expenses?

Answer: _____

Next, turn to page 110 to see if you identified the pattern correctly. Why might Sara or any child adopt such a procedure?

Error Pattern P-P-2

Steve is having difficulty solving percent questions. Can you find an error pattern in his paper?

Name *Steve*

A. What number is 30% of 180?

$$
\begin{array}{r}
180 \\
\times\ .30 \\
\hline
000 \\
540 \\
\hline
54.00
\end{array}
$$

Answer: _____ 54

B. 15% of what number is 240?

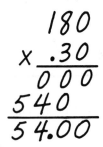

$$
\begin{array}{r}
240 \\
\times\ .15 \\
\hline
1200 \\
240 \\
\hline
36.00
\end{array}
$$

Answer: _____ 36

C. What percent of 40 is 28?

$$
\begin{array}{r}
40 \\
\times\ .28 \\
\hline
320 \\
80 \\
\hline
11.20
\end{array}
$$

Answer: _____ 11.2

When you have found Steve's error pattern, use it to solve these examples.

D. What number is 80% of 54?   Answer:_____

E. Seventy is 14% of what number?   Answer:_____

F. What percent of 125 is 25?   Answer:_____

Now, turn to page 112 to learn if you found Steve's error pattern. How would you help a child using this procedure?

Error Pattern S-M-1

Margaret is having difficulty with computation involving measurement. Can you find an error pattern in her work?

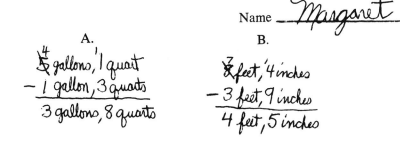

Name _Margaret_

A.
$$\overset{4}{\cancel{5}} \text{ gallons, } \overset{1}{1} \text{ quart}$$
$$- 1 \text{ gallon, } 3 \text{ quarts}$$
$$3 \text{ gallons, } 8 \text{ quarts}$$

B.
$$\overset{7}{\cancel{8}} \text{ feet, } \overset{1}{4} \text{ inches}$$
$$- 3 \text{ feet, } 9 \text{ inches}$$
$$4 \text{ feet, } 5 \text{ inches}$$

   Check yourself by using Margaret's erroneous pattern to complete these examples.

C.
6 yards, 1 foot
— 2 yards, 2 feet

D.
3 quarts, 1 cup
— 1 quart, 3 cups

   After you have finished examples C and D, turn to page 113 to see if you have accurately identified Margaret's error pattern. Why might Margaret or any other child use such a procedure?

In Appendix B, sample error patterns are shown for other areas of mathematics: numeration, problem solving, integers, algebra, and geometry. Practice your diagnostic skills by identifying the patterns illustrated.

Chapter 4

Analyzing Error Patterns in Computation

In this chapter error patterns are described and analyzed. Accompanying many of the patterns is a discussion which focuses upon the question of why some children learn to compute with error patterns. In many cases an erroneous computational procedure sometimes produces the correct answer, thereby confirming the validity of the pattern in the mind of the child. Evidences of purely mechanical procedures will abound. Such procedures cannot be explained by the child through mathematical principles or with physical aids. Children who use mechanical procedures "push symbols around" whenever there are examples to be computed and right answers to be determined. Many of the children represented here have been introduced to the standard short-form algorithms too soon; some lack very basic understandings of the operations themselves; others have become careless and confused. Each child has practiced his or her erroneous procedure and uses the procedure regularly.

As you read about an error pattern you will have an opportunity to suggest corrective or remedial instruction. Remember, these boys and girls may be in your classroom soon. What will you do to help them?

Keep in mind the suggestions included in Chapter 1 as you propose specific activities. Remember that some children may have special problems with language or in relating concepts, representations, and symbols. Frequently, children who are having difficulty computing with whole numbers do not have an adequate understanding of numeration.

Error Pattern A-W-1

>   *used by Mike on page 38.*

Using the error pattern, examples E and F would be computed as they appear
below.

E.
$$
\begin{array}{r}
43 \\
+\ 65 \\
\hline
108
\end{array}
$$

F.
$$
\begin{array}{r}
88 \\
+\ 39 \\
\hline
1117
\end{array}
$$

If your responses are the same as these, you were able to identify Mike's
erroneous computational procedure. The ones were added and recorded, then the
tens were added and recorded (or vice versa). The sum of the ones and the sum of
the tens were each recorded without regard to place value in the sum. Note that
Mike may have applied some knowledge of place value in his work with the two
addends, *i.e.,* he may have treated the 88 in example F as 8 tens and 8 ones, and
his answer as 11 tens and 17 ones. It is also true that Mike may have merely
thought "8 plus 9 equals 17, and 8 plus 3 equals 11." I have found many students
who think through such a problem in this way; some of these students also
emphasize that you add 8 and 9 first because "you add the ones first."

Mike has the idea of adding ones with ones—possibly from work with
bundles of sticks and single sticks. He apparently knows he should consider all of
the single sticks together. He *may* know a rule for exchanging or regrouping ten
single sticks for one bundle of ten, but, if he does, he has not applied the rule to
these examples. Previous instruction may not have given adequate emphasis to
the mechanics of recording sums.

Cox found in her study of systematic errors among children in regular
second- through sixth-grade classrooms that 67 percent of the children who made
systematic errors when adding two two-digit numbers with renaming made this
particular error.[1]

If you were Mike's teacher, what remedial steps might you take? Describe
two instructional activities which would hopefully correct the error pattern.

1. _____

_____

_____

---

[1] L. S. Cox, "Systematic Errors in the Four Vertical Algorithms in Normal and Handicapped
Populations," *Journal for Research in Mathematics Education* 6, no. 4 (November 1975): 202–20.

2. _____

_____

When you have completed your responses, turn to page 116 to see if your suggestions are among the alternatives described.

Error Pattern A-W-2

from Mary's paper on page 39.

If you used Mary's error pattern, you completed examples E and F as they are shown below.

E.
$$\begin{array}{r} 254 \\ + 535 \\ \hline 789 \end{array}$$

F.
$$\begin{array}{r} 3\ 2 \\ 618 \\ + 782 \\ \hline 1112 \end{array}$$

This pattern is a reversal of the procedure used in the usual algorithm—without regard for place value. Addition is performed from left to right, and, when the sum of a column is ten or greater, the left figure is recorded and the right figure is placed above the next column to the right.

You probably noted that example A on page 39 and example E above are correct. In these two examples, Mary's use of a left-to-right procedure was reinforced, for she computed the correct sum. In such cases, use of an erroneous procedure is very apt to go unnoticed by the classroom teacher; yet the erroneous pattern, or at least part of it, is practiced and "mastered."

You may want to determine if Mary's left-to-right orientation is from reading instruction, especially if she is in a remedial program. She may need help in taking a "global look" at numerals to identify place values.

If you were Mary's teacher, what corrective procedures might you follow? Describe two instructional activities which would hopefully help Mary add correctly.

1. _____

_____

2. _____

_____

When your responses are complete, turn to page 117 and see if your suggestions are among the alternatives described.

Error Pattern A-W-3

from Carol's paper on page 40.

If you found Carol's error pattern, your results are the same as the erroneous computation shown below.

F.
$$26$$
$$+\ \ 3$$
$$\overline{11}$$

G.
$$60$$
$$+\ 24$$
$$\overline{84}$$

H.
$$74$$
$$+\ 5$$
$$\overline{16}$$

Carol misses examples in which one of the addends is written as a single digit. When working such examples, she adds the three digits as if they were all units. When both addends are two-digit numbers, she appears to add correctly. However, it is quite probable that Carol is not applying any knowledge of place value with either type of example. She may be merely adding units in every case. (When both addends are two-digit numbers, she adds units in straight columns. When one addend is a one-digit number, she adds the three digits along a curve.) If this is the way Carol is thinking, she will probably experience even more failure and frustration when she begins addition and subtraction requiring regrouping.

Carol needs help. How would you help her? Describe at least two instructional activities you believe would correct Carol's error pattern.

1. _____

_____

2. _____

_____

After you have described at least two activities, turn to page 118 and compare your suggestions with the suggestions listed there.

Error Pattern A-W-4

from Dorothy's paper on page 41.

Using Dorothy's error pattern, examples E and F would be computed as they appear on the following page.

Dorothy is not having difficulty with her basic addition facts, but higher decade addition situations are confusing her. She tries to use the regular addition algorithm; however, when she adds the tens column she adds in the one-digit number again.

E.
$$\overset{\text{\tiny 1}}{4}6$$
$$+\ \ 8$$
$$\overline{134}$$

F.
$$\overset{\text{\tiny 1}}{9}8$$
$$+\ \ 3$$
$$\overline{131}$$

If Dorothy has been introduced to the multiplication algorithm, she may persist in seeing similar patterns for computation whenever numerals are arranged as she has seen them in multiplication examples. Changing operations when the arrangement of numerals is similar is difficult for some children. An interview with Dorothy may help you determine if she really knows how to add problems like these. When working with a child who tends to carry over one situation into his perception of another, avoid extensive practice at a given time on any single procedure.

In her study of children adding a two-digit number and a one-digit number with renaming, Cox found that 11 percent of the children in regular classrooms who made systematic errors made this particular error. Furthermore, in special education classrooms 60 percent of the children with systematic errors had adopted this procedure.[2]

How would you help Dorothy? Describe at least two instructional activities which would help Dorothy replace her erroneous pattern with a correct procedure.

1. _____

_____

2. _____

_____

When both activities are described, turn to page 119 and compare your suggestions with the suggestions recorded there.

Error Pattern S-W-1

from Cheryl's paper on page 42.

Using the error pattern, examples E and F would be computed as they appear on the following page.

---

[2] Cox, *Ibid.*

E. $\begin{array}{r} 458 \\ -\ 372 \\ \hline 126 \end{array}$ F. $\begin{array}{r} 241 \\ -\ 96 \\ \hline 255 \end{array}$

Did you identify the error pattern? As a general rule, the ones are subtracted and recorded, then the tens are subtracted and recorded, etc. Apparently Cheryl is considering each position (ones, tens, etc.) as a separate subtraction problem. In example E she probably did not think of the numbers 458 and 372, but only of 8 and 2, 5 and 7, and 4 and 3. Further, in subtracting single-digit numbers, she does not conceive of the upper figure (minuend) as the number in a set and the lower figure (subtrahend) as the number in a subset. When subtracting ones Cheryl may think of the larger of the two numbers as the number of the set, and the smaller as the number to be removed from the set. Or she may merely compare the two single-digit numbers much as she would match sets one to one or place rods side by side to find a difference. In example F she would think "1 and 6, the difference is 5." She uses the same procedure when subtracting tens and hundreds. Cheryl may have merely over-generalized commutativity for addition, and assumed that subtraction is also commutative.

Note that example A on page 42 is correct. This example includes much smaller numbers than the other examples. It may be that Cheryl counted from 16 to 32, or she may have used some kind of number line. If she did think of 32 as "20 plus 12" in order to subtract, it may be the case that she applies renaming procedures only to smaller numbers which she can somehow conceptualize, but she breaks up larger numbers in the manner described above.

Has Cheryl heard rules in the classroom or at home which she is applying in her own way? Perhaps she has heard, "Always subtract the little number from the big one" and "Stay in the column when you subtract."

Children frequently adopt this error pattern. For children in regular classrooms who are subtracting a two-digit number from a two-digit number with renaming, Cox found that 83 percent of the children with systematic errors used this particular procedure.[3]

If you were Cheryl's teacher, what remedial steps might you take? Describe two instructional activities which would hopefully help Cheryl correct the error pattern.

1. _____

_____

_____

[3] Cox, *Ibid.*

2. _____

_____

After you have finished writing your responses, turn to page 120 to see if your suggestions are among the alternatives described.

Error Pattern S-W-2

from George's paper on page 43.

Did you identify the error pattern George used?

D.
$$
\begin{array}{r}
2\,\overset{6}{\cancel{7}}\,\overset{1}{3} \\
-\ \ 38 \\
\hline
235
\end{array}
$$

E.
$$
\begin{array}{r}
2\,\overset{7}{\cancel{8}}\,\overset{1}{5} \\
-\ \ 63 \\
\hline
2112
\end{array}
$$

George has learned to borrow or regroup in subtraction. In fact he regroups whether he needs to or not. It is possible that George would be able to interpret regrouping in terms of renaming a 10 as 10 ones, and it is also possible that he could interpret the answer (in example E) as 12 ones, 1 ten, and 2 hundreds. At any rate, his final answer does not take account of conventional place value notation.

You have no doubt observed that the answer to example D is correct. George's procedure is correct paper-and-pencil procedure for a problem such as example D. However, George does not distinguish between problems in which regrouping is required and problems which do not require regrouping; the fact that some of his answers are correct may positively reinforce the pattern he is using as appropriate for all subtraction problems.

Many children rename the minuend when it is unnecessary. In Cox's study, when children in regular classrooms subtracted a two-digit number from a two-digit number with no renaming, 75 percent of the children who used a systematic erroneous procedure did rename the minuend although it was inappropriate to do so.[4]

George has a problem. How would you help him? Describe two instructional activities which would help George replace his error pattern with a correct computational procedure.

1. _____

_____

_____

[4] Cox, *Ibid.*

2. _____

_____

After you complete your two descriptions, turn to page 121 and compare what you have written with the suggestions presented there.

Error Pattern S-W-3

from Donna's paper on page 44.

Did you find Donna's error pattern?

E.
$$\begin{array}{r} 446 \\ -\ 302 \\ \hline 104 \end{array}$$

F.
$$\begin{array}{r} 760 \\ -\ 230 \\ \hline 530 \end{array}$$

Although Donna uses the subtraction fact $0 - 0 = 0$ correctly, she consistently writes "0" for the missing addend whenever the known addend (subtrahend) is zero. She regularly misses nine of the 100 basic subtraction facts because of this one difficulty.

We ought to be able to help Donna with a problem of this sort. How would you help her? Describe two instructional activities you think would enable Donna to subtract correctly.

1. _____

_____

2. _____

_____

Did you describe at least two activities? (It is important to have more than one possible instructional procedure in mind when working remedially with a child.) If so, turn to page 122 and compare your suggestions with the suggestions described there.

Error Pattern S-W-4

from Barbara's paper on page 45.

Did you find Barbara's error pattern?

Barbara appeared to be doing well with subtraction until recently, when regrouping or renaming more than once was introduced. She apparently had been

E.
$$\begin{array}{r} \overset{3}{\cancel{4}}\overset{1}{3}6 \\ -\ 172 \\ \hline 264 \end{array}$$

F.
$$\begin{array}{r} \overset{4}{\cancel{6}}\overset{1}{2}\overset{1}{5} \\ -\ 348 \\ \hline 187 \end{array}$$

thinking something like "Take 1 from 4 and put the 1 in front of the 3" (example E). Now she has extended this procedure so that, in example F, she thinks, "In order to subtract (*i.e.*, in order to use a simple subtraction fact), I need a 1 in front of the 5 and a 1 in front of the 2. Take *two* 1's from the 6. . . ." Note that if Barbara had not been showing her work with crutches of some sort, it would have been much more difficult to find the pattern.

Help is needed, and promptly—before she reinforces her error pattern with further practice. How would you help her? Describe two instructional activities you think would make it possible for Barbara to subtract correctly, even in examples such as these.

1. _____

_____

2. _____

_____

When you have described two instructional activities, turn to page 124 and compare your suggestions with the suggestions listed there.

Error Pattern S-W-5

from Sam's paper on page 46.

Did you find Sam's error patterns?

E.
$$\begin{array}{r} \overset{4}{\cancel{5}}\overset{7}{\cancel{8}}5 \\ -\ 322 \\ \hline 153 \end{array}$$

F.
$$\begin{array}{r} \overset{7}{\cancel{8}}\overset{3}{\cancel{4}}0 \\ -\ 626 \\ \hline 110 \end{array}$$

Whenever the digits in the minuend and the subtrahend are the same, Sam borrows "so he will be able to subtract." However, his procedure is simply "Take one from here and add it here." It is not meaningful regrouping. You may also have noted that Sam has difficulty with zeros in the minuend. Rather than regrouping so he can subtract, he merely records a zero.

How would you help Sam if you had the opportunity? Describe at least two instructional activities which you believe would help Sam subtract whole numbers correctly.

1. _____

_____

2. _____

_____

After you have written both descriptions, turn to page 125 and see if your suggestions are among the suggestions listed there.

Error Pattern M-W-1

used by Bob on page 47.

Did you find the error pattern Bob used?

D.
$$
\begin{array}{r}
\overset{4}{} \\
98 \\
56 \\
\hline
588 \\
490 \\
\hline
5488
\end{array}
$$

E.
$$
\begin{array}{r}
\overset{3}{} \\
86 \\
45 \\
\hline
430 \\
354 \\
\hline
3970
\end{array}
$$

Consider example E. When multiplying 5 ones times 6 ones, Bob recorded the 3 tens as a crutch above the 8 tens to remind him to add 3 tens to the product of 5 and 8 tens. However, the crutch recorded when multiplying by ones was *also* used when multiplying by tens.

Note that the answers to example B on page 47 and example D above are correct. Bob's error pattern may have gone undetected because he gets enough correct answers, enough positive reinforcement, to convince him that he is using a correct procedure. There may have been enough correct answers to cause Bob's busy teacher to conclude that Bob was merely careless. But Bob *is* consistently applying an erroneous procedure.

How would you help Bob with his problem? Describe two instructional activities which would help Bob replace this error pattern with a correct computational procedure.

1. _____

_____

2. _____

_____

When you have written descriptions of two instructional activities, turn to page 127 and compare what you have written with the suggestions presented there.

Error Pattern M-W-2

from Bill's paper on page 48.

The examples below illustrate Bill's error pattern.

$$
\text{E.} \quad \overset{1}{} \\
\begin{array}{r} 35 \\ \times\ 3 \\ \hline 95 \end{array}
\qquad\qquad
\text{F.} \quad \overset{3}{} \\
\begin{array}{r} 28 \\ \times\ 4 \\ \hline 82 \end{array}
$$

Bill simply does not add the number of tens he records with a crutch. Perhaps he knows he should add, but don't be too sure. He forgets consistently!

You ought to be able to help Bill with a problem of this sort. How would you help him? Describe two activities you think would enable Bill to complete the multiplication correctly.

1. _____

_____

2. _____

_____

Are both activities described? Then turn to page 129 and compare what you have written with the suggestions listed there.

Error Pattern M-W-3

from Joe's paper on page 49.

Did you find the error pattern Joe uses?

D.   ⁴68
    × 5
    500

E.   ²29
    × 3
    127

Joe is using an erroneous procedure which is all too frequently adopted by children. He adds the number associated with the crutch *before* multiplying the tens figure, whereas the algorithm requires that the tens figure be multiplied first. In example D, he thought "6 plus 4 equals 10 and 5 times 10 equals 50" instead of "5 times 6 equals 30 and 30 plus 4 equals 34." It may be that when Joe learned the addition algorithm involving regrouping, his teacher reminded him repeatedly, "The first thing you do is to add the number you carry." Many teachers drill children on such a rule, and it is little wonder that children sometimes apply the rule in inappropriate contexts.

Cox found in her study that, for examples of this type, 43 percent of the children in regular classrooms who used an erroneous procedure systematically used this particular error pattern.[5]

The fact that children frequently use Joe's procedure does not lessen your obligation to help Joe multiply correctly. How would *you* help him? Describe two different instructional activities you think would enable Joe to replace his error pattern with a correct computational procedure.

1. _____

_____

2. _____

_____

When you have finished writing both descriptions, turn to page 130 and compare what you have written with the suggestions offered there.

Error Pattern M-W-4

from Doug's paper on page 50.

Did you find Doug's error pattern? If so, you completed examples E and F as they are shown.

The procedure used by Doug is a blend of the algorithm for multiplying by a one-digit multiplier and the conventional addition algorithm. Each column is

---

[5] Cox, *Ibid.*

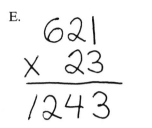

E.
$$\begin{array}{r} 621 \\ \times\ 23 \\ \hline 1243 \end{array}$$

F.
$$\begin{array}{r} 5\overset{2}{1}7 \\ \times\ 463 \\ \hline 2081 \end{array}$$

approached as a separate multiplication; when the multiplicand has more digits than the multiplier, the left-most digit of the multiplier continues to be used.

You may meet Doug in your own classroom. How would you help him? Describe at least two instructional activities you believe would enable Doug to multiply by two- and three-digit numbers correctly.

1. _____

_____

2. _____

_____

After your descriptions are written, turn to page 131 and see if your suggestions are among the suggestions listed there.

Error Pattern D-W-1

used by Jim on page 51.

Did you find the erroneous procedure Jim used?

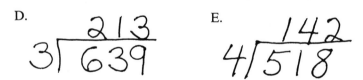

D.
$$3\overline{)639}\ \ 213$$

E.
$$4\overline{)518}\ \ 142$$

Example D is correct and it does not give many clues to Jim's thinking. However, the fact that example D *is* correct is a reminder that erroneous procedures sometimes produce correct answers, thereby reinforcing the procedure as far as the student is concerned and making the error pattern more difficult for the teacher to identify.

Example E illustrates Jim's thinking more completely. Apparently Jim ignores place value in the dividend and quotient, and he thinks of each digit as "ones." Furthermore, he considers one digit of the dividend and the one-digit divisor as two numbers "to be divided." The larger of the two (whether the divisor or a digit within the dividend) is divided by the smaller and the result recorded. Jim has probably learned that a smaller number "goes-into" a larger number. Interestingly, the remainder is ignored.

Did you notice that no numerals were recorded below the dividend? This lack in itself is a sign of possible trouble. It may well be that someone (a teacher, a parent, a friend) tried to teach Jim the "short" division procedure.

How would you help Jim with his problem? Describe two instructional activities which you think would help Jim replace this erroneous procedure with a correct computational procedure.

1. _____

_____

2. _____

_____

After you have written descriptions of two appropriate instructional activities, compare your activities with the suggestions on page 133.

Error Pattern D-W-2

from Gail's paper on page 52.

Using Gail's incorrect procedure, examples E and F would be computed as shown below.

E.
$$\begin{array}{r} 52 \\ 3\overline{)75} \\ 60 \\ \hline 15 \\ 15 \\ \hline \end{array}$$

F.
$$\begin{array}{r} 68 \\ 6\overline{)516} \\ 480 \\ \hline 36 \\ 36 \\ \hline \end{array}$$

Did you find the error pattern? In the ones column Gail records the first quotient figure she determines, and in the tens column she records the second digit she determines. In other words, the answer is recorded right to left. In the usual algorithms for addition, subtraction, and multiplication of whole numbers, the answer is recorded right to left; perhaps Gail assumes it is appropriate to do the same with the division algorithm.

The fact that example A is correct illustrates again that correct answers are sometimes obtained with incorrect procedures, thereby positively reinforcing an error pattern.

It is quite probable that, for example E, Gail thinks "7 divided by 3" (or perhaps "3 times what number is 7") rather than "75 divided by 3." The quotient for a shortcut expression such as "7 divided by 3" would indeed be 2 units. Shortcuts in thinking and the standard algorithm for division may have been introduced too soon.

What would you do if you were Gail's teacher? What corrective steps might you take? Describe two instructional activities which you believe would help Gail correct the erroneous procedure.

1. _____

_____

2. _____

_____

If you have finished your responses, turn to page 135 and see if your suggestions are among the alternatives listed there.

Error Pattern D-W-3

from John's paper on page 53.

If you found John's error pattern, you completed examples E and F as they are shown below.

E.

$$\begin{array}{r} 32r3 \\ 9\overline{)2721} \\ \underline{27} \\ 21 \\ \underline{18} \\ 3 \end{array}$$

F.

$$\begin{array}{r} 78r2 \\ 6\overline{)4250} \\ \underline{42} \\ 50 \\ \underline{48} \\ 2 \end{array}$$

John is missing examples, which include a zero in the tens place of the quotient. Whenever he brings down and cannot divide he brings down again, but without recording a zero to show that there are no tens. He may believe that "zero is nothing." Also, careless placement of figures in the quotient may contribute to John's problem.

It is also possible that a careful transition was not made from an algorithm used earlier. For example, John may bring down all remaining digits from the dividend because that is what he did when he used the subtractive form of division, the Greenwood algorithm. It is so important that transition from one form of division to another be made carefully, step-by-step.

Children commonly compute this way. Cox found that for children with systematic errors in regular classrooms who computed similar examples (but with three-digit dividends) 72 percent used this procedure. In special education classrooms 90 percent of those with systematic errors had adopted this error pattern.[6]

How would you help John? Describe at least two instructional activities you believe would help John correct his pattern of error.

1. _____

_____

2. _____

_____

When you have completed both descriptions, turn to page 136 and compare your suggestions with the suggestions listed there.

Error Pattern D-W-4

from Anita's paper on page 54.

If Anita's procedure is used, examples E and F would be completed as shown.

E.

$$6\overline{)4818} \quad \begin{array}{r} 830 \\ \hline \end{array}$$
$$\underline{4800}$$
$$18$$
$$\underline{18}$$

F.

$$7\overline{)3525} \quad \begin{array}{r} 530 \text{ R4} \\ \hline \end{array}$$
$$\underline{3500}$$
$$25$$
$$\underline{21}$$
$$4$$

Like John, Anita is having difficulty with examples which include a zero in the tens place of the quotient. If she "brings down" and cannot divide, she "brings down" again; but she does not record a zero to show that there are no tens. However, she is careful to align her work in columns of hundreds, tens, etc., so that the quotient is obviously incomplete as she finishes her computation. Therefore, a zero is inserted in the remaining position—the ones place.

---

[6] Cox, *Ibid.*

The extensive use of zeros in the computation (*e.g.,* the 4800 in example E) sometimes helps a child if the child consciously multiplies in terms of the total values involved. In example E, 800 × 6 = 4800. However, Anita also indicated that 30 × 6 = 18, which is not true. It may be the case that zeros are being written all the way across just because it is the thing to do. An interview with Anita, letting her think out loud while computing, may be helpful in determining what is actually happening.

What would *you* do to help Anita? Describe at least two instructional activities you believe would help her correct the pattern of error.

1. _____

_____

2. _____

_____

When both activities have been described, turn to page 137 and compare your suggestions with the suggestions recorded there.

Error Pattern E-F-1

from Greg's paper on page 55.

If Greg's procedure is used, examples E and F would be completed as follows:

E. $\dfrac{16}{64} = \dfrac{1}{4}$ F. $\dfrac{14}{42} = \dfrac{1}{2}$

If the same digit appears in both numerator and denominator, Greg uses a cancellation procedure similar to what he has apparently learned to apply whenever both expressions are written as products of two numbers. Though the procedure is erroneous, examples A and E are both correct, and Greg may find it difficult to believe his method is not satisfactory.

We ought to be able to help Greg. How would you help him? Describe two instructional activities you believe would help Greg correct his pattern of error.

1. _____

_____

2. _____

_____

   After two activities have been described, turn to page 139 and compare what you have written with the suggestions listed there.

Error Pattern E-F-2

from Jill's paper on page 56.

Did you find Jill's error pattern?

E. $\dfrac{3}{4} = \dfrac{1}{2}$ F. $\dfrac{2}{8} = \dfrac{1}{4}$

   Jill's computation appears almost random though, interestingly, several answers are correct. She obviously does not recognize which fractions are already in simplest terms. She explains her procedure as follows:

> "4 goes to 2, and 9 goes to 3"
> "3 goes to 1, and 9 goes to 3"

For examples E and F,

> "3 goes to 1, and 4 goes to 2"
> "2 goes to 1, and 8 goes to 4"

Jill simply associates a specific whole number with each given numerator or denominator. *All* 3's become 1's and *all* 4's become 2's when fractions are to be reduced or changed to simplest terms. This procedure is a very mechanical one, requiring no concept of a fraction; however, it does produce correct answers part of the time.

   Jill has a very real problem. How would you help her? Describe two instructional activities which would help Jill replace this erroneous procedure with a correct procedure.

1. _____

_____

2. _____

_____

   After two activities have been described, turn to page 140 and compare what you have written with the suggestions listed there.

Error Pattern E-F-3

from Sue's paper on page 57.

Did you correctly identify Sue's pattern of error? Many teachers would assume she had responded randomly.

G. $\dfrac{3}{6} = \dfrac{2}{6}$ H. $\dfrac{6}{4} = \dfrac{1}{6}$

Sue considers the given numerator and denominator as two whole numbers, and divides the larger by the smaller to determine the new numerator (ignoring any remainder); then the largest of the two numbers is copied as the new denominator. Perhaps she has observed that the denominator is usually the larger of the two numbers in the fractions she sees.

How would you help Sue? She is not unlike many other children who develop mechanistic and unreasonable procedures in arithmetic classes. Describe at least two instructional activities which you believe would help Sue learn to correctly change fractions to lowest or simplest terms.

1. _____

_____

2. _____

_____

When you have described at least two activities, turn to page 142 and compare your suggestions with the suggestions listed there.

Error Pattern A-F-1

from Robbie's paper on page 58.

Did you find Robbie's error pattern?

E. $\dfrac{3}{4} + \dfrac{1}{5} = \dfrac{4}{9}$ F. $\dfrac{2}{3} + \dfrac{5}{6} = \dfrac{7}{9}$

Robbie adds the numerators to get the numerator for the sum, then he adds the denominators to get the denominator for the sum. Lankford, in the research described in Chapter 1, found this procedure to be a "most prevalent practice."[7] It is likely that Robbie has already learned to multiply fractions, and he appears to be following a similar procedure for adding fractions.

Robbie has a problem. How would you help him? Describe two instructional activities which would help Robbie replace his error pattern with a correct computational procedure.

1. _____

_____

2. _____

_____

After you complete your two descriptions, turn to page 143 and compare what you have written with the suggestions presented there.

Error Pattern A-F-2

from Dave's paper on page 59.

Did you find the error pattern Dave is using?

D.
$$9\tfrac{1}{3} = \tfrac{3}{9}$$
$$+5\tfrac{5}{9} = \tfrac{5}{9}$$
$$\overline{\quad\quad \tfrac{8}{9}}$$

E.
$$16\tfrac{3}{4} = \tfrac{3}{4}$$
$$+23\tfrac{1}{2} = \tfrac{2}{4}$$
$$\overline{\quad\quad \tfrac{5}{4} = 1\tfrac{1}{4}}$$

Dave apparently becomes so involved with the process of renaming fractions that he forgets to add the whole numbers. He has probably been taught the following algorithm or one similar to it.

F.
$$9\tfrac{1}{3} = 9\tfrac{3}{9}$$
$$+5\tfrac{5}{9} = 5\tfrac{5}{9}$$
$$\overline{\quad\quad 14\tfrac{8}{9}}$$

G.
$$16\tfrac{3}{4} = 16\tfrac{3}{4}$$
$$+23\tfrac{1}{2} = 23\tfrac{2}{4}$$
$$\overline{\quad\quad 39\tfrac{5}{4} = 40\tfrac{1}{4}}$$

---

[7] Francis G. Lankford, Jr., *Some Computational Strategies of Seventh Grade Pupils,* U.S. Department of Health, Education, and Welfare, Office of Education, National Center for Educational Research and Development (Regional Research Program) and The Center for Advanced Study, The University of Virginia, October 1972, p. 30. (Project number 2-C-013, Grant number OEG-3-72-0035)

In the algorithm shown with examples F and G, required rewriting of mixed numerals sometimes results in carelessness on the part of children. They all too frequently write incorrect statements such as

$$9\frac{1}{3} = \frac{3}{9}$$

and

$$16\frac{3}{4} = \frac{3}{4}$$

How would you help Dave with his problem? Describe two instructional activities which you think would help Dave replace his error pattern with a correct computational procedure.

1. _____

_____

2. _____

_____

When you have finished describing both instructional activities, turn to page 144 and compare your suggestions with those listed there.

Error Pattern A-F-3

from Allen's paper on page 60.

Did you find Allen's error pattern?

D.
$$\frac{1}{4} + \frac{1}{5} = \frac{5}{9} + \frac{4}{9} = \frac{9}{9}$$

E.
$$\frac{2}{5} + \frac{1}{2} = \frac{2}{7} + \frac{10}{7} = \frac{12}{7}$$

Allen has learned a very mechanical procedure for changing two fractions so they will have the same denominator. Someone may have tried to teach him a rather common shortcut which includes rules for adding and multiplying different numerators in an apparently arbitrary pattern. However, what Allen actually learned was a very different pattern of additions and multiplications, a mechanical procedure he uses to "get an answer" when required to do so by a teacher. He first adds the unlike denominators to get a common denominator, then he multiplies the numerator and denominator of the first fraction to get a numerator for the new second fraction. Similarly, he multiplies the numerator and denominator of the second fraction to get a numerator for the new first fraction. (Apparently, he adds like fractions correctly.) If Allen has been practicing addition of unlike fractions, it is this erroneous procedure he has been reinforcing.

Can we help Allen with a problem of this sort? How would you help him? Describe at last two instructional activities you think would enable Allen to add unlike fractions correctly.

1. _____

_____

2. _____

_____

Have you described at least two activities? Remember, it is important to have more than one possible instructional procedure in mind when working remedially with a child. If so, turn to page 145 and compare your suggestions with the suggestions noted there.

Error Pattern A-F-4

from Robin's paper on page 61.

Did you find Robin's procedure?

D. $\dfrac{3}{4} = \dfrac{3}{4}$

$+\dfrac{1}{2} = \dfrac{1}{4}$

$\dfrac{4}{4}$

E. $\dfrac{4}{5} = \dfrac{4}{20}$

$+\dfrac{1}{4} = \dfrac{1}{20}$

$\dfrac{5}{20}$

Robin is able to determine the least common denominator and she uses it when changing two fractions so they will have the same denominator. However, she merely copies the original numerator. Apparently, Robin is able to add like fractions correctly.

How would you help Robin with her difficulty? Describe two instructional activities which you believe would help her learn to add unlike fractions correctly.

1. _____

_____

2. _____

_____

When you have described both activities, turn to page 146 and compare your suggestions with those listed there.

Error Pattern S-F-1

from Andrew's paper on page 62.

Did you find Andrew's error patterns?

E.
$$5\frac{1}{5}$$
$$-\ 3\frac{3}{5}$$
$$\overline{\quad 2\frac{2}{5}}$$

F.
$$1$$
$$-\ \frac{1}{3}$$
$$\overline{\quad 1\frac{1}{3}}$$

In every case the whole numbers are subtracted as simple subtraction problems, perhaps even before attention is given to the column of common fractions. Where only one fraction appears in the problem (examples A and C), the fraction is simply "brought down." If two fractions appear, Andrew records the difference between them, ignoring whether the subtrahend or the minuend is the larger of the two.

How would you help Andrew? (You may want to review Error Pattern S-W-1 for ideas.) Describe two instructional activities you think would help Andrew correct his erroneous procedures.

1. _____

_____

2. _____

_____

When both descriptions are completed, turn to page 148 and compare your suggestions with the suggestions listed there.

Error Pattern S-F-2

from Don's paper on page 63.

If Don's procedure is used, examples D and E would be completed as they are shown below.

D.

$$6\frac{5}{8} = 6\frac{5}{8}$$
$$-3\frac{1}{4} = 3\frac{2}{8}$$
$$\overline{\phantom{-3\frac{1}{4}=}3\frac{3}{8}}$$

E.

$$4\frac{3}{8} = \cancel{4}^{3}\,\cancel{3}^{8}_{8}$$
$$-1\frac{1}{2} = 1\frac{4}{8}$$
$$\overline{\phantom{-1\frac{1}{2}=}2\frac{4}{8} = 2\frac{1}{2}}$$

Don appears to be able to subtract mixed numbers whenever no regrouping is necessary, and renaming fractions to higher and lower terms does not appear to be a problem for him. However, when renaming a mixed number in order to subtract, Don subtracts one whole or unit without properly adding an equivalent amount to the fraction. In every case, the numerator of the fraction is crossed out and the same number as the denominator is written in place of the numerator (rather than being added to the numerator). This may be, in part, confusion with the form of the unit (*i.e.*, $\frac{n}{n}$) which should be added to the existing fraction.

What would you do to help Don? Describe at least two instructional activities you believe would help him correct his pattern or errors.

1. _____

_____

2. _____

_____

When both activities have been described, turn to page 149 and compare your suggestions with the suggestions listed there.

Error Pattern S-F-3

from Chuck's paper on page 64.

Did you find Chuck's error pattern?

E.

$$6\frac{2}{3} - 3\frac{1}{6} = 3\frac{1}{3}$$

F.

$$4\frac{5}{8} - 1\frac{3}{4} = 3\frac{2}{4}$$

Chuck is subtracting by first finding the difference between the two whole numbers and recording that difference as the new whole number. He then finds the difference between the two numerators and records that difference as the new numerator. Finally, he finds the difference between the two denominators and records that number as the new denominator. The procedure is similar to addition as seen in Error Pattern A-F-1. However, children using this procedure for subtraction necessarily ignore the order of the minuend and the subtrahend.

Someone needs to come to Chuck's aid. How would you help him? Describe two instructional procedures you believe would help Chuck subtract correctly when given examples such as these.

1. _____

_____

2. _____

_____

When you have described two instructional activities, turn to page 150 and compare your suggestions with the suggestions listed there.

Error Pattern S-F-4

from Ann's paper on page 65.

Did you find the pattern?

$$\text{D.} \quad 5\frac{3}{8} = 5\frac{43}{8}$$
$$-2\frac{1}{2} = 2\frac{5}{8}$$
$$\overline{\quad\quad\quad 3\frac{38}{8}}$$

$$\text{E.} \quad 4\frac{1}{3} = 4\frac{13}{15}$$
$$-1\frac{4}{5} = 1\frac{9}{15}$$
$$\overline{\quad\quad\quad 3\frac{4}{15}}$$

Ann's difficulty is with changing mixed numbers to equivalent mixed numbers which have a common denominator. She does determine a common denominator, but she computes each new numerator by multiplying the original denominator times the whole number and adding the original numerator. She merely copies the given whole number.

You probably recognize part of the procedure as the way to find the new numerator when changing a mixed number to a fraction, but doing this makes no sense when changing a mixed number to an equivalent mixed number with a specified denominator.

How would you help Ann? Describe two instructional activities you believe will help her subtract correctly when she encounters examples such as these.

1. _____

_____

2. _____

_____

    If you have described two activities, turn to page 150 and compare what you have written with the suggestions recorded there.

Error Pattern M-F-1

from Dan's paper on page 66.

Did you find Dan's error pattern?

E. $\dfrac{3}{4} \times \dfrac{2}{3} = 89$ F. $\dfrac{4}{9} \times \dfrac{2}{5} = 200$

    Dan begins by multiplying the first numerator and the second denominator and recording the units digit of this product. If there is a tens digit, he remembers it to add later (as in multiplication of whole numbers). He then multiplies the first denominator and the second numerator, adds the number of tens remembered, and records this as the number of tens in the answer. The procedure involves a sort of cross multiplication and the multiply-then-add sequence from multiplication of whole numbers.
    Dan uses this error pattern consistently; he has somehow learned to multiply fractions this way. How would you help him learn the correct procedure? Describe two instructional activities you believe would help.

1. _____

_____

2. _____

_____

    After two activities have been described, turn to page 152 and compare what you have written with the suggestions listed there.

Error Pattern M-F-2

from Grace's paper on page 67.

Did you identify the error pattern Grace is using?

D. $\dfrac{2}{3} \times \dfrac{3}{4} = \dfrac{2}{3} \times \dfrac{4}{3} = \dfrac{8}{9}$

E. $\dfrac{5}{7} \times \dfrac{3}{8} = \dfrac{5}{7} \times \dfrac{8}{3} = \dfrac{40}{21}$

Grace has learned to invert and multiply, and she is using this division procedure to multiply fractions.

How would you help Grace? Describe two instructional activities which would help her replace this error pattern with the correct computational procedure.

1. _____

_____

2. _____

_____

After you complete your two descriptions, turn to page 153 and compare what you have written with the suggestions recorded there.

Error Pattern M-F-3

from Lynn's paper on page 68.

Did you find the procedure Lynn is using?

E. $\dfrac{3}{8} \times 4 = \dfrac{12}{32}$ F. $\dfrac{5}{6} \times 2 = \dfrac{10}{12}$

Lynn has learned that when you are multiplying and you have a fraction, you have to multiply *both* the numerator and the denominator of the fraction. Of course, when multiplying both terms by the same number she is actually multiplying the fraction by *one* rather than by the whole number in the example. It may be that she multiplied both numerator and denominator by the same number when she practiced changing a fraction to higher terms, and she continues to use this familiar pattern.

How would you help Lynn? Describe two activities which you believe would enable her to multiply correctly.

1. _____

_____

2. _____

_____

If you have described two such activities, turn to page 153 and compare your suggestions with the ideas listed there.

Error Pattern D-F-1

from Linda's paper on page 69.

Did you find the error pattern Linda is using?

$$\text{E.} \quad \frac{4}{12} \div \frac{4}{4} = \frac{1}{3} \qquad \text{F.} \quad \frac{13}{20} \div \frac{5}{6} = \frac{2}{3}$$

Linda divides the first numerator by the second numerator and records the result as the numerator for the answer. She then determines the denominator for the answer by dividing the first denominator by the second denominator. In both divisions she ignores remainders. Note that examples A, B, and E are correct. It may be that she learned her procedure while the class was working with such examples. The common denominator method of dividing fractions may be part of the background, for her procedure is similar; however, she fails to change the fractions to equivalent fractions with the same denominator before dividing.

This is a tricky error pattern, producing both correct answers and absurd answers with zero numerators and denominators. Linda obviously needs help. How would you help her? Describe two instructional activities you think would enable her to replace her error pattern with a correct computational procedure.

1. _____

_____

2. _____

_____

When you have noted your descriptions, turn to page 154 and compare them with the suggestions listed there.

Error Pattern D-F-2

from Joyce's paper on page 70.

Did you find the procedure Joyce is using?

D.
$$\frac{5}{8} \div \frac{2}{3} = \frac{8}{5} \times \frac{2}{3} = \frac{16}{15}$$

E.
$$\frac{1}{2} \div \frac{1}{4} = \frac{2}{1} \times \frac{1}{4} = \frac{2}{4}$$

Joyce knows to "invert and multiply," but she inverts the dividend (or product) instead of the divisor. It *does* make a difference!

Dividing fractions seems to involve such an arbitrary rule. How would *you* help Joyce? Describe two instructional activities you believe would help her divide correctly.

1. _____

_____

2. _____

_____

When you have described both activities, turn to page 155 and compare your ideas with the activities described there.

Error Pattern A-D-1

from Harold's paper on page 71.

Did you find Harold's error pattern?

Harold seemingly adds these decimal fractions as he would add whole numbers. The placement of the decimal point in the sum is a problem, but in every case he merely places the decimal point at the left of the sum.

E.

$$+\frac{.3}{.5}$$
$$\overline{.8}$$

F.

$$+\frac{.7}{.7}$$
$$\overline{.14}$$

We ought to be able to help Harold with a problem of this sort. How would *you* help him? Describe at least two instructional activities you believe would enable Harold to add such examples correctly.

1. _____

_____

2. _____

_____

After you have recorded both activities, turn to page 156 and compare your suggestions with the suggestions listed there.

Error Pattern S-D-1

from Les's paper on page 72.

Did you determine the procedure Les is using?

D. $60 - 1.35 = ?$

$$\begin{array}{r} 60 \\ -\ 1.35 \\ \hline 59.35 \end{array}$$

E. $24.8 - 2.26 = ?$

$$\begin{array}{r} 24.8 \\ -\ 2.26 \\ \hline 22.66 \end{array}$$

When presented with "ragged" decimals such as these, Les simply brings down the extra digits at the right. (This procedure produced an acceptable result when he added similar decimals!) Apparently, when there are no ragged decimals he is able to subtract correctly.

What would you do to help Les? Describe two activities you believe would help him subtract correctly when confronted with ragged decimals.

1. _____

_____

2. _____

_____

When your activities have been described, turn to page 158 and compare your ideas with the suggestions listed there.

Error Pattern M-D-1

from Marsha's paper on page 73.

If you used Marsha's error pattern, you completed examples E and F as they are shown below.

E.
$$
\begin{array}{r}
4\,0.5 \\
\times\quad .6 \\
\hline
24.30
\end{array}
$$

F.
$$
\begin{array}{r}
6.7 \\
\times\quad 3 \\
\hline
2.01
\end{array}
$$

In her answer, Marsha places the decimal point by counting over from the left instead of from the right. She frequently gets the correct answer (examples A, B, and E), but much of the time her answer is not the correct product.

If you were Marsha's teacher, what corrective procedures might you follow? Describe two instructional activities which you think would help Marsha multiply decimals correctly.

1. _____

_____

2. _____

_____

When your responses are complete, turn to page 159 and see if your suggestions are among the alternatives described.

Error Pattern D-D-1

from Ted's paper on page 74.

If you found Ted's error pattern, your results are the same as the erroneous computation shown on the following page.

Ted misses examples because of the way he handles remainders. If division does not "come out even" when taken as far as digits given in the dividend, Ted writes the remainder as an extension of the quotient. He may believe this is the

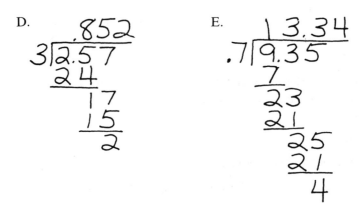

D.
$$3\overline{\smash{)}2.57} \;\; .852$$

E.
$$.7\overline{\smash{)}9.35} \;\; 13.34$$

same as writing R2 after the quotient for a division problem with whole numbers. Some children, having studied division with decimals, thereafter use a procedure similar to Ted's when dividing whole numbers. For example, 400 divided by 7 is computed as 57.1.

Ted needs help. How would you help him? Describe at least two instructional activities you believe would correct his error pattern.

1. _____

_____

2. _____

_____

After you have described at least two activities, turn to page 159 and compare your suggestions with the suggestions listed there.

Error Pattern P-P-1

from Sara's paper on page 75.

If you used Sara's error pattern, you completed the three percent problems as shown.

D. Brad earned $400 during the summer, and saved $240 from his earnings. What percent of his earnings did he save?

$$\frac{240}{400} = \frac{x}{100}$$

Answer: ___60%___

E. Barbara received a gift of money on her birthday. She spent 80% of the money on a watch. The watch cost her $20. How much money did she receive as a birthday gift?

$$\frac{20}{80} = \frac{x}{100}$$

Answer: $25

F. The taffy sale brought in a total of $750, but 78% of this was used for expenses. How much money was used for expenses?

$$\frac{78}{750} = \frac{x}{100}$$

Answer: $10.40

Sara successfully solved percent problems when the class first solved them, but as different types of problems were encountered she began to have difficulty. She *is* correctly solving the proportion she writes for the problem.

However, Sara uses a procedure that often does not accurately represent the ratios described in the problem. She is using the following proportion for every problem encountered:

$$\frac{\text{smaller number in the problem}}{\text{larger number in the problem}} = \frac{x}{100}$$

She appears to have abstracted the procedure from initial experiences with problems like A and D, with percents of less than 100. In each of the problems encountered, the first ratio was the smaller number over the larger number; this was always equal to x/100. Interestingly, the procedure also seems to work with problems of the type illustrated by B and E, even though different ratios are suggested; however, the procedure does not work with problems of the type illustrated by C and F.

How would you help Sara? Describe at least two instructional activities you believe would help her correctly solve percent problems.

1. _____

_____

2. _____

_____

After you have described at least two activities, turn to page 161 and compare your suggestions with the suggestions listed there.

Error Pattern P-P-2

from Steve's paper on page 76.

If you found Steve's error pattern, your results are as follows:

D. What number is 80% of 54?

$$54$$
$$\times\ .80$$
$$\overline{00}$$
$$432$$
$$\overline{43.20}$$

Answer: ___43.2___

E. Seventy is 14% of what number?

$$70$$
$$\times\ .14$$
$$\overline{280}$$
$$70$$
$$\overline{9.80}$$

Answer: ___9.8___

F. What percent of 125 is 25?

$$125$$
$$\times\ .25$$
$$\overline{625}$$
$$250$$
$$\overline{31.25}$$

Answer: ___31.25___

Steve's solutions are correct when he is finding the percent of a specified number (problems A and D). However, his solutions are incorrect when the percent is known and he is to find a number (problems B and E) and when he is to find what percent one number is of a specified number (problems C and F).

Usually, the first percent problems a student encounters involve finding the percent of a number. Steve probably developed his procedure while solving such problems, but he is also using a somewhat adapted version of it when he attempts to solve other types of percent problems. When the percent is given, he changes it to a decimal, then multiplies this number times the other number given. When the percent is not given, he treats the smaller of the two given numbers as if it were a decimal and proceeds similarly.

How would you help Steve? Describe at least two instructional activities you believe would help him correctly solve percent problems.

1. _____

_____

2. _____

_____

After you have written at least two descriptions, turn to page 162 and check your suggestions against those listed there.

Error Pattern S-M-1

from Margaret's paper on page 77.

Using Margaret's error pattern, examples C and D would be completed as they appear below.

C.
$$\overset{5}{\cancel{6}} \text{ yards, } \overset{1}{}1 \text{ foot}$$
$$- 2 \text{ yards, } 2 \text{ feet}$$
$$\overline{3 \text{ yards, } 9 \text{ feet}}$$

D.
$$\overset{2}{\cancel{3}} \text{ quarts, } \overset{1}{}1 \text{ cup}$$
$$- 1 \text{ quart, } 3 \text{ cups}$$
$$\overline{1 \text{ quart, } 8 \text{ cups}}$$

Margaret is regrouping in order to subtract just as she does when subtracting whole numbers expressed with base 10 numeration. She always crosses out the left figure and writes one less above it, then places a one in front of the right figure. This technique produces a correct result when the relationship between the two measurement units is a base 10 relationship, but the results are incorrect whenever other relationships exist.

How would *you* help Margaret? Describe at least two instructional activities you believe would make it possible for Margaret to subtract correctly in measurement situations.

1. _____

_____

2. _____

_____

After you have written at least two descriptions, turn to page 163 and see if any of your activities are among the suggestions listed there.

Chapter 5

Helping Children Correct Error Patterns in Computation

Whenever an error pattern is identified within a child's written work, corrective or remedial instruction needs to be provided so he will be able to replace his erroneous procedure with a useful algorithm. Only then can he make adequate use of computational procedures as tools. When a child solves mathematical problems and explores topics of interest, skill in computation permits him to expand his horizons conceptually.

In Chapter 2 a list of guidelines for instruction was presented. The following chapter contains descriptions of instructional activities which may be useful in helping children correct specific patterns of error. It is always important for the teacher to have in mind more than one instructional strategy; therefore, several activities are suggested for each error pattern. As you examine an error pattern, consider your own suggestions for providing remedial instruction. Do you find your suggestions among those recorded on the succeeding pages?

Selected materials that can be used in remedial instruction are described in Appendix E. Many of these materials are referred to in the following pages.

Also, numerous specific ideas for remedial instruction can be found in the references listed after this chapter.

Error Pattern A-W-1

from pages 38 and 80.

What instructional activities did you suggest to help correct the error pattern illustrated? See if your suggestions are among those listed below.

E.
$$
\begin{array}{r}
43 \\
+\ 65 \\
\hline
108
\end{array}
$$

F.
$$
\begin{array}{r}
88 \\
+\ 39 \\
\hline
1117
\end{array}
$$

Note: Be sure to extend your diagnosis by interviewing the student. Let Mike "think out loud" for you. Unless you do this you will not even know if he is adding the ones or the tens first.

1. *Use bundles of ten and single sticks.* Show both addends, then "make a ten" as may have been done in past instruction. Emphasize that we always need to start with the single sticks. Apply a rule for exchanging or regrouping if it is possible. Then make ten bundles of ten, if possible, and apply the rule again. With paper and pencil, record what is done *step-by-step*.

2. *Show both addends on a computing abacus.* Proceed as above.

3. *Provide the student with a set of numerals (0–9) and a frame for the answer.* Each box of the frame should be of a size which will enclose only one digit. Let the student use the cardboard or plastic numerals to record sums for problems. This activity should help the student remember to apply the rule for exchanging.

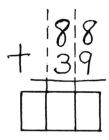

4. *Play chip-trading games.* To develop the idea for exchanging many for one, play games in which the values of chips are defined in terms of our numeration place-value pattern. However, it is easier to begin with bases less than ten. A child rolls a die and receives as many units as indicated on the die. He then exchanges for higher valued chips according to the rule of the game (five for one if base five, ten for one if base ten). Play proceeds similarly. The first child to get a specific

chip of a high value wins. Such games are described in *Chip Trading Activities, Book I* (See Appendix E.)

Error Pattern A-W-2

from pages 39 and 81.

What instructional activities do you suggest to help Mary correct the error pattern illustrated? See if your suggestions are among those described below.

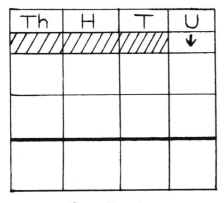

1. *Estimate sums.* Even *before* computing, the sum can be estimated. For instance, in example F it can be determined in advance that the sum is more than 1300.

2. *Use a game board and a bank.*[1] Help children understand place values and begin computation with units by making the algorithm a record of moves in a game (or a problem to solve). If base ten blocks are used on a gameboard, the object of the game is to show the amount of wood on the board with as few pieces as possible. To compute example F, the child would place 6 hundreds, 1 ten, and 8 unit blocks in the upper row. Then she sorts blocks for 782 in the second row. Beginning with the units (at the arrow), the child collects 10 units

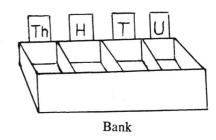

Bank

Game Board

---

[1] Lauren B. Resnick is developing a similar mapping procedure to help children link the semantics of the base system with the semantics of the algorithm. See her "Syntax and Semantics in Learning to Subtract" in Thomas P. Carpenter, James M. Moser, and Thomas A. Romberg (eds.), *Addition and Subtraction: A Cognitive Perspective* (Hillsdale, N.J.: Lawrence Erlbaum Assoc., Pub., 1982), pp. 136–55.

if she can (for this is a base ten game) and moves all remaining units below the heavy line. If she has been able to collect 10 units, they are traded at the bank for 1 ten; the ten is then placed above the other tens in the shaded place. (At first many children want to verify the equivalence of what goes into the bank and what comes out by placing the 10 units in a row and matching them with 1 ten.) As the child continues, she collects 10 tens if she can, and then moves all remaining tens below the heavy line. If she has been able to collect 10 tens, they are traded at the bank for 1 hundred, and the hundred is placed above the other hundreds in the shaded place. Finally, the child collects 10 hundreds if she can and moves all remaining hundreds below the heavy line. If she has been able to collect 10 hundreds they are traded at the bank for 1 thousand, and the thousand is placed in the shaded area at the top of the column for thousands. As it is not possible to collect 10 thousands, the one remaining thousand is brought below the heavy line. As the child computes the sum on paper, she records the number of blocks in each region every time trading is completed. (Making the record can be likened to writing a story.) When the record is finished, the algorithm is completed.

Error Pattern A-W-3

from pages 40 and 82.

You have written suggestions for helping Carol, who was using the error pattern illustrated. Are your suggestions among those listed below?

F.
$$\begin{array}{r} 26 \\ + \ 3 \\ \hline 11 \end{array}$$

G.
$$\begin{array}{r} 60 \\ +24 \\ \hline 84 \end{array}$$

H.
$$\begin{array}{r} 74 \\ + \ 5 \\ \hline 16 \end{array}$$

Note: An interview with the child may provide very helpful information. Is the child able to explain the examples which were worked correctly? Does the child identify tens and units and reason that units must be added to units and tens must be added to tens?

1. *Play "Pick-a-Number."* This game stresses the different values a digit may signify in various positions. Use cards with 0–9. Each player makes a form like this:

One player picks a card and reads the number, and each player writes that number in one of the spaces. Repeat until all blanks are full. The player showing the largest number wins.

2. *Show each addend with base ten blocks.* After the child shows both addends, have her collect the units and record the total number of units. She can then collect the tens and record the total number of tens.

3. *Show addends with sticks or toothpicks.* Bundles of ten and single sticks (or toothpicks) can be used. Proceed as with base ten blocks.

4. *Draw a line to separate tens and units.* This procedure may help with the mechanics of notation if the child understands the need to add units to units and tens to tens.

$$
\begin{array}{c|c} T & U \\ & 3 \\ +\ 2 & 6 \\ \hline 2 & 9 \end{array}
\qquad
\begin{array}{c|c} T & U \\ 6 & 0 \\ +\ 2 & 4 \\ \hline 8 & 4 \end{array}
\qquad
\begin{array}{c|c} T & U \\ 7 & 4 \\ +\ & 5 \\ \hline 7 & 9 \end{array}
$$

Error Pattern A-W-4

from pages 41 and 82.

You have suggested instructional activities for helping Dorothy or any child using this error pattern. Are your suggestions among those listed below?

E.
$$
\begin{array}{r} \overset{1}{4}6 \\ +\ 8 \\ \hline 134 \end{array}
$$

F.
$$
\begin{array}{r} \overset{\cdot}{9}8 \\ +\ 3 \\ \hline 131 \end{array}
$$

Note: The following suggestions assume that the child is *not* confusing these higher decade situations with multiplication.

1. *Explain the addition with ones and tens.*   Have the child explain the addition to you in terms of ones (or units) and tens. If her understanding of place value is adequate, this procedure may be sufficient to clear up the problem. It may be necessary to have the child use base ten blocks, a place-value chart, or an abacus to work out the problem.

2. *Label tens and units.*   Have the child label each column. The use of squared paper may also help if only one digit is written in each square.

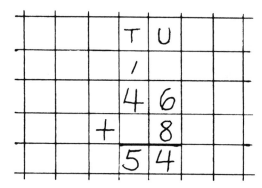

3. *Make higher decade sequences.*   Help the child discover the pattern illus-trated, then have her complete similar sequences. She may want to make up a few patterns all on her own.

$$\begin{array}{c} 6 \\ +\ 8 \\ \hline 14 \end{array} \quad \begin{array}{c} 16 \\ +\ 8 \\ \hline 24 \end{array} \quad \begin{array}{c} 26 \\ +\ 8 \\ \hline 34 \end{array} \quad \begin{array}{c} 36 \\ +\ 8 \\ \hline 44 \end{array} \ldots$$

Have you examined the papers in Appendix A that involve adding whole numbers? See if you can find the error patterns.

Error Pattern S-W-1

from pages 42 and 83.

You have described instructional activities to help correct the error pattern illustrated. Are your activities among those described?

Note: Be sure to extend your diagnosis by interviewing the child and letting her think out loud as she works similar examples. Does she use the erroneous procedure only with larger numbers? Does the child, on her own initiative,

E.
$$
\begin{array}{r}
458 \\
-\ 372 \\
\hline
126
\end{array}
$$

F.
$$
\begin{array}{r}
241 \\
-\ 96 \\
\hline
255
\end{array}
$$

question the reasonableness of her answers? (In example F, the result is larger than the sum.)

1. *Use bundles of 100, bundles of ten and single sticks.*   Let the student show the "number altogether," the sum. Pose the problem of removing the number of sticks shown by the lower numeral. Trading or exchanging as needed could be done at a trading post or a bank. Any verbal problems presented in this context should describe "take-away" rather than comparison situations. Eventually, guidance should be provided to help the student remove ones first, then tens, etc.

2. *Use base ten blocks.*   Proceed as above.

3. *Use a place-value chart.*   Proceed similarly.

4. *Use an abacus.*   Proceed as above. However, trading will not be for the same number of sticks or the same amount of wood. Trading will be based upon the more abstract notion of equal value.

Error Pattern S-W-2

from pages 43 and 85.

You have described two instructional procedures for helping a child using this error pattern. Are the activities you suggested for George similar to any of the activities described below?

D.
$$
\begin{array}{r}
2\overset{6}{\cancel{7}}\overset{1}{3} \\
-\ 38 \\
\hline
235
\end{array}
$$

E.
$$
\begin{array}{r}
2\overset{7}{\cancel{8}}\overset{1}{5} \\
-\ 63 \\
\hline
2112
\end{array}
$$

Note: Helpful instruction will emphasize (1) the ability to distinguish between subtraction problems requiring regrouping in order to use basic subtraction facts and subtraction problems not requiring regrouping, and (2) mechanics of notation.

1. *Use a physical representation for the minuend (sum).* If the minuend of example E is represented physically (with base blocks or bundles of sticks), questions can be posed such as "Can I take away 3 units *without* trading?" "When do I need to trade and when is it not necessary for me to trade?"

2. *Replace computation with* yes *or* no. Focus on the critical skill of distinguishing by presenting a row of subtraction problems for which the differences are *not* to be computed. Have the child simply write yes or no for each example to indicate the decision whether regrouping is or is not needed. If this is difficult, physical materials should be available for the child to use. (See activity 1 above.)

3. *Use squared paper.* Have the student use squared paper for computation with the rule that only one digit can be written within each square. Before computing each example it may be helpful to review the place value of each column of squares.

4. *Estimate differences.* Before each problem is solved, have the student estimate the answer. Encourage statements like "more than 300" or "less than 500" rather than exact answers.

Error Pattern S-W-3

from pages 44 and 86.

You have described two instructional activities you think would help children like Donna with this zero difficulty. Are any of your suggestions among those listed below?

E.
$$446$$
$$-302$$
$$\overline{104}$$

F.
$$760$$
$$-230$$
$$\overline{530}$$

1. *Use sets and record number sentences.* In a demonstration with simple subtraction facts show the sum with a set of objects. Next, remove a subset of as many objects as the known addend. Finally, record the missing addend as the number of objects remaining. After demonstrating the process, let the child having difficulty remove a subset from a set of 9 objects or less while you record the number sentence as a record of what is done. Encourage the child to remove the empty set. Then reverse the process and you demonstrate while the child records with a number sentence. Include many examples of removing the empty set.

2. *Use base blocks or bundled sticks to picture the computation.* Show the sum of a given subtraction problem. Sit beside the child and arrange the materials so that units are to the right and hundreds to the left as in the algorithm. For example

$$\begin{array}{r} 446 \\ -302 \\ \hline \end{array}$$

or

E, beginning with the units, remove the number (of sticks or blocks) shown by the given addend. After removing a subset of 2 units, record the fact that 4 units remain. After removing an empty set of tens, record the fact that 4 tens remain, etc. For another example, let the child remove the subsets while *you* record the number remaining each time.

3. *Try a sorting game.* If the child has been introduced to the multiplication facts for zero, there may be confusion between the zero property for multiplication and the zero properties for other operations. For the zero facts of arithmetic, cards can be prepared showing open number sentences similar to the ones shown.

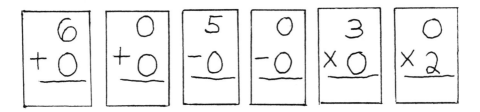

(Vertical notation is suggested in this case because it appears in the algorithm. It may be appropriate to include division number sentences as well, *e.g.,* $0 \div 3 = ?$) As an individual activity or as a game for two, the cards can be sorted into two sets—those with zero for the answer and those which do not have zero for an answer.

4. *Use a calculator.* Have the child try many examples of adding a zero, subtracting a zero, and multiplying by a zero. Then ask the child to state a generalization or rule for each operation. Also have the child compare the rules to see how they are alike or different.

Error Pattern S-W-4

from pages 45 and 86.

Do you find, among the suggestions listed below, your suggestions for helping Barbara, who has the difficulty illustrated?

E.
$$
\begin{array}{r}
\overset{3}{\cancel{4}}\overset{1}{3}6 \\
-\ 172 \\
\hline
264
\end{array}
$$

F.
$$
\begin{array}{r}
\overset{4}{\cancel{6}}\overset{1}{2}\overset{1}{5} \\
-\ 348 \\
\hline
187
\end{array}
$$

Note: Asking a child to check his computation may accomplish little in this situation. "Adding up" may only confirm that individual subtraction facts have been correctly completed. (In example F, $7 + 8 = 15$, $8 + 4 = 12$, and $1 + 3 = 4$.) The following activities are suggested to help the child keep in mind the *total quantity* from which a lesser number is being subtracted.

1. *Use base ten blocks to show the sum (minuend).* Pointing to the subtrahend, ask, "What trading must we do so we can take away this many?" As appropriate, trade a ten for ones and *immediately* record the action; then trade a hundred for tens and record that action. Stress the need to proceed step by step. Have the child trade and remove blocks while you record the action, then reverse the process. While you trade and remove blocks, let the child make the record.

2. *Use a place-value chart.* Proceed in a manner similar to that suggested for base ten blocks.

3. *Use bundles of 100, bundles of ten and single sticks.* Proceed as above.

4. *Use an abacus.* Again, proceed similarly.

5. *Use expanded notation.* Have the child rename the sum to a name which makes possible the use of basic subtraction facts. In this example, $600 + 20 + 5$ was renamed as $600 + 10 + 15$, then $600 + \underline{10} + 15$ was renamed as $\underline{500} + \underline{110} +$ 15. Base ten blocks can be used to verify such equivalences.

$$
\begin{array}{r}
625 = \\
-\ 348 =
\end{array}
\quad
\begin{array}{l}
\overset{500}{\cancel{600}} + \overset{\overset{110}{\cancel{70}}}{\cancel{20}} + \overset{15}{\cancel{5}} \\
300 + 40 + 8 \\
\hline
200 + 70 + 7 = 277
\end{array}
$$

Error Pattern S-W-5

from pages 46 and 87.

Are your suggestions for helping Sam among the suggestions listed below? He has the illustrated difficulties.

$$
\text{E.} \quad
\begin{array}{r}
\overset{4}{\cancel{3}}\ \overset{7}{\cancel{8}} 5 \\
-\ 3\ 2\ 2 \\
\hline
1\ 5\ 3
\end{array}
\qquad
\text{F.} \quad
\begin{array}{r}
\overset{7}{\cancel{6}}\ \overset{3}{\cancel{4}} 0 \\
-\ 6\ 2\ 6 \\
\hline
1\ 1\ 0
\end{array}
$$

Note: Suggestions 3 and 4 are primarily for dealing with the zero difficulty illustrated in this error pattern.

1. *Use base blocks or bundled sticks to picture the sum (minuend).* Specific procedures are outlined with Error Pattern S-W-4.

2. *Estimate before computing.* Have the child estimate his answer. A number line showing at least hundreds and tens may be helpful for this purpose. Ask, "Will the answer be more than a hundred? . . . less than a hundred?"

3. *Use a learning center for renaming.* For Sam and others with similar difficulties, a simple learning center could be set up to help them rename a minuend and select the most useful name for that number in a specific subtraction problem. One

possibility is to have a sorting task in which the child decides which cards show another name for a given number and which show an entirely different number. A second task would be to consider all the different names for the given number and decide which of the names would be most useful for computing subtraction problems having the given number for the minuend. Ask, "Which name will let us use the subtraction facts we know?"

4. *Use a game board and a bank.* Make the subtraction algorithm a record of moves in a game-like activity that can be presented as a problem to solve: the student is to show the amount of wood that will remain. Use the game board and bank pictured with Error Pattern A-W-2 but have the child picture *only the minuend* with base blocks or similar materials. The subtrahend should be shown with numeral cards to indicate how much wood is to be removed from the minuend set of wood. Begin with units and trade one ten for ten units if necessary; then place the units card and as many unit pieces of wood aside. The units that remain should be brought below the heavy line. For the tens, repeat by trading one hundred for ten tens if needed in order to have enough tens pieces to go with the numeral card below. Set aside the numeral card and the indicated number of tens; then bring the remaining tens below the line and continue the procedure. Make a step-by-step record of the child's moves in the game by recording each move with the written algorithm. Later, let the child record your moves or those of another child.

Th	H	T	U
////	////	////	↓
	□ □	/ / /	▫ ▫ ▫
	1	8	5

Game Board Used for Subtraction

Have you examined the papers in Appendix A that involve subtracting whole numbers? See if you can find the error patterns.

Error Pattern M-W-1

from pages 47 and 88.

How would you help a student such as Bob correct the error pattern illustrated? Are the activities you described similar to any of those below?

D.
$$\begin{array}{r} \overset{4}{9}8 \\ \times\ 56 \\ \hline 588 \\ 490 \\ \hline 5488 \end{array}$$

E.
$$\begin{array}{r} \overset{3}{8}6 \\ \times\ 45 \\ \hline 430 \\ 354 \\ \hline 3970 \end{array}$$

Note: The following activities emphasize place value, the distributive property, and proper mechanics of notation.

1. *Use more partial products and no crutch.* The following algorithm can be related to an array which is partitioned twice. When the student is able to use this algorithm with ease, let him try to combine the first two partial products (and also the last two) by *remembering* the number of tens and the number of hundreds. Do not encourage the use of a crutch in this situation.

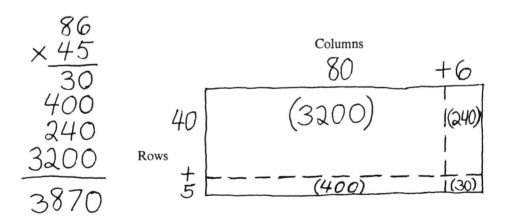

2. *Make two problems.* When the student is able to compute the product in this way, encourage him to try remembering his crutch "because such crutches are sometimes confusing in multiplication and division problems." When he can compute easily without recording the crutch, convert to a more standard algorithm by placing the same partial products *under* the example.

3. *Record tens within partial products.* Instead of writing "crutch" numerals above the example, use lightly written, half-sized numerals within each of the partial products to record the number of tens to be remembered.

$$
\begin{array}{r} 86 \\ \times\,45 \\ \hline \end{array}
\;\longrightarrow\;
\begin{array}{r} 86 \\ \times\,45 \\ \hline {}^{3}0 \end{array}
\;\longrightarrow\;
\begin{array}{r} 86 \\ \times\,45 \\ \hline 4\overset{3}{3}0 \end{array}
$$

$$
\longrightarrow
\begin{array}{r} 86 \\ \times\,4\overset{}{5} \\ \hline 4\overset{3}{3}0 \\ {}^{2}4 \end{array}
\;\longrightarrow\;
\begin{array}{r} 86 \\ \times\,45 \\ \hline 4\overset{3}{3}0 \\ 344 \end{array}
\;\longrightarrow\;
\begin{array}{r} 86 \\ \times\,45 \\ \hline 4\overset{3}{3}0 \\ 344 \\ \hline 3870 \end{array}
$$

4. *Apply the commutative and associative principles.* This technique should be especially helpful if the student has difficulty in processing open number sentences like 5 × 80 = ?; 40 × 6 = ?; and 40 × 80 = ? These number sentences are parts of example E and suggest a prerequisite skill for such examples; namely, application of the commutative and associative principles where one of the factors is a multiple of a power of ten. The error pattern may result, in part, from thinking of all digits as ones and the inability to think of tens, hundreds, etc., when using basic multiplication facts. After the associative principle is introduced with one-digit factors (perhaps with the aid of a three-dimensional arrangement of cubic units) let the student think through examples such as:

$$
\begin{aligned}
40 \times 6 &= (4 \times 10) \times 6 \\
&= (10 \times 4) \times 6 \\
&= 10 \times (4 \times 6) \\
&= 10 \times 24 \\
&= 240
\end{aligned}
$$

When the student generalizes this procedure, he will be able to compute the product of a one-digit number and a multiple of a power of ten *in one step.*

Cautions

In general, written crutches are to be encouraged if they are useful and help the child understand what he is doing. However, they can be confusing when multiplying a two-digit multiplier. Also, problems such as $5 \times 86 = ?$ occur within division algorithms where use of a written crutch is impractical. For these reasons, students should be encouraged to remember such crutches.

There is a very real danger in proceeding to a standard algorithm too quickly. A new, more efficient procedure is best introducd as a shortcut of an already understood algorithm. Zeros help a student think in terms of place value. Do not insist that the units zero in the second and succeeding partial products be dropped. (Pencil lead is not that expensive!)

Error Pattern M-W-2

from pages 48 and 89.

In the error pattern illustrated below, the child forgets to add the number of tens recorded as a crutch. Which of the instructional activities you suggested as help for this child are similar to activities described below?

E.
$$\begin{array}{r} 1 \\ 35 \\ \times\ 3 \\ \hline 95 \end{array}$$

F.
$$\begin{array}{r} 3 \\ 28 \\ \times\ 4 \\ \hline 82 \end{array}$$

1. *Use partial products.*   Introduce the following algorithm, possibly as a record of multiplying with parts of a partitioned array. If the child has previously used this algorithm and he uses it successfully, it may still be wise to return to the longer procedure so that instruction can proceed from a position of strength. Before returning to the standard algorithm, it may be helpful to have the child encircle the numeral to be remembered.

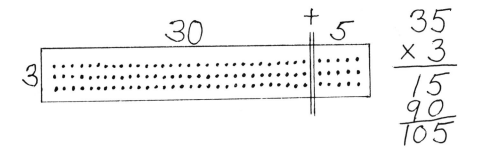

2. *Record a reminder below the bar.* Instead of a small numeral written above the multiplicand, introduce the idea that a reminder can be recorded as follows:

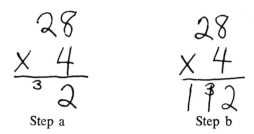

Step a   Step b

This procedure is a convenient bridge between the algorithm using partial products and the standard algorithm.

$$
\begin{array}{r}
27 \\
\times\ 3 \\
\hline
21 \\
60 \\
\hline
81
\end{array}
\quad\longrightarrow\quad
\begin{array}{r}
27 \\
\times\ 3 \\
\hline
81
\end{array}
\quad\longrightarrow\quad
\begin{array}{r}
27 \\
\times\ 3 \\
\hline
81
\end{array}
$$

Error Pattern M-W-3

from pages 49 and 89.

You have described two instructional activities for helping Joe and other students who have adopted the error pattern illustrated. Are your suggestions included in the activities described below?

D.
$$
\begin{array}{r}
\overset{4}{6}8 \\
\times\ 5 \\
\hline
500
\end{array}
$$

E.
$$
\begin{array}{r}
\overset{2}{2}9 \\
\times\ 3 \\
\hline
127
\end{array}
$$

1. *Use partial products.* Such an algorithm is easily developed as a step-by-step record of what is done when an array is partitioned. Help the child determine the order in which the multiplication and addition occur; lead him to generalize and state the sequence. In the example above, the 2 tens are multiplied by the 4; later the 1 ten is added to the 8 tens.

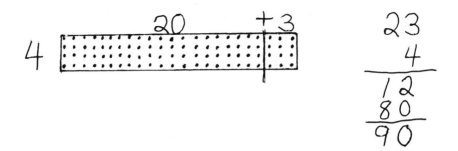

2. *Write the crutch below the bar.* Instead of the child writing a reminder in the conventional way, have him make a small numeral below the bar to remind him to add *just before* recording a product.

3. *Practice examples of the form (a × b) + c.* Sometimes a child appears to understand the algorithm and can verbalize the proper procedure correctly, but while using the algorithm he adopts careless procedures. Such a child may be helped by practicing examples such as (4 × 2) + 1 = ? and (3 × 6) + 2 = ?, thereby reinforcing the proper sequence. The child should be helped to relate this kind of practice to his difficulty in the multiplication algorithm.

4. *Introduce Aunt Sally.* This may be the time to introduce My Dear Aunt Sally (*m*ultiply, then *d*ivide, then *a*dd, then *s*ubtract).

Error Pattern M-W-4

from pages 50 and 90.

Are either of the instructional activities you suggested among those listed below?

E.
$$\begin{array}{r} 621 \\ \times\ 23 \\ \hline 1243 \end{array}$$

F.
$$\begin{array}{r} 5\overset{2}{1}7 \\ 463 \\ \hline 2081 \end{array}$$

1. *Use the distributive property.*   Have the child rewrite each problem as two problems. Later relate each partial product to the partial products in the conventional algorithm.

$$\begin{array}{r} 621 \\ \times\ 23 \\ \hline \end{array} \longrightarrow \begin{array}{r} 621 \\ \times\ 20 \\ \hline ? \end{array} + \begin{array}{r} 621 \\ \times\ 3 \\ \hline ? \end{array}$$

    If the child does not understand why the sum of the two multiplication problems is the same number as the product in the original problem, partition an array and label the parts. If the child does not understand the concept of an array, begin with small numbers.

2 × 3

$$2\left\{ \overbrace{\begin{array}{ccc} \bullet & \bullet & \bullet \\ \bullet & \bullet & \bullet \end{array}}^{3} \right.$$

Then use rectangles to represent arrays with large numbers.

23 × 621

	621
20 +	(20 × 621)
3	(3 × 621)

2. *Use a paper mask.*   Cover the multiplier so only one digit will show at a time. After multiplication by the units digit is completed, the mask can be moved to the left so that only the tens digit is visible. Later, the hundreds digit can be highlighted. With each digit, emphasize the need to do a complete multiplication problem. Also stress proper placement of each partial product.

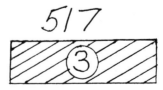

3. *Use a calculator.*   Use a calculator to compute each partial product.

Have you examined the papers in Appendix A that involve multiplying whole numbers? See if you can find the error patterns.

Error Pattern D-W-1

from pages 51 and 91.

How might you help Jim correct the erroneous procedure in the illustration? Are the instructional activities you described similar to any of the activities listed below?

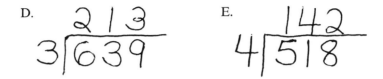

D. $$3\overline{)639} \quad 213$$

E. $$4\overline{)518} \quad 142$$

Note: To help the student who has adopted such an error pattern, activities need to emphasize place value in the dividend and the total quantity of the dividend. Procedures which can be understood in relation to concrete referents are needed instead of an assortment of rules to be applied in a mechanical way. In essence, a reintroduction to a division algorithm is needed.

1. *Use number rods to redevelop the algorithm.* Teach the child a computational procedure as a step-by-step record of activity with objects. For the problem 54 ÷ 3 = ?, the child can show the dividend as 5 ten-rods and 4 unit-rods using base ten blocks, Cuisenaire rods, or Unifix materials. Interpret the divisor as the number of equivalent sets to be formed. For example, in 54 ÷ 3 = ?, objects are to be distributed among three sets. (Single sticks and bundles can be used similarly.)

Step a   Step b   Step c

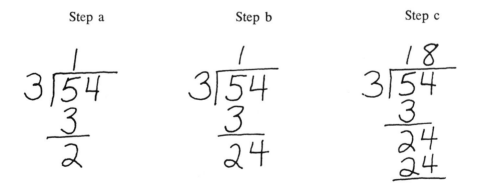

To begin, 1 ten-rod is placed in each of the three sets. Then a record is made to show this has been done. The record should also show that a total of 3 ten-rods has been removed from the dividend set (Step a). As the 2 remaining ten-rods cannot be distributed among three sets, they are traded for 20 units and joined with the other 4 unit-rods. This procedure is shown by "bringing down" the 4

(Step b). The 24 unit-rods are then distributed equally among the three sets and the record is completed (Step c).

2. *Estimate quotient figures.*   Use open number sentences such as $3 \times ? \leq 65$ with the rule that the number to be found is the largest multiple of a power of 10 which will make the number sentence true. To record the resulting partial quotients, one of the following algorithms would be especially useful:

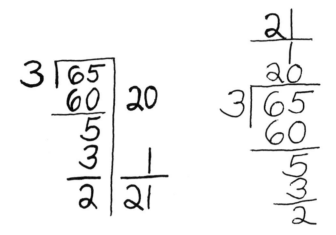

3. *Focus on skill in multiplying multiples of powers of ten by a single digit.*   This skill, used in the above activities, may need to be developed independently of a division algorithm. Patterns can be observed from such data as the following display.

$2 \times 3 = 6$ $2 \times 3 = 6$
$2 \times 30 = 60$ $20 \times 3 = 60$
$2 \times 300 = 600$ $200 \times 3 = 600$

It is possible to present a more detailed explanation related to a $2 \times 3 \times 10$ rectangular prism of unit cubes or to an application of mathematical principles.

$$2 \times 30 = 2 \times (3 \times 10)$$
$$= (2 \times 3) \times 10$$
$$= 6 \times 10$$
$$= 60$$

Error Pattern D-W-2

from pages 52 and 92.

Below are illustrations of Gail's error pattern in division of whole numbers. Are the instructional activities you suggested to help this child among those described?

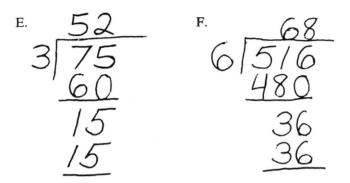

E.

$$3\overline{)75}$$ quotient 52, 60, 15, 15

F.

$$6\overline{)516}$$ quotient 68, 480, 36, 36

1. *Emphasize place value in estimating quotient figures.* Have the child use open number sentences such as $3 \times ? \le 70$ and $3 \times ? \le 15$ while thinking through example E. Number sentences should be completed using the following rule: When dividing 7 tens, the missing number is the largest multiple of ten which will make the number sentence true. For $3 \times ? \le 70$, $? = 20$. Similarly, when dividing 15 ones the missing number is the largest multiple of one which will make the number sentence true. For larger numbers, similar rules apply.

2. *Use a different algorithm.* At least temporarily, choose an algorithm that will show the value of each partial quotient. In each of the algorithms shown, the 8 in the quotient of example F is shown as 80, thereby emphasizing proper placement of quotient figures. After the student is able to use such algorithms, a transition to the standard computational procedure can be made, if desired, by recording quotients differently. In example F, the first quotient figure would be recorded as 8 in the tens place instead of as 80.

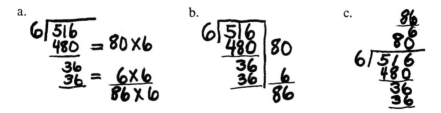

a.

$$6\overline{)516}$$
$$480 = 80 \times 6$$
$$36$$
$$36 = 6 \times 6$$
$$86 \times 6$$

b.

$$6\overline{)516}$$
$$480 \mid 80$$
$$36$$
$$36 \mid 6$$
$$86$$

c.

$$86$$
$$6$$
$$80$$
$$6\overline{)516}$$
$$480$$
$$36$$
$$36$$

3. *Develop skill in multiplying multiples of powers of 10.* This skill is necessary for rational use of any of the division algorithms illustrated. Exercises can be written to facilitate observation of patterns by the student.

$$6 \times 4 = 24$$
$$6 \times 40 = 240$$
$$6 \times 400 = 2400$$

Or, a more detailed explanation can be developed.

$$6 \times 400 = 6 \times (4 \times 100)$$
$$= (6 \times 4) \times 100$$
$$= 24 \times 100$$
$$= 2400$$

4. *Estimate the quotient before computing.* Frequently, quotients resulting from the erroneous algorithm are quite unreasonable. If intelligent estimating is followed by computing, and the estimate and the quotient are then compared, the student may rethink his computational procedure.

Error Pattern D-W-3

from pages 53 and 93.

You have suggested activities for helping John, who was using the error pattern illustrated. Are your suggestions among those listed below?

E.
$$
\begin{array}{r}
32\ r\,3 \\
9\overline{\smash)2721} \\
27 \\
\hline
21 \\
18 \\
\hline
3
\end{array}
$$

F.
$$
\begin{array}{r}
78\ r\,2 \\
6\overline{\smash)4250} \\
42 \\
\hline
50 \\
48 \\
\hline
2
\end{array}
$$

1. *Use lined paper turned 90°.* It may be that having the child use vertically lined paper (or cross-sectioned paper) will clear up the problem. The omission of one digit becomes very obvious when such forms are used for practice.

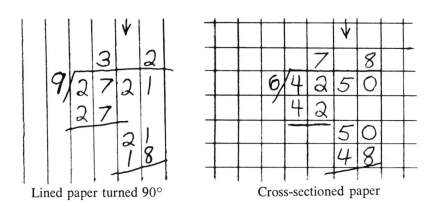

Lined paper turned 90°　　　　　　Cross-sectioned paper

2. *Use the pyramid algorithm.* At least temporarily, use an algorithm that emphasizes place value. If the pyramid algorithm has been learned by the child earlier in the instructional program, ask him to solve some of the troublesome examples using it in order to see if he can figure out why he is having difficulty now. If the pyramid algorithm is new to the child, he may enjoy trying a new procedure which is a bit easier to understand.

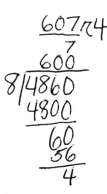

3. *Estimate the quotient before beginning computation.* The practice of recording an estimated quotient before computing may be sufficient to overcome the problem, especially if the error is not present in every such example and careless writing of quotient figures is a major cause of the difficulty.

Error Pattern D-W-4

from pages 54 and 94.

Are your suggestions for helping a child like Anita with the error pattern shown on the following page among those suggestions listed?

E.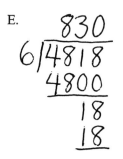

F.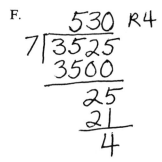

1. *Develop skill in multiplying multiples of powers of ten by a single-digit number.* Patterns such as this one can be observed. As the pattern is generalized and skill in such multiplication is developed, help the child see specific points within the division algorithm where this skill is applied.

$$3 \times 6 = 18 \qquad\qquad 7 \times 3 = 21$$
$$30 \times 6 = 180 \qquad\quad 7 \times 30 = 210$$
$$300 \times 6 = 1800 \qquad 7 \times 300 = 2100$$

2. *Use the pyramid algorithm.* Using an algorithm with partial quotients may adequately demonstrate the need for a zero in the tens place of the quotient.

$$
\begin{array}{r}
8 0 3 \\
3 \\
8 0 0 \\
6\overline{)4818} \\
4800 \\
\hline
18 \\
18 \\
\hline
\end{array}
$$

3. *Use base ten blocks.* In the example 4818 ÷ 6 = ?, have the child show 4818 with 4 thousand-blocks, 8 hundred-blocks, 1 ten-block, and 8 unit-blocks. Write the problem, and interpret the problem as partitioning the blocks into 6 sets of equal number. As it is not possible to parcel out 4 thousand-blocks among 6 sets, it is necessary to exchange the 4 thousand-blocks for an equal amount of wood, *i.e.*, for 40 hundred-blocks. The 48 hundred-blocks are then parcelled out evenly among 6 sets. The 8 in the hundreds place is recorded to show that 8 hundred-blocks have been placed in each of the 6 sets, and the 4800 is written in the algorithm to show how many blocks have been taken from the initial pile of blocks. (The initial pile of blocks can be called the dividend pile.) After subtract-

ing to see how many blocks remain in the initial pile, the resulting 18 should be compared with the 1 ten-block and 8 unit-blocks remaining to verify that the record (the algorithm) accurately describes what remains.

   The next task is to parcel out ten-blocks among the 6 sets; however, the 1 ten-block cannot be partitioned among 6 sets. It is therefore necessary to ex-change the 1 ten-block for an equal number—for 10 unit-blocks. Before exchang-ing, *have the child record in the algorithm with a zero that no ten-blocks are being partitioned* among the 6 sets. Finally, proceed to partition the 18 unit-blocks and complete the algorithm.

Paper 27 in Appendix A involves division with whole numbers. Can you find the error pattern?

Error Pattern E-F-1

   from pages 55 and 95.

When attempting to change a fraction to lower terms, Greg used his own cancella-tion procedure. Which of the instructional activities you suggested as help for this child are similar to activities described below?

E.
$$\frac{16}{64} = \frac{1}{4}$$

F.
$$\frac{14}{42} = \frac{1}{2}$$

   Note: You will probably want to extend your diagnosis to see if the child can interpret a fraction with some form of physical representation. If not, instruction should focus first of all upon the meaning or meanings of a fraction. The activities which follow are suggested with the assumption that the student has a basic understanding of the fraction idea.

1. *Emphasize prime factorizations.*   Show that both the numerator and the de-nominator can be renamed as products. If the unique name for a number we call the prime factorization is used, common factors can be noted and the greatest common factor can be determined easily. When the fraction is rewritten with prime factorizations, the child's cancellation procedure *is* appropriate.

2. *Use the multiplicative identity to "go both ways."*   Have the child use names for one of the form n/n when multiplying to rename a common fraction to higher terms. Then explore the question, How can we change the fraction back to the way it was? Show that both numerator and denominator can be divided by the same number without changing the value of the fraction.

3. *Interpret a fraction as a ratio of disjoint sets.*   Construct disjoint sets to show both numerator and denominator and compare them. For the unit fraction ¼ and

any fraction which is equivalent to ¼, the denominator is four times as great as the numerator. Have the child evaluate his written work keeping this relationship in mind.

Error Pattern E-F-2

from pages 56 and 96.

The error pattern illustrated was explained: "3 goes to 1, and 4 goes to 2." Are the instructional activities you suggested similar to any of the activities described below?

E.
$$\frac{3}{4} = \frac{1}{2}$$

F.
$$\frac{2}{8} = \frac{1}{4}$$

Note: It may be wise to extend the diagnosis to determine if the student is able to interpret a fraction as parts of a region or a set. If the student cannot, instruction should begin with a concept of a fraction. The following activities assume the student has such a basic understanding of a fraction even though a mechanical rule for changing a fraction to simplest terms was adopted.

1. *Use fractional parts of regions.* Begin with reference to the unit, then show the given number with fractional parts. Do *not* restrict the instruction to pie shapes, but use rectangular shapes as well. Pose the question, "Can we use larger parts to cover what we have exactly?" Record several "experiments" and note which are already in simplest terms. Then look for a mathematical rule for changing, *i.e.*, dividing both numerator and denominator by the same number.

$$\frac{4}{6}$$

2. *Build an array with fractional parts of a set.* With discs of two colors, make a row for a given fraction.

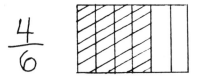

Then, build an array by forming additional rows of discs—rows identical to the first. As each row is formed, count the columns and the discs. Record the equivalent fractions.

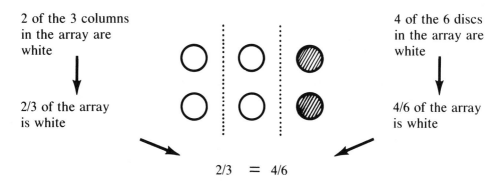

2 of the 3 columns in the array are white

2/3 of the array is white

4 of the 6 discs in the array are white

4/6 of the array is white

2/3 = 4/6

3. *Look for a pattern in a list.* Present a list of *correct* examples similar to the following ones. (Equivalent fractions can be thought of as two pictures of the same number, but wearing different clothes.) Have the student look for a pattern (a mathematical rule) for changing. Test out the suggested pattern on other examples. When a correct procedure is found, use it to help determine which fractions can be changed to simpler terms and which are already in simplest terms.

$$\frac{6}{8} = \frac{3}{4}$$

$$\frac{4}{6} = \frac{2}{3}$$

4. *Make sets of equivalent fractions.* Children can do this by successively subdividing regions. Record the resulting sets of equivalent fractions, with the smallest whole numbers first and larger numbers in order; then use the sets for finding simplest terms. Look for a relationship between any one fraction and the first fraction in the set.

$$\left\{ \frac{2}{3}, \frac{4}{6}, \frac{6}{9}, \frac{8}{12}, \circ \circ \circ \right\}$$

5. *Have a race.* Play a board game in which players race their pieces forward along a track made up of sections, each of which is partitioned into twelfths. Players roll special dice, draw cards with fraction numerals, or draw unit regions for fractions. Possible fractions include ½, ⅔, ⅚, ¾, and so forth. Moves forward are for the equivalent number of twelfths. An example of this kind of game can be found in the Introductory Cards of the Fraction Bars program (see Appendix E).

Error Pattern E-F-3

from pages 57 and 97.

In order to change to lowest terms, Sue divided the larger number by the smaller to determine the new numerator, and copied the larger number as the new denominator. Which of the remedial instructional activities you suggested are among the activities described below?

$$\text{G. } \frac{3}{6} = \frac{2}{6} \qquad\qquad \text{H. } \frac{6}{4} = \frac{1}{6}$$

Note: There is some evidence that this child is only manipulating symbols in a mechanistic way and not even interpreting fractions as parts of unit regions. For example, the child's statement that ⅜ = ⅔ suggests that an understanding of ⅜ or ⅔ as parts of a unit just is not present, or, if it is, it is a behavior associated with something like fraction pies, and it is not applied in other contexts. It may be wise to interview the child to determine how the child conceptualizes fractions before planning any remedial instruction.

1. *Match numerals with physical or diagrammatic representations.* To encourage the interpretation of a fraction in terms of real world referents, help the child learn and reinforce two behaviors:

   a. When given a physical or diagrammatic representation for a fraction, the child writes the fraction or picks out a numeral card showing "how much." In an activity of this sort, be sure the child understands the given frame of reference, *i.e.,* the unit.
   b. When given a fractional numeral, the child makes a representation for the fraction with blocks, parts of a unit region, sets, etc.; or draws an appropriate diagrammatic representation.

2. *Order fraction cards.* Give the child a set of cards, each with a different fraction having the same denominator. Have the child sequence the cards, thereby focusing on the fact that ⅜ ≠ ⅔. (It may be necessary to emphasize that the equality sign means "is the same as.") Encourage the child to refer to physical or diagrammatic representations as necessary to verify any decisions.

3. *Play "Can you make a whole?"* The child needs to recognize fractions which can be changed to a mixed number. Give the child a set of cards with a fraction on each card. Some of the cards should have proper or common fractions; others should have improper fractions. The child plays the game by sorting the cards into two piles: those which will "make a whole" (those equal to or greater than 1) and those which will not "make a whole." A playing partner or teacher then picks two of the sorted cards to challenge, and the child uses physical representations to prove that the challenged fractions are sorted correctly. If two children are

playing, they should take turns assuming sorting and challenging roles. More specific game rules and scoring procedures (if any) can be agreed upon by the children involved.

Additional suggestions for remedial activities are listed for pattern E-F-2. They are apt to be appropriate if the child is able to do the activities listed in items 1 through 3.

Error Pattern A-F-1

from pages 58 and 97.

What instructional activities do you suggest to help Robbie correct the error pattern illustrated? See if your suggestions are among those illustrated below.

E. $\dfrac{3}{4} + \dfrac{1}{5} = \dfrac{4}{9}$ F. $\dfrac{2}{3} + \dfrac{5}{6} = \dfrac{7}{9}$

Note: You should extend your diagnosis by having the child complete a variety of tasks which assess subordinate skills for adding unlike fractions. Appendix D is a hierarchy of such tasks. If you prepare a diagnostic instrument with the hierarchy as a guide, order your examples from simple to complex. You may want to put them on cards or in a learning center. Because the error pattern is so similar to the multiplication algorithm, this may be a child who tends to carry over one situation into his perception of another. If so, avoid extensive practice at a given time on any single procedure.

1. *Emphasize both "horizontal" and "vertical."* When adding *un*like fractions, it is usually best to write the example vertically so the renaming can be recorded more easily. Have the child practice deciding which of the several examples should be written vertically to facilitate computation and which can be computed horizontally.

2. *Use unit regions and parts of unit regions.* Have the child first represent each addend as fractional parts of a unit region. It will be necessary for the child to exchange some of the fractional parts so they are all of the same size (same denominator). The fractional parts can then be used to determine the total number of units. This procedure should be related step-by-step to the mechanics of notation in a written algorithm, probably an example written vertically so the renaming can be noted more easily.

3. *Discuss counting as a strategy.* Show how counting is appropriate when the denominators are the same, but not appropriate when they are different.

4. *Estimate answers before computing.* This may require some practice locating fractions on a number line and ordering fractions written on cards. Use phrases

like "almost a half" and "a little less than one" when discussing problems. In example F, more than a half is added to a little less than one. The result should be about one and a half.

After examining the research, Suydam states: "It seems apparent that we need to shift emphasis from having students learn rules for operations on fractions to helping them develop a conceptual base for fractions."[2]

Error Pattern A-F-2

from pages 59 and 98.

How would you help a student such as Dave who uses the error pattern illustrated below? Are your suggestions included among the activities described?

D.
$$9\frac{1}{3} = \frac{3}{9}$$
$$+ \ 5\frac{5}{9} = \frac{5}{9}$$
$$\frac{8}{9}$$

E.
$$16\frac{3}{4} = \frac{3}{4}$$
$$+ \ 23\frac{1}{2} = \frac{2}{4}$$
$$\frac{5}{4} = 1\frac{1}{4}$$

1. *Estimate answers before computing.* Have the child record an estimated answer before he computes. Attention is thereby focused upon addition of the whole numbers. In example E, the child could note that a number greater than 16 added to a number greater than 23 will be a number greater than 39. Similarly, a number less than 17 added to a number less than 24 will be a number less than 41. The sum must be between 39 and 41.

2. *Emphasize the meaning of "equals."* Tell (or remind) the child that the equality sign means "is the same as." Have the child point to each equality sign in his work and explain why the numerals on either side of the sign are both names for the same number.

3. *Use unit regions and parts of unit regions.* This procedure should not be necessary for most students using the error pattern under consideration, but it can help some students become much more conscious of the whole numbers involved. If this procedure is to be followed, have the child first represent each addend with physical aids, *e.g.,* as a number of unit regions and as fractional parts of a region. It may then be necessary for the child to exchange some of the fractional parts so they are all of the same size (same denominator). The fractional parts can then be joined together and the unit regions can also be joined. Whenever it is possible, another unit region should be formed from the collection of fractional parts. This

---

[2] Marilyn N. Suydam, "Fractions," *The Arithmetic Teacher* 31, no. 7 (March 1984): 64.

procedure should be related step-by-step to the mechanics of notation in the written algorithm.

Error Pattern A-F-3

from pages 60 and 99.

You have described at least two instructional activities you think would help Allen or any child with the difficulty illustrated. Are any of your suggestions among those listed below?

D
$$\frac{1}{4} + \frac{1}{5} = \frac{5}{9} + \frac{4}{9} = \frac{9}{9}$$

E.
$$\frac{2}{5} + \frac{1}{2} = \frac{2}{7} + \frac{10}{7} = \frac{12}{7}$$

Note: Doctoring up an erroneous mechanical procedure by trying to substitute other purely mechanical procedures frequently results in a further confusion of arbitrary and meaningless procedures. Remediation should help the student use procedures which make sense to him.

1. *Find the l.c.m. (lowest common multiple) of two whole numbers.* To help the child find the least common denominator for two fractions, work separately with the denominators as whole numbers. First make sure the child can generate sets of multiples for each whole number. If the student is able to identify the intersection set of two given sets, he will be able to find a set of *common* multiples. Finally, he can note which common multiple is *least* in value. This least common multiple is the most useful common denominator for adding the two fractions. To reinforce this skill, give the student examples where he only finds the least common denominator.

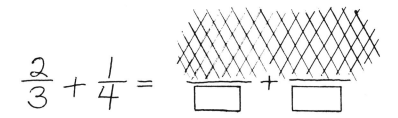

2. *Use the property of one for multiplication and the idea of many names for a number.* When the student can determine the least common denominator he will probably need specific help in changing one fraction to an equivalent fraction with

a specified denominator. This is a specific skill which can be developed apart from the larger example.

$$\frac{2}{3} = \frac{\square}{12}$$

If the child knows or can be taught how to multiply simple fractions, the property of one can be applied in renaming. The question posed is "*Which* name for one is useful?"

The useful name
for one

$$\frac{2}{3} \times 1 = \frac{\square}{12} \qquad \frac{2}{3} \times \frac{\triangle}{\triangle} = \frac{\square}{12} \qquad \frac{2}{3} \times \frac{4}{4} = \frac{\square}{12}$$

Clue: $3 \times \triangle = 12$

3. *Change to a vertical algorithm.* A vertical algorithm permits the student to write simple equivalence statements for each renaming of a fraction.

$$
\begin{aligned}
\frac{2}{3} &= \frac{2}{3} \times \frac{4}{4} = \frac{8}{12} \\
+ \quad \frac{1}{4} &= \frac{1}{4} \times \frac{3}{3} = \frac{3}{12} \\
&\qquad\qquad\qquad\quad \frac{11}{12}
\end{aligned}
$$

Error Pattern A-F-4

from pages 61 and 100.

Robin uses the error pattern illustrated. Are your suggestions for helping Robin among the activities described?

D. $\dfrac{3}{4} = \dfrac{3}{4}$

$+\dfrac{1}{2} = \dfrac{1}{4}$

$\dfrac{4}{4}$

E. $\dfrac{4}{5} = \dfrac{4}{20}$

$+\dfrac{1}{4} = \dfrac{1}{20}$

$\dfrac{5}{20}$

Note: Apparently Robin can find the least common denominator. She can also add like fractions. Corrective instruction should focus on the specific process of changing a fraction to higher terms, to a fraction with a designated denominator; e.g., $\frac{3}{4} = \frac{?}{20}$.

1. *Show that two fractions are or are not equal.* The equals sign tells us that numerals or numerical expressions on either side are names for the same number (the same fractional part, the same point on a number line). Help Robin find ways to tell if two different fractions name the same number; have her "prove" in *more than one way* that both fractions show the same amount. Examples of varied procedures which can be used include: stacking fractional parts of a unit region, using a number line which is labelled with different fractions (halves, thirds, fourths, etc.), finding a name for one (*n/n*) which could be used to change one of the fractions to the other, and for *a/b* = *c/d* showing that *ad* = *bc*.

2. *Use the multiplicative identity.* Emphasize the role of one by outlining *n/n* with the numeral "1" as illustrated. Have the child note that *both* terms of a fraction are multiplied, and therefore, both terms in the new fraction are different than the original fraction.

$$\dfrac{3}{4} = \dfrac{3 \times \boxed{2}}{4 \times \boxed{2}} = \dfrac{6}{8}$$

3. *Use games involving equivalent fractions.* Have the child play games in which equivalent fractions are matched, possibly adaptations of rummy or dominoes. Such games provide an excellent context for discussing how to determine if two fractions name the same number.

4. *Use a shield.* Within the algorithm, use a shield as illustrated to help the child focus on the task of changing a fraction to higher terms. Help the child see that the procedure for changing a fraction is the same as that used *within* this algorithm.

Appendix A includes other papers that involve adding with fractions. See if you can find the error patterns.

Error Pattern S-F-1

from pages 62 and 101.

Are your suggestions for helping Andrew with the difficulty illustrated below among the suggestions listed?

E.
$$5\tfrac{1}{5}$$
$$-\ 3\tfrac{3}{5}$$
$$\overline{\quad 2\tfrac{2}{5}\quad}$$

F.
$$1$$
$$-\ \tfrac{1}{3}$$
$$\overline{\quad 1\tfrac{1}{3}\quad}$$

Note: You will want to interview the child and have him think out loud as he works similar examples. Does the child question the reasonableness of his answers? In example F, the result is larger than the sum (minuend).

1. *Use fractional parts of a unit region.* Interpret the example as "take-away" subtraction and use fractional parts to show *only* the sum. If the child subtracts the whole numbers first, demonstrate that this procedure does not work; not enough remains so the fraction can be subtracted. Conclude that the fraction must be subtracted first. Have the child exchange one of the units for an equivalent set of fractional parts in order to take away the quantity indicated by the subtrahend.

2. *Use crutches to facilitate renaming.* Record the exchange of fractional parts (suggested above) as a renaming of the sum. The sum is renamed so the fraction can be subtracted easily.

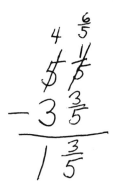

3. *Practice specific prerequisite skills.* Without computing, the child can decide which examples require renaming and which do not. The skill of renaming a mixed number in order to subtract can also be practiced. You will get ideas for other prerequisite skills from Appendix D, for most, if not all, of the tasks in the addition hierarchy found there apply equally to subtraction.

$$2\tfrac{1}{3} = 1\tfrac{4}{3} \qquad\qquad 3\tfrac{1}{2} = 2\tfrac{3}{2}$$

Error Pattern S-F-2

from pages 63 and 102.

You have described activities for helping Don, who is using the error pattern illustrated. Are your suggestions among those listed below?

D.
$$6\tfrac{5}{8} = 6\tfrac{5}{8}$$
$$- 3\tfrac{1}{4} = 3\tfrac{2}{8}$$
$$\overline{\qquad 3\tfrac{3}{8}}$$

E.
$$4\tfrac{3}{8} = \cancel{4}\,\overset{3}{\underset{}{}}\tfrac{8}{8}$$
$$-1\tfrac{1}{2} = 1\tfrac{4}{8}$$
$$\overline{\qquad 2\tfrac{4}{8} = 2\tfrac{1}{2}}$$

1. *Use fractional parts of a region.* The child can rename mixed numbers by exchanging a unit region for fractional parts. For example, in problem E, he can exchange 1 of the unit regions for 8 eighths and place them with the 3 other eighths. He should record his findings by writing 4⅜ = 3¹¹⁄₈.

2. *Find many names for a mixed number.*   Have the child make several names for a given number. For example, $4\frac{3}{8} = 3\frac{11}{8} = 2\frac{19}{8} = 1\frac{27}{8}$. For each unit subtracted it is necessary to add $\frac{8}{8}$ in order to keep the same numerical value for the mixed number. Guide the child in applying this skill in subtraction by asking the questions: "Do I need to rename? What name will be most useful?"

Error Pattern S-F-3

from pages 64 and 102.

Do you find among the suggestions listed below your suggestions for helping Chuck who has the difficulty illustrated?

E. $6\frac{2}{3} - 3\frac{1}{6} = 3\frac{1}{3}$ F. $4\frac{5}{8} - 1\frac{3}{4} = 3\frac{2}{4}$

Note: Extended diagnosis is probably wise. Most of the subordinate skills suggested in the addition hierarchy found in Appendix D apply equally to subtraction.

1. *Emphasize both "horizontal" and "vertical."*   When subtracting with unlike fractions and with mixed numerals, it is usually best to write the example vertically so the renaming can be recorded more easily. Have the child practice deciding which of several examples should be written vertically to facilitate computation and which can be computed horizontally.

2. *Use fractional parts of a unit region.*   Use fractional parts to show *only* the sum, then cover or set apart the amount indicated by the known addend. The child will soon discover that it is necessary to deal with the fraction before the whole number. Have the child exchange as necessary in order to cover or set apart the amount required. Such a procedure will help the child relate the problem more adequately to the operation of subtraction. However, it can become a cumbersome procedure, so choose examples carefully. (An appropriate example might be $3\frac{1}{6} - 1\frac{2}{3}$.) Step-by-step, relate the activity with fractional parts to the vertical algorithm.

3. *Reteach and/or practice specific prerequisite skills.*   Consider the tasks listed in Appendix D. Suggestions for instructional activities have already been described for many of these. For example, for Error Pattern A-F-3 activities are suggested which are appropriate for subtraction as well as for addition of unlike fractions. These activities are concerned with least common multiples, the identity element, and the like.

Error Pattern S-F-4

from pages 65 and 103.

Are your suggestions for helping Ann with the difficulty illustrated among the suggestions listed?

D. $\quad 5\frac{3}{8} = 5\frac{43}{8}$

$\quad -2\frac{1}{2} = 2\frac{5}{8}$

$\quad\quad\quad\quad 3\frac{38}{8}$

E. $\quad 4\frac{1}{3} = 4\frac{13}{15}$

$\quad -1\frac{4}{5} = 1\frac{9}{15}$

$\quad\quad\quad\quad 3\frac{4}{15}$

Note: Corrective instruction should focus on changing a mixed number to an equivalent mixed number, one in which the fraction has a specified denominator. Ann will need to understand *why* it is frequently necessary to rename mixed numbers with the algorithm.

1. *Prove that mixed numbers are or are not equal.* Emphasize that the whole number and fraction together constitute *a* mixed number, and that "equals" written between two mixed numbers says that they name the same number (show the same amount, name the same point on a number line). Two mixed numbers can be shown to be equal with unit regions and fractional parts, or with an appropriately labelled number line.

2. *Make many names for a mixed number.* With the help of an aid such as unit regions and fractional parts, have the child generate as many names as possible for a given mixed number. For example:

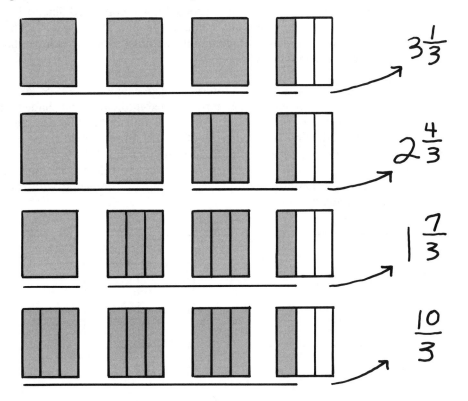

Then, for an example like 3⅓ − 1⅔ = ☐ ask, "Which is the most useful name for 3⅓?"

3. *Point to different trading patterns.*   Liken the regrouping within this algorithm to the regrouping done with whole numbers when different bases are used. Chip trading activities with varied trading rules have a structure similar to the process of changing a mixed number to an equivalent mixed number.

Appendix A includes other papers that involve subtracting with fractions. See if you can find the error patterns.

Error Pattern M-F-1

from pages 66 and 104.

How would you help a student such as Dan correct the error pattern illustrated? Are the activities you described similar to any of those below?

E. $\dfrac{3}{4} \times \dfrac{2}{3} = 89$ F. $\dfrac{4}{9} \times \dfrac{2}{5} = 200$

    Note: The child's product is most unreasonable, and continued diagnosis is wise. Does the child understand the equals sign as meaning "the same"? What kind of meaning does he associate with common fractions? Does he believe that products are *always* larger numbers?

1. *Use fractional parts of unit regions.*   Interpreting an example like ¾ × ⅔ = ? as ¾ of ⅔ = ?, picture a rectangular region partitioned into thirds and shade two of them. This represents ⅔ of one. Next, partition the unit so the child can see ¾ of the ⅔. What part of the unit is shown as ¾ of ⅔? Be sure the child relates the answer to the unit rather than just the ⅔. Record the fact that ¾ of ⅔ = ⁶⁄₁₂ and solve other problems with drawings. Then redevelop the rule for multiplying fractions by observing a pattern among several examples completed with fractional parts of unit regions.

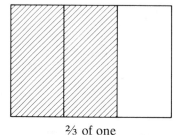

⅔ of one

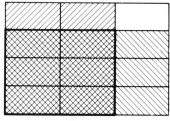

¾ of ⅔

2. *Estimate before computing.* Children often assume that the result of multi-plying will be a larger number. Ask if ⅔ is less than one or more than one. Is ¼ of ⅔ less than one or more than one? ¾ of ⅔? ¾ of ⅔? Will ¾ of ⅔ be less than ⅔ or more than ⅔? It will be helpful if the child expects his answer to be less than ⅔. Of course, a child must understand fraction concepts before he can be expected to learn to estimate.

Error Pattern M-F-2

from pages 67 and 105.

What instructional activities do you suggest to help Grace correct the error pattern illustrated? See if your suggestions are among those illustrated below.

D. $\dfrac{2}{3} \times \dfrac{3}{4} = \dfrac{2}{3} \times \dfrac{4}{3} = \dfrac{8}{9}$

E. $\dfrac{5}{7} \times \dfrac{3}{8} = \dfrac{5}{7} \times \dfrac{8}{3} = \dfrac{40}{21}$

1. *Emphasize the meaning of "equals."* *Equals* means "the same," and the expressions on either side of an equals sign should show the same number. Of course, when working with fractions, it is necessary to keep in mind the fact that a given number can be expressed with many equivalent fractions, but all equivalent fractions name the same number as labels on a number line will show. Have the child examine work that has been completed and compare the expressions on both sides of the equals sign to see if they are the same number. For example, in D the ⅔ is multiplied by less than one on one side of the equals sign and by more than one on the other side.

2. *Replace computation with* yes *and* no. Note that the student multiplied correctly after the second factor had been inverted. Focus on the question, "Do I invert or not?" Give the child a mixture of multiplication and division examples to write *yes* or *no* by each.

Error Pattern M-F-3

from pages 68 and 105.

How would you help Lynn correct the error pattern illustrated? Are your ideas similar to those listed below?

E. $\dfrac{3}{8} \times 4 = \dfrac{12}{32}$

F. $\dfrac{5}{6} \times 2 = \dfrac{10}{12}$

1. *Make the whole number a fraction.* Show Lynn that when multiplying both terms by the same number, she is multiplying by one (in the form *n/n*) and not by the number given. Have her put a one under the whole number. Both numbers will be fractions and the child can then use the procedure for multiplying fractions, e.g., ⅜ × ⁴⁄₁ = ¹²⁄₈.

2. *Use a number line.* On a number line which is labelled appropriately, have the child draw arrows to show the multiplication. Emphasize that the product tells how many sixths (or whatever denominator is being used). For 2 × ⅚ or for ⅚ × 2:

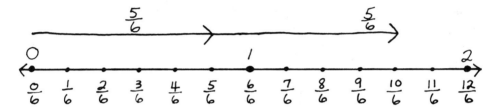

3. *Use addition.* Reverse the factors and have the child solve the addition problem suggested.

$$\frac{3}{8} \times 4 = 4 \times \frac{3}{8}$$

$$4 \times \frac{3}{8} = \frac{3}{8} + \frac{3}{8} + \frac{3}{8} + \frac{3}{8} = \frac{12}{8}$$

Appendix A includes other papers that involve multiplying with fractions. See if you can find the error patterns.

Error Pattern D-F-1

from pages 69 and 106.

What instructional activities do you suggest to help Linda correct the error pattern illustrated? See if your suggestions are among those described below.

E. $$\frac{4}{12} \div \frac{4}{4} = \frac{1}{3}$$ F. $$\frac{13}{20} \div \frac{5}{6} = \frac{2}{3}$$

Note: Selection of appropriate remedial activities will depend somewhat upon which algorithm for division with fractions the child was taught originally.

1. *Introduce an alternative algorithm.* Complex fraction, common denominator, and invert and multiply are frequently taught algorithms for division with fractions. Introduce a procedure different from the one previously studied by the child.

2. *Discover a pattern.* Introduce the invert and multiply rule by presenting a varied selection of examples complete with correct answers, e.g., $\frac{7}{12} \div \frac{3}{5} = \frac{35}{36}$. Have the child compare the problems and answers and look for a pattern among the examples. Be sure each hypothesized rule is tested by checking it against all examples in the selection. After the pattern has been found, have the child verbalize the rule and make up a few examples to solve.

3. *Estimate answers with paper strips and a number line.* Using a number line and the measurement model for division, make a strip of paper about as long as the dividend and another about as long as the divisor. Ask how many strips the length of the divisor strip can be made from the dividend strip. For $\frac{5}{8} \div \frac{2}{5} = ?$, the answer might be "about one and a half." For example F, the estimate might be "a little less than one."

Error Pattern D-F-2

from pages 70 and 107.

How would you help a student such as Joyce who uses the error pattern illustrated below? Are your suggestions included among those listed?

D. $\dfrac{5}{8} \div \dfrac{2}{3} = \dfrac{8}{5} \times \dfrac{2}{3} = \dfrac{16}{15}$

E. $\dfrac{1}{2} \div \dfrac{1}{4} = \dfrac{2}{1} \times \dfrac{1}{4} = \dfrac{2}{4}$

Note: Determine whether the student consistently inverts the dividend, or alternates between the divisor and the dividend. You may also want to make sure the student has no difficulty distinguishing between right and left.

1. *Compare results.* Have the student determine if both procedures produce the same result. Then explain that it is the divisor "there on the right" which is to be inverted. Have the student suggest a way of remembering to invert the fraction on the right and not the other fraction when dividing. (Be careful. Remember the child in Chapter 1 who used the piano?)

2. *Use parts of a unit region.* Because inverting the dividend and inverting the divisor produce different answers, the student can use a manipulative aid to

determine which result is correct. Parts of a unit region may be appropriate if the example is interpreted as measurement division. For example, for ½ ÷ ¼ = ☐, have the child first place ½ of a unit on top of a unit region. This shows the dividend or product. Then explain that just as 6 ÷ 2 = ☐ asks "How many 2's are in 6?" so ½ ÷ ¼ = ☐ asks "How many ¼'s are in ½?" Have the student cover the ½ of a unit with ¼'s of a unit. In all, exactly *two* ¼'s are equal to ½. The correct result is two and not ¾; it is the result obtained by inverting the divisor on the right.

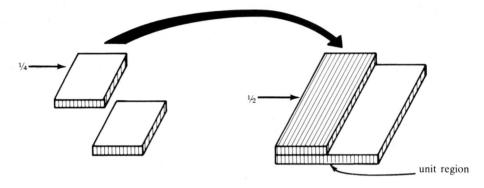

¼

½

unit region

3. *Use paper strips and a number line.* These can be used as described in the previous error pattern, but used in this case to determine which fraction should be inverted for the correct result.

Papers 40 and 41 in Appendix A involve dividing with fractions. See if you can find the error patterns.

Error Pattern A-D-1

from pages 71 and 107.

You have described two activities for helping Harold with the difficulty illustrated below. Are either of your suggestions among those listed?

E.
$$+ \begin{array}{r} .3 \\ .5 \\ \hline .8 \end{array}$$

F.
$$+ \begin{array}{r} .7 \\ .7 \\ \hline .14 \end{array}$$

Note: Some teachers will be tempted to simply tell the child that in problems like example F the decimal point should go *between* the two digits in the sum. However, such directions only compound the problem. The child needs a greater understanding of decimal numeration and the ability to apply such knowledge.

Research has shown that much of the difficulty children have with decimals stems from a lack of conceptual understanding.[3]

Further diagnosis is probably wise. When the addends also include units, does the child regroup tenths as units, or does he think of two separate problems—one to the right and one to the left?

$$
\begin{array}{r}
\overset{1}{6}.7 \\
8.5 \\
\hline
15.2
\end{array}
\qquad \text{or} \qquad
\begin{array}{r}
6.7 \\
8.5 \\
\hline
14.12
\end{array}
$$

1. *Use blocks or rods.* Define one size as a unit. Then have the child show each addend with blocks or rods one-tenth as large as the unit. After he combines the two, have him exchange tenths for a unit if possible. He should compare the results of this activity with his erroneous procedure.

2. *Use a number line.* Mark units and tenths clearly on a number line and show addition with arrows. Compare the sum indicated on the number line with the sum resulting from computation.

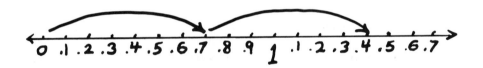

3. *Use vertically lined or cross-sectioned paper.* Theme paper can be turned 90° to use as vertically lined paper. Have the child compute using the rule that only one digit can be placed in a column. If cross-sectioned paper is used, only one digit should be written within each square.

4. *Use metersticks.* Use metersticks to reintroduce decimals and the names for the value of each place.[4]

Papers 42 and 43 in Appendix A also involve adding with decimals. See if you can find the error patterns.

---

[3]Thomas P. Carpenter et al., "Decimals: Results and Implications from National Assessment," *The Arithmetic Teacher* 28, no. 8 (April 1981): 34–37.

[4]See Robert Ashlock, "Introducing Decimal Fractions with the Meterstick," *The Arithmetic Teacher* 23, no. 3 (March 1976): 201–6.

Error Pattern S-D-1

from pages 72 and 108.

You described ways to help Les or other students who subtract as illustrated when they encounter ragged decimals. Are your suggestions among those listed?

D. $60 - 1.35 = ?$ E. $24.8 - 2.26 = ?$

$$\begin{array}{r} 60 \\ -1.35 \\ \hline 59.35 \end{array}$$

$$\begin{array}{r} 24.8 \\ -2.26 \\ \hline 22.66 \end{array}$$

Note: Usually the need to add or subtract decimals arises from measurement situations, and measurements should always be expressed in the same units and with the same precision if they are to be added or subtracted. Ragged decimals are inappropriate. At the same time, ragged decimals sometimes occur in situations with money (e.g., $4 − $.35). They also appear on some standardized tests, and many teachers believe students need to be taught a procedure for computing with them even if examples are somewhat contrived.

1. *Use a place value chart.* A place value chart can be relabelled for use with decimals (e.g., tens, ones, tenths, and hundredths). For a given example, have the student first show the sum (minuend) and then work through the regrouping necessary to subtract as would be done with whole numbers. Point out that the regrouping is being done *as if* additional zeros were written to the right of the decimal point. Suggest that by affixing zeros appropriately the examples can be computed without the confusion of ragged decimals. If it will simplify things, encourage the student to affix zeros when adding as well as when subtracting. (Be sure students *affix* zeros; they do not add them.)

2. *Use base ten blocks.* For use with decimals, the unit must be defined differently from the way it is used with whole numbers, so you may choose to use blocks that are not lined. Use them as the place value chart is to be used.

3. *Use a computing abacus.* Place values on an abacus can also be adapted to decimals and should be so labelled when this is done. Use them as the place value chart is to be used.

4. *Use money.* Use pennies, dimes, dollar bills, and ten-dollar bills much as you would use a place value chart. Stress the fact that the dollar bill is the unit; the dimes and pennies are tenths and hundredths of one dollar.

Error Pattern M-D-1

from pages 73 and 109.

Below are illustrations of Marsha's error pattern in multiplication of decimals. Are the instructional activities you suggested to help this child among those described?

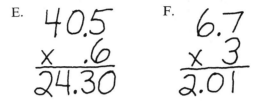

E.
$$\begin{array}{r} 40.5 \\ \times\ .6 \\ \hline 24.30 \end{array}$$

F.
$$\begin{array}{r} 6.7 \\ \times\ 3 \\ \hline 2.01 \end{array}$$

1. *Estimate before computing.* Use concepts like less than and more than in estimating the product before computing. For example E, a bit more than 40 is being multiplied by about a half. The product should be a bit more than 20. There is only one place where the decimal point could go if the answer is to be a bit more than 20. Similarly, in example F, 6.7 is between 6 and 7; therefore, the answer should be between 18 and 21. Again, there is only one place the decimal point can be placed for the answer to be reasonable. For 3.452 × 4.845, it can be easily seen that the product must be between 12 (i.e., 3 × 4) and 20 (i.e., 4 × 5), and there will be only one sensible place to write the decimal point.

2. *Look for a pattern.* Introduce the rule for placing the decimal point in the product by presenting a varied selection of examples complete with correct answers. Have the child compare the problems and answers and look for a pattern among the examples. Be sure the child checks her rule against all examples in the selection. When the correct rule has been established, have the child verbalize the rule and use it with a few examples she makes up herself.

Error Pattern D-D-1

from pages 74 and 109.

Are your suggestions for helping Ted among the suggestions listed below? He has the illustrated difficulty.

D.
$$\begin{array}{r} .852 \\ 3\overline{)2.57} \\ 24 \\ \hline 17 \\ 15 \\ \hline 2 \end{array}$$

E.
$$\begin{array}{r} 13.34 \\ .7\overline{)9.35} \\ 7 \\ \hline 23 \\ 21 \\ \hline 25 \\ 21 \\ \hline 4 \end{array}$$

1. *Label columns on lined paper.*   Turn theme paper 90° and write each column of digits between two vertical lines. Then label each column with the appropriate place value. This may help discourage moving digits around mechanically. In example D, 2 hundredths is not the same as 2 thousandths.

2. *Study alternatives for handling remainders.*   By using simple examples and story problems, first show that for division of *whole* numbers there are at least three different ways to handle remainders:

   a. As the amount remaining after distributing. Either a measurement or partitioning model for division can be used. The amount left over is expressed with a whole number.

$$\begin{array}{r} 64 \\ 6\overline{)387} \\ 36 \\ \hline 27 \\ 24 \\ \hline 3 \end{array}$$

Answer: 64 (groups, or in each group) with 3 left over

   b. As a common fraction within the quotient expressed as a mixed number. A partitioning model for division is usually used here.

$$\begin{array}{r} 93\tfrac{1}{4} \\ 4\overline{)373} \\ 36 \\ \hline 13 \\ 12 \\ \hline 1 \end{array}$$

Answer: 93¼ for each of the 4

   c. As an indicator that the quotient should be rounded up by one, often in relation to the cost of an item. For example, pencils priced 3 for 29¢ would sell for 10¢ each.

$$\begin{array}{r} 9 \\ 3\overline{)29} \\ 27 \\ \hline 2 \end{array}$$

Answer: 10¢ each

Next, consider remainders for division of decimals similarly. If the remainder in example D is viewed as the amount left over after distributing, 0.02 would remain. If it is viewed as a common fraction within the quotient, the quotient would be 0.85⅔ or 0.857.

Error Pattern P-P-1

from pages 75 and 110.

What instructional activities did you suggest to help Sara correctly solve percent problems? See if your suggestions are among the following.

Note: When you assign percent problems, ask to see all of the work done on each problem. You need to see what ratios are derived from the problem, and if the proportion itself is correctly derived. This particular student is correctly processing the proportion once it is derived and does *not* need instruction concerning cross multiplication. For this student, corrective instruction should focus on the concepts of percent, relating data in a problem to ratios (to fractions), and possibly equal ratios.

1. *Use 10 × 10 squares of graph paper.* Redevelop the meaning of percent as "per hundred." Therefore, *n*% is always *n*/100. For example:

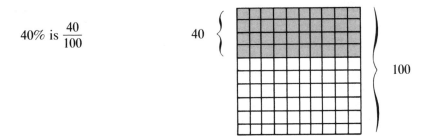

$$40\% \text{ is } \frac{40}{100}$$

2. *Use base ten blocks.* A flat block of 100 can be partially covered with long blocks of 10 and with unit blocks of one to redevelop the meaning of percent.

3. *Identify what is being "counted."* Ask: "Do I know how many there are in the whole set? Do I know how many are in part of the set?" Show these numbers with a fraction:

$$\frac{\text{number in part of the set}}{\text{number in the whole set}}$$

In Problem B, for example, you are counting students. You know there are 12 students in part of the class, but you do not know how many students are in the whole class. Therefore, the fraction is

$$\frac{12}{n}$$

4. *Use number lines to show equivalent ratios.* Sketch a number line for the fraction in which both numbers are known.

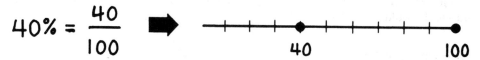

$$40\% = \frac{40}{100}$$

Then sketch another line just below it for the other fraction. Align the number that is known with the counterpart in the other fraction. Have the child estimate the unknown.

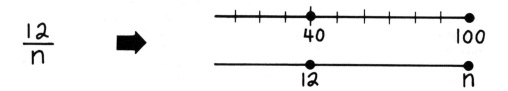

$$\frac{12}{n}$$

Error Pattern P-P-2

from pages 76 and 112.

What activities did you suggest to help Steve correctly solve percent problems of different types? See if your suggestions are among those that follow.

Note: Emphasizing a rule like "percent times a number equals percentage" is not likely to be helpful, for this is actually the rule Steve is attempting to apply. Many children find it difficult to identify the three types of percent problems; they also confuse the terms *percent* and *percentage*. Instead, it may be helpful to develop a strategy that is basically the same for all three types of percent problems, possibly the proportion method.

1. *Show equal fractions.* Write a proportion for each problem: one fraction equal to another. With one fraction show what the problem tells about percent, and with the other show what the problem tells about the number of things. Use n whenever you are not told a number.

For example: 70 is 14% of what number?

$$\text{percent} \left\{ \frac{14}{100} = \frac{70}{n} \begin{array}{l} \leftarrow \text{part of the set} \\ \leftarrow \text{the whole set} \end{array} \right.$$

2. *Build arrays for equations.* To help the child understand and solve equations like $2n = 12$, count out 12 items and build a $2 \times ?$ array. Gradually use larger numbers, and conclude that the missing factor can be determined by dividing.

3. *Cross multiply.* After the student is able to write a proportion for a percent problem, suggest that the two products indicated by an X are equal. Have the child supply several pairs of fractions known to be equal, and cross multiply each

$$\frac{1}{2} = \frac{4}{8} \qquad 1 \times 8 = 2 \times 4$$
$$8 = 8$$

$$\frac{14}{100} = \frac{70}{n}$$

$$14 \cdot n = 100 \times 70$$
$$14 \cdot n = 7000$$
$$n = 500$$

pair to see if the rule holds for them. Then, apply cross multiplication to percent problems.

Error Pattern S-M-1

from pages 77 and 113.

You have suggested instructional activities for helping Margaret, who is using the error pattern illustrated. Are any of your suggestions among those listed below?

C.
$$\begin{array}{r} 5 \\ 6 \text{ yards, } 1 \text{ foot} \\ - \ 2 \text{ yards, } 2 \text{ feet} \\ \hline 3 \text{ yards, } 9 \text{ feet} \end{array}$$

D.
$$\begin{array}{r} 2 \\ 3 \text{ quarts, } 1 \text{ cup} \\ - \ 1 \text{ quart, } 3 \text{ cups} \\ \hline 1 \text{ quart, } 8 \text{ cups} \end{array}$$

1. *Use measuring devices.* First, have the child show the minuend with measuring devices. In example C it could be shown with yardsticks and foot rulers. Then have the child take away as much length (volume, etc.) as is suggested by the subtrahend. In the process it will be necessary to exchange. Be sure to point out that the exchanges are not always with ones and a ten; many other kinds of exchanges occur with measurement situations.

2. *Regroup in many different number bases.* Use multibase blocks, chip trading activities, place value charts, or sticks and bundles of sticks to learn to regroup in different number bases. A game-rule orientation in which the rule for exchanging changes from game to game may help the child generalize the regrouping pattern. For base four games and activities the rule would be "Exchange a 4 for ones"; in base twelve games the rule would be "Exchange a 12 for ones," etc. Follow such activities with computation involving measurement and emphasize that the regrouping is similar to that encountered in other number bases.

3. *Identify number base relationships.* Have the child determine the number base relationship which obtains in specific computation situations involving measurement.

Conclusion

Diagnosis is a continuous process. It continues even during remedial activity as you observe a child at work and note patterns.

During instruction, make sure each child is aware of his strengths. Help the child take note of progress as it is made. Proceed in very small steps, if necessary, to insure successful experiences. It is important that your sessions with the child be varied and include games and puzzles which are enjoyable. Remedial teaching should first of all build upon the child's strengths. As confidence is gained and as the activities associated with mathematics become enjoyable, the child will be much more open to your continued efforts to remediate specific difficulties.

Selected References

References Focusing on Diagnosis and Remediation

Abbott, Gypsy A., and Elizabeth McEntire. *Effective Remediation Strategies in Mathematics: Characteristics of an Effective Remedial Mathematics Teacher; Effective Remedial Math Teacher Checklist; Math Remediation Methods Questionnaire.* Occasional Papers in Educational Policy Analysis, 1985, No. 417 (ERIC Document Reproduction Service No. ED 262 459). The authors have prepared tools for assessing remedial mathematics teaching.

Ashcraft, Mark H. "Is It Farfetched That Some of Us Remember Our Arithmetic Facts?" in the *Journal for Research in Mathematics Education* 16 (March 1985):99–105. Ashcraft argues that older children and adults actually retrieve basic facts that are stored in memory, rather than reconstructing answers as Baroody claims.

Ashlock, Robert R. "Testing Understanding of Concepts with Paper-and-Pencil Items," in *Focus on Learning Problems in Mathematics* 9 (Fall 1987): 49–54. The author illustrates three types of items: word statements, symbolizations, and portrayals. The limitations of each are discussed.

Backmon, Carl A. "Analyzing Children's Work Procedures," in Suydam, Marilyn N., and Reys, Robert E., eds. *Developing Computational Skills* (Reston, VA: National Council of Teachers of Mathematics, 1978 Yearbook): 177–95. Backmon identifies and discusses several categories of answer patterns; implications for instruction are noted.

Barclay, Tim. "Buggy," in *Classroom Computer News* 2 (March/April 1982): 25–27. The author describes a microcomputer program for helping students identify and describe error patterns in computation.

Baroody, Arthur J. "Children's Difficulties in Subtraction: Some Causes and Cures," in *The Arithmetic Teacher* 32 (November 1984): 14–19. Baroody emphasizes the need for us to diagnose a child's informal subtraction procedures so we can plan specific remedial instruction.

Baroody, Arthur J. "Mastery of Basic Number Combinations: Internalization of Relationships or Facts?" in the *Journal for Research in Mathematics Education* 16 (March 1985): 83–98. Baroody emphasizes the role of learned principles and procedures as a person attempts to recall basic number facts, and contrasts his position with that of Ashcraft.

Beattie, Ian D., and Janet K. Scheer. "Diagnosis and Remediation of Iconic Knowing in Elementary Mathematics" in *Focus on Learning Problems in Mathematics* 7 (Spring 1985): 23–28. The authors argue that iconic knowing is a key element in meaningful instruction and assessment of that learning, and they illustrate ways stamps of iconic representations can be used with children during diagnosis and remediation.

Beattie, John and Bob Algozzine. "Testing for Teaching," in *The Arithmetic Teacher* (September 1982): 47–51. The authors illustrate tests that highlight error patterns, and describe remedial activities.

Behr, Merlyn J. et al. "Order and Equivalence of Rational Numbers: A Clinical Teaching Experiment," in *Journal for Research in Mathematics Education* (November 1984): 323–41. The authors describe both correct and erroneous strategies used by students, with implications for instruction.

Behr, Merlyn, Stanley Erlwanger, and Eugene Nichols. "How Children View the Equals Sign," in *Mathematics Teaching* 92 (September 1980): 13–15. Interviews with six- and seven-year-old children reveal varied concepts associated with the equals sign in number sentences.

Bloom, Robert B., and Linda Bourdon. "Types and Frequencies of Teachers' Written Instructional Feedback" in *Journal of Educational Research* 74 (September/October 1980): 13–15. The authors found that teachers make very limited use of feedback strategies which are positively associated with student achievement.

Bright, George W. "Computer Diagnosis of Errors," in *School Science and Mathematics* 84 (March 1984): 208–19. Bright describes the challenge and remediation of computational errors.

Borasi, Raffaella. "Using Errors As Springboards For The Learning of Mathematics: An Introduction" in *Focus on Learning Problems in Mathematics* 7 (Summer and Fall 1985): 1–14. The author believes that, even apart from remediation, errors can have a positive role in a student's learning of mathematics.

Braswell, James S., and Alicia A. Dodd. *Mathematics Tests Available in the United States and Canada* (Reston, VA: National Council of Teachers of Mathematics, 1988). Tests are classified by targeted grade levels and courses. Descriptions and information on availability are given.

Bright, George W. "Computers for Diagnosis And Prescription in Mathematics," in *Focus on Learning Problems in Mathematics* 9 (Spring 1987): 29–41. Bright describes two general approaches to computer diagnosis of error patterns.

Brown, John S., and Richard R. Burton. "Diagnostic Models for Procedural Bugs in Basic Mathematical Skills," in *Cognitive Science* 2 (1978): 155–92. Attempts to form diagnostic models of students' misconceptions about arithmetic skills are described, and related pedagogical issues are discussed.

Brown, John Seely, and Kurt VanLehn. "Towards a Generative Theory of 'Bugs'," in Thomas P. Carpenter, James M. Moser, and Thomas A. Romberg, eds., *Addition and Subtraction: A Cognitive Perspective* (Hillsdale, NJ: Lawrence Erlbaum Assoc., Pub., 1982): 117–35. The authors describe their research with computer systems for diagnosing systematic student errors (specifically, BUGGY and DEBUGGY) and with explanations for error patterns—why and how they are formed.

Brueckner, Leo J. *Diagnostic and Remedial Teaching in Arithmetic* (Philadelphia: John C. Winston Co., 1930). A classic in the area of diagnosis and treatment of disabilities in mathematics. Much of this book is based on early studies of the errors pupils make in computation.

Brumfield, Robert D., and Bobby D. Moore. "Problems with the Basic Facts May Not Be the Problem," in *The Arithmetic Teacher* 33 (November 1985): 17–18. The authors classify observed errors in addition and subtraction and suggest remediation that focuses on types of errors.

Burton, Grace M., and Marcee J. Meyers. "Teaching Mathematics to Learning Disabled Students in the Secondary Classroom," in *The Mathematics Teacher* 80 (December 1987): 702–747. The authors focus on ways to modify mathematics instruction for learning disabled students.

Callahan, Leroy. "Remedial Work with Underachieving Children," in *The Arithmetic Teacher* 9 (March 1962): 138–40. Callahan describes a three-month individual diagnostic and remedial program which significantly reduced the underachievement of participants.

Callahan, Leroy G., and Mary L. Robinson. "Task-Analysis Procedures in Mathematics Instruction of Achievers and Underachievers," in *School Science and Mathematics* 73 (October 1973): 578–84. The authors report research suggesting that, when the task-analysis procedures of Gagné are combined with learning of subordinate tasks in a hierarchy, learning of a mathematical task can be quite effective.

Carpenter, Thomas P. et al. "Decimals: Results and Implications from National Assessment," in *The Arithmetic Teacher* 28 (April 1981): 34–47. The authors found that much of the difficulty with decimals lies in a lack of conceptual understanding.

Carpenter, Thomas P. et al. "Subtraction: What Do Students Know?" in *The Arithmetic Teacher* 22 (December 1975): 653–57. Selected data from the 1972–73 NAEP mathematics assessment are presented, and errors are discussed.

Carry, L. Ray et al. *Psychology of Equation Solving: An Information Processing Study, Final Technical Report* (Austin, TX: Department of Curriculum and Instruction, University of Texas, 1979). (ERIC Document Reproduction Service No. ED 186 243). In this NSF-sponsored research, the investigators sought to identify and classify difficulties college students had in solving algebraic equations. Three types of errors are identified. Sections of the report are devoted to kinds of knowledge in algebra, meaning in algebra, errors and the psychology of skill, and characteristics of good solvers.

Cawley, John F., ed. *Cognitive Strategies and Mathematics for the Learning Disabled* (Rockville, MD: Aspen Systems Corp., 1985). A guide for construct-

ing a classroom test of mathematics learning by disabled children is followed
by suggestions for instruction.

Cawley, John F., ed. *Practical Mathematics: Appraisal of the Learning Disabled*
(Rockville, MD: Aspen Systems Corp., 1985). This book is an in-depth
treatment of assessment and diagnosis of learning disabled students.

Charles, Randall, Frank Lester, and Phares O'Daffer. *How to Evaluate Progress
in Problem Solving* (Reston, VA: National Council of Teachers of Mathematics, 1987). The authors describe evaluation techniques for various levels
of instruction and suggest ways to use the results.

Clark, H. Clifford. "How to Check Elementary Mathematics Papers," in *The
Arithmetic Teacher* 34 (September 1986): 37–38. Clark suggests a way to
have more time for careful diagnosis and evaluation of those students that
need it.

Clement, John. "Algebra Word Problem Solutions: Thought Processes Underlying a Common Misconception," in *Journal for Research in Mathematics
Education* 13 (January 1982): 16–30. Clement's research identifies two conceptual sources of reversal errors: one syntactic and the other semantic.

Clements, M. A. "Analyzing Children's Errors on Written Mathematical Tasks,"
in *Educational Studies in Mathematics* 11 (1980). Newman's hierarchy of
error causes is emphasized. Data are included on errors made by children
on verbal arithmetic problems.

Cooney, Thomas J., and Edward J. Davis. "Teaching Concepts and Generalizations in Mathematics and Science," in *School Science and Mathematics* 76
(March 1976): 215–20. The authors stress that in diagnosing students' learning difficulties we need to distinguish between concepts and generalizations.
Strategies for instruction can be based on whether a child's difficulty is with
concepts or with the generalization itself.

Cooper, Martin. "The Dependence of Multiplicative Reversal on Equation Format," in *The Journal of Mathematical Behavior* 5 (August 1986): 115–120.
Cooper found that whether a multiplication sign was actually used or not
made a significant difference even among secondary students.

Cox, L. S. "Diagnosing and Remediating Systematic Errors in Addition and Subtraction Computations," in *The Arithmetic Teacher* 22 (February 1975): 151–
57. Cox emphasizes that teachers must look for patterns in the work they
collect from pupils having difficulty with computation. She describes three
categories of errors which can be noted.

Cox, L. S. "Systematic Errors in the Four Vertical Algorithms in Normal and
Handicapped Populations," in *Journal for Research in Mathematics Education* 6 (November 1975): 202–20. The author documents the fact that many
children use specific erroneous procedures. Data on the frequency of selected error patterns is included.

Crouse, R. J., and C. W. Sloyer. *Mathematical Questions from the Classroom*
(Boston: Prindle, Weber, and Schmidt, Inc., 1977). The authors illustrate
faulty algorithms used to solve problems in arithmetic and algebra.

Davis, Robert B. "The Convergence of Cognitive Science and Mathematics Education," in *The Journal of Mathematics Behavior* 5 (December 1986): 323–

329. In this stimulating article Davis discusses types of learning, knowledge, and memory storage. Implications for diagnosis abound.

Davis, Robert B. "Learning Mathematical Concepts: The Case of Lucy," in *The Journal of Mathematical Behavior* 4 (October 1985): 135–153. Davis focuses on one secondary student having difficulty in a calculus course, because he believes that teachers can learn the most from students having difficulty.

DeCorte, Erik, and Lieven Verschaffel. "Beginning First Graders' Initial Representation of Arithmetic Word Problems," in *The Journal of Mathematical Behavior* 4 (April 1985): 3–21. The authors analyze children's errors in word problem solving, and point to the main difficulty as construction of a mental problem representation that reflects the correct understanding of the story.

Deloche, G., and X. Seron, eds. *Mathematical Disabilities* (Hillsdale, NJ: Lawrence Erlbaum Associates, 1987). The authors have assembled articles on acalculia and number-processing disorders. The neuropsychological approach to mathematical cognition is emphasized.

Easley, J. A., Jr. *On Clinical Studies in Mathematics Education* (Champaign, IL: University of Illinois, 1977). Examples from clinical research studies are used to illustrate the value of interviews to researchers and classroom teachers.

Easterday, Kenneth. "Student Error Patterns in Studying Square Root," in *School Science and Mathematics* 80 (February 1980): 141–47. The author identifies ten error patterns.

Engelhardt, Jon M. "Analysis of Children's Computational Errors: A Qualitative Approach," in *British Journal of Educational Psychology* 47 (1977): 149–54. Errors are classified into eight types: basic fact error, grouping error, inappropriate inversion, incorrect operation, defective algorithm, incomplete algorithm, identity error, and zero error. The distribution of errors among the types is examined and tentative generalizations are presented.

Engelhardt, Jon M. "Using Computational Errors in Diagnostic Teaching," in *The Arithmetic Teacher* 29 (April 1982): 16–19. The author focuses on diagnosis and remediation of four types of errors: mechanical, careless, conceptual, and procedural. Research related to conceptual errors is described.

Engelhardt, Jon, Robert Ashlock, and James Wiebe. *Helping Children Understand and Use Numerals* (Boston: Allyn and Bacon, Inc., 1984). The authors identify specific numeration concepts and describe diagnostic and remedial activities.

Erlwanger, S. H. "Benny's Conception of Rules and Answers in IPI Mathematics," in *Journal of Children's Mathematical Behavior* 1 (1975): 157–281. The author's case studies show that there are children who conceive of arithmetic as arbitrary procedures to be used in arbitrary ways.

Feghali, I. *Interviews with Students of High Confidence and Low Achievement* (Vancouver, B.C.: Mathematics Education Diagnostic and Instructional Centre, British Columbia University, 1976). (ERIC Document Reproduction Service No. ED 128 230). Students making errors in computation often have great confidence in their faulty techniques.

Fennell, Francis M. *Elementary Mathematics Diagnosis and Correction Kit* (West Nyack, NY: Center for Applied Research in Education, Inc.,

1981). Chapters on diagnosing achievement and attitudes are followed by chapters on correcting difficulties in major areas of elementary school mathematics.

Fowler, Mary Anne. "Diagnostic Teaching for Elementary School Mathematics," in *Arithmetic Teacher* 27 (March 1980). The author emphasizes the importance of careful and accurate diagnoses of children's work in mathematics. Specific difficulties are discussed.

Gagné, Robert M. "Learning and Proficiency in Mathematics," in *The Mathematics Teacher* 56 (December 1963): 620–26. Gagné describes a method of analyzing desired pupil behaviors into subordinate behaviors.

Garofalo, Joe, and Frank K. Lester, Jr. "Metacognition, Cognitive Monitoring, and Mathematical Performance," in *Journal for Research in Mathematics Education* 16 (May 1985): 163–176. The authors define and discuss metacognition in relation to mathematical performance. A framework for the study of performance is included, as well as a discussion of the role of metacognition in instruction.

Ginsburg, Herbert. *Children's Arithmetic: The Learning Process* (New York: D. Van Nostrand Co., 1977). The author describes the process of learning arithmetic by young children, emphasizing competencies that often go unnoticed. Most chapters close with a statement of useful principles.

Goodstein, Henry A. "Are the Errors We See the True Errors? Error Analysis in Verbal Problem Solving," in *Topics in Learning and Learning Disabilities* (October 1981): 31–45. The author explores the range of possible causes for errors in verbal problem solving among learning disabled students.

Graeber, Anna O., and Lisa Wallae. *Identification of Systematic Errors: Final Report* (Philadelphia: Research for Better Schools, Inc., 1977). (ERIC Document Reproduction Service No. ED 139 662). For completed Individually Prescribed Instruction (IPI) tests, this study reports on the use of faulty algorithms by students in grades 1–6.

Hansen, Randall S., Joan McCann, and Jerome L. Myers. "Rote Versus Conceptual Emphases in Teaching Elementary Probability," in *Journal for Research in Mathematics Education* 16 (November 1985): 364–374. The authors observed patterns of errors across students that reflect the degree of their understanding of concepts under study.

Helm, Hugh and Joseph D. Novak. *Proceedings of the International Seminar on Misconceptions in Science and Mathematics* (Ithaca, NY: Cornell University, July 1983). (ERIC Document Reproduction Service No. ED 242 553). Included in this extensive compilation of technical conference presentations are many descriptions of erroneous mathematical learnings and suggestions for instruction that might avoid such misconceptions.

Hiebert, James. "Children's Mathematics Learning: The Struggle to Link Form and Understanding," in *The Elementary School Journal* 84 (May 1984): 497–513. Hiebert stresses the need to teach so that understanding and forms (such as paper-and-pencil algorithms) are linked, and he describes ways to do this.

Hiebert, James, ed. *Conceptual and Procedural Knowledge: The Case of Mathematics.* (Hillsdale, NJ: Lawrence Erlbaum Associates, 1986). In this book, which is based on a colloquium series at the University of Delaware, there is an attempt to relate knowledge of the symbols and syntax of mathematics to the knowledge of relationships.

Hopkins, Marty H. "The Diagnosis of Learning Styles in Arithmetic," in *The Arithmetic Teacher* 25 (April 1978). In the author's view, diagnosis must attend to many factors, including the child's most effective learning style (auditory, visual, tactile, etc.).

Hynes, Michael C., ed. *An Annotated Bibliography of Periodical Articles Relating to the Diagnostic and Prescriptive Instruction of Mathematics* (Kent, OH: Research Council for Diagnostic and Prescriptive Mathematics, 1979). Extensive annotations are provided for the serious student of diagnosis and prescriptive instruction in mathematics.

Inskeep, James E., Jr. "Diagnosing Computational Difficulty in the Classroom," in Suydam, Marilyn N., and Robert E. Reys, eds., *Developing Computational Skills,* 1978 Yearbook (Reston, VA: National Council of Teachers of Mathematics, 1978): 163–76. Inskeep describes a procedure for teachers to follow when preparing and interpreting classroom tests of skill in computation.

Jansson, Lars C. "Judging Mathematical Statements in the Classroom," in *The Arithmetic Teacher* 18 (November 1971): 463–66. The author alerts us to ways children often interpret statements in the mathematics lesson and suggests judgments teachers need to make when evaluating such statements.

Kalin, Robert. "How Students Do Their Division Facts," in *The Arithmetic Teacher* 31 (November 1983): 16–20. The author describes a diagnostic test and interview and illustrates how using the question, "How do you know?" enables the interviewer to determine level of mastery or understanding.

Kent, David. "The Dynamic of Put," in *Mathematics Teaching* 82 (1978): 32–36. The author discusses explanations students offer for the erroneous algebraic techniques they use.

Kent, David. "Some Processes Through Which Mathematics Is Lost," in *Educational Research* 21 (1978): 27–35; and "More About the Processes Through Which Mathematics Is Lost," in *Educational Research* 22 (1979): 22–31. In both of these articles, the author discusses mistakes of secondary school students. The mistakes are considered as a source for learning about the students' thought processes.

Kerslake, Daphne. *Fractions: Children's Strategies and Errors.* (Windsor, Berkshire: The NFER-NELSON Publishing Company Ltd., 1986). The author reports research conducted in conjunction with the Strategies and Errors in Secondary Mathematics Project at Chelsea College, University of London. Interviews, teaching experiments, and classroom trials of instructional procedures all contributed to conclusions about children's difficulties with fractions. Detailed evaluations of errors are included.

Kilian, Lawrence et al. "Errors That Are Common in Multiplication," in *The Arithmetic Teacher* 27 (January 1980): 22–25. The authors report data on types of errors made as children multiply: procedural errors that involve zeros and carrying and calculation errors that involve multiplication facts of tables over five.

Laursen, K. W. "Errors in First Year Algebra," in *The Mathematics Teacher* 71 (1978): 194–95. The author describes some of the common errors in elementary algebra.

Lepore, Angela V. "A Comparison of Computational Errors Between Educable Mentally Handicapped and Learning Disability Children," in *Focus on Learning Problems in Mathematics* 1 (January 1979): 12–33. The author concludes that computational errors are similar for the two groups if mental age is examined, and states that remediation for errors should be mental-age specific rather than disability specific.

Liedtke, Werner. "Diagnosis in Mathematics: The Advantages of an Interview," in *The Arithmetic Teacher* 36 (November 1988): 26–29. The author includes interview strategies and specific interview protocols.

Liedtke, Werner. "Learning Difficulties: Helping Young Children with Mathematics—Subtraction," in *The Arithmetic Teacher* 30 (December 1982): 21–23. The author focuses on diagnosis of difficulties with subtraction facts.

Lindquist, Mary Montgomery. "Assessing through Questioning," in *The Arithmetic Teacher* 35 (January 1988): 16–18. The author gives examples of questions that can help us know what a child understands, but recognizes it is better not to ask some questions.

MacKay, I. D. *A Comparison of Students' Achievement in Arithmetic with their Algorithmic Confidence* (Vancouver, B.C.: Mathematics Education Diagnostic and Instructional Centre, British Columbia University, 1975). (ERIC Document Reproduction Service No. ED 128 228). Many of the students in grades 5–8 are reported to place substantial confidence in their erroneous procedures for solving problems on the four operations.

Marshall, Sandra P. "Sex Differences in Mathematical Errors: An Analysis of Distracter Choices," in *Journal for Research in Mathematics Education* 14 (November 1983): 325–36.

Matz, M. "Towards a Process Model of High School Algebra Errors," in Sleeman, D. H. and J. S. Brown, eds. *Intelligent Tutoring Systems* (London: Academic Press, 1981). The author includes evidence of error patterns in the work of students doing algebra.

Mestre, Jose and William Gerace. "The Interplay of Linguistic Factors in Mathematical Translation Tasks," in *Focus on Learning Problems in Mathematics* (Winter 1986): 59–72. From their study the authors note the need to help students understand the difference between labels and variables.

Mitchell, Charles E. "The Non-Commutativity of Subtraction," in *School Science and Mathematics* 83 (February 1983): 133–39. Many children ignore order when subtracting, and the author discusses possible explanations. The need for instruction stressing the non-commutativity of subtraction is emphasized.

Movshovitz-Hadar, Nitsa, Shlomo Inbar, and Orit Zaslavsky. "Students' Distortions of Theorems," in *Focus on Learning Problems in Mathematics* 8 (Winter 1986): 49–57. The authors describe and illustrate two types of errors: distortions of antecedent and distortions of the consequent. Recommendations for prevention and remediation are included.

Movshovitz-Hadar, Nitsa, Orit Zaslavsky, and Shlomo Inbar. "An Empirical Classification Model for Errors in High School Mathematics," in the *Journal for Research in Mathematics Education* 18 (January 1987): 3–14. The authors analyzed errors and developed an error classification system with six categories of errors.

Moyer, Margaret B. and John C. Moyer. "Ensuring That Practice Makes Perfect: Implications for Children with Learning Disabilities" in *The Arithmetic Teacher* 33 (September 1985): 40–42. The authors recommend focusing on substeps; they use subtraction with regrouping as an example.

Okey, James R. and John McGarity. "Classroom Diagnostic Testing with Microcomputers," in *Science Education* 66 (July 1982): 571–77. The authors discuss testing with a microcomputer and present a BASIC program designed for this purpose.

Orr, Eleanor W. *Twice As Less: Black English and the Performance of Black Students in Mathematics and Science* (New York, NY: W. W. Norton & Co., 1987). Orr illustrates how differences between black English vernacular and standard English cause difficulties for black students as they solve problems involving quantitative relationships.

Pincus, Morris et al. "If You Don't Know How Children Think, How Can You Help Them?" in *The Arithmetic Teacher* 22 (November 1975): 580–85. Specific errors in computation are illustrated and recommendations for remediation are made.

Post, Thomas R. "Fractions: Results and Implications from National Assessment," in *The Arithmetic Teacher* 28 (May 1981): 26–31. The author shows that many students use rote procedures; he recommends an emphasis on estimation with fraction operations.

Quintero, Ana H. "Conceptual Understanding in Solving Two-Step Word Problems with a Ratio," in *Journal for Research in Mathematics Education* 14 (March 1983): 102–112. Quintero found that the meanings of concepts and relationships was the major source of difficulty in solving the problems; the concept of ratio was the key source of difficulty.

Radatz, Hendrik. "Error Analysis in Mathematics Education," in *Journal for Research in Mathematics Education* 10 (May 1979): 163–72. The author describes a scheme for classifying errors in performing mathematical tasks. The errors are categorized in terms of their apparent causes (e.g., difficulty in processing iconic information, application of irrelevant rules).

Rees, Jocelyn M. *Error Descriptions for Math Test: User's Guide.* 1986 (ERIC Document Reproduction Service No. ED 274 563). Rees has prepared a computer program for generating a description of items missed on the KeyMath Diagnostic Arithmetic Test.

Reisman, Fredricka K. *A Guide to the Diagnostic Teaching of Arithmetic,* 3rd ed. (Columbus, OH: Charles E. Merrill Publishing Co., 1982). Reisman includes sample diagnostic tools for the teacher and thought-provoking case studies.

Reisman, Fredricka K., and Samuel H. Kauffman. *Teaching Mathematics to Children with Special Needs* (Columbus, OH: Charles E. Merrill Publishing Co., 1980). The children referred to have special cognitive, psychomotor, sensory, physical, social or emotional needs. The authors provide background information and specific help for both diagnosis and remediation of their problems in learning mathematics.

Resnick, Lauren B. "Syntax and Semantics in Learning to Subtract," in Carpenter, Thomas P., James M. Moser, and Thomas A. Romberg, eds., *Addition and Subtraction: A Cognitive Perspective* (Hillsdale, NJ: Lawrence Erlbaum Assoc., Pub., 1982): 136–55. The author has found that although children know much about our base ten numeration system, many are unable to apply this knowledge to written arithmetic procedures. She focuses on teaching methods that will help students link place value knowledge with the sequenced steps of computation.

Reys, Robert E. "Evaluating Computational Estimation," in Schoen, Harold L., and Marilyn J. Zweng, eds., *Estimation and Mental Computation.* (Reston, VA: National Council of Teachers of Mathematics, 1986 Yearbook): 225–238. The author discusses sample test items, and suggests guidelines for testing estimation.

Richbart, Lynn A. "Remedial Mathematics Program Considerations," in *The Arithmetic Teacher* 28 (November 1980): 22–23. Richbart raises questions to be answered by anyone setting up a remedial program.

Roberson, E. Wayne, and Debra J. Glowinski. *Computer Assisted Diagnostic Prescriptive Program in Reading and Mathematics: An Exemplary Micro-Computer Program and a Developer/Demonstrator Project,* National Diffusion Network, January 1986. (ERIC Document Reproduction Service ED 272 148). The authors have developed a data based curriculum management system which produces customized prescriptions for each participating student.

Rogan, John M. "Conceptual Mapping as a Diagnostic Aid," in *School and Science and Mathematics* 88 (January 1988): 50–59. The author found that conceptual maps produced by students provided useful information about each individual's understanding of specific concepts.

Rudnitsky, Alan N., Priscilla Drickamer, and Roberta Handy. "Talking Mathematics with Children," in *The Arithmetic Teacher* 28 (April 1981): 14–17. Strategies are presented so that teachers can learn through interviews what a child knows about both concepts and procedures.

Sadowski, Barbara. "Sentence-Solving Strategies of Elementary School Children," in *School Science and Mathematics* 85 (April 1985): 317–329. The author found that students following a strategy which is 80 percent successful for solving open number sentences were not likely to abandon it for a strategy that is 100 percent successful.

Sadowski, Barbara R., and Delayne Houston McIlveen. "Diagnosis and Remediation of Sentence-solving Error Patterns," in *Arithmetic Teacher* 31 (January 1984): 42–45. The author's analysis of errors in sentence-solving (with some surprises) is followed by suggestions for instruction. Students profit from identifying addends, sums, factors, and products before finding the missing number.

Scheer, Janet K. "The Etiquette of Diagnosis," in *The Arithmetic Teacher* 27 (May 1980): 18–19. Twelve guidelines for diagnosis are presented.

Schoenfeld, Alan H. "Beyond the Purely Cognitive: Metacognition and Social Cognition As Driving Forces in Intellectual Performance," in *Cognitive Science* 7 (December 1983): 329–363. The author explores the role of meta-cognitions and social cognitions as "driving forces" behind ostensibly "purely cognitive" behavior.

Schoenfeld, Alan H. "Making Sense of 'Out Loud' Problem-Solving Protocols," in *The Journal of Mathematical Behavior* 4 (October 1985): 171–191. Schoenfeld argues that the circumstances in which people generate "out loud" solutions often affect those solutions in a variety of ways.

Sharma, Mahesh C. "Dyscalculia and Other Learning Problems in Mathematics: A Historical Perspective," in *Focus on Learning Problems in Mathematics* 8 (Summer/Fall 1986): 7–45. In addition to describing scholarship which has focused through the years on persons unable to perform the operations of arithmetic, Sharma also presents an extensive reference list of special interest to anyone studying the history of this aspect of education.

Shaw, Robert A., and Philip A. Pelosi. "In Search of Computational Errors," in *The Arithmetic Teacher* 30 (March 1983): 50–51. The authors illustrate the need to conduct individual interviews in addition to paper-and-pencil diagnostic procedures.

Siders, James A., Jane Z. Siders, and Rebecca M. Wilson. "A Screening Procedure to Identify Children Having Difficulties in Arithmetic," in *Journal for Research in Mathematics Education* 16 (November 1985): 356–363. Rate-of-response measures were found to be reliable predictors.

Steinberg, Ruth M. "Instruction on Derived Facts Strategies in Addition and Subtraction," in *Journal for Research in Mathematics Education* 16 (November 1985): 337–55. The authors found that rate-of-response measures with first graders were effective predictors of achievement in arithmetic over a two-year period.

Suydam, Marilyn N. "Addition and Subtraction—Processes and Problems," in *The Arithmetic Teacher* 33 (December 1985): 20. Suydam summarizes research findings concerning difficulties students experience when learning to add and subtract.

Suydam, Marilyn N. *Evaluation in the Mathematics Classroom: From What and Why to How and Where,* Revised Edition (Columbus, OH: The Ohio State University, 1986). (ERIC Document Reproduction Service No. ED 284 717). Suydam not only helps the reader develop better paper-and-pencil tests, but she suggests other approaches to evaluation as well.

Suydam, Marilyn N. "What Research Says: Helping Low-Achieving Students in Mathematics," in *School Science and Mathematics* 84 (May–June 1984): 437–41. Suydam lists guidelines supported by both practice and research.

Tatsuoda, Kikumi K. et al. *A Psychometric Approach to Error Analysis on Response Patterns* (Research Report 80-3 ONR). Urbana, IL: University of Illinois, Computer-based Education Research Laboratory, 1980. (ERIC Document Reproduction Service No. ED 195 577). The authors used a test of signed-number operations to examine response patterns on achievement tests. They used multi-dimensional binary vectors for error analysis and found that some problems were correct for the wrong reasons.

Thornton, Carol A., Graham A. Jones, and Margaret A. Toohey. "A Multisensory Approach to Thinking Strategies for Remedial Instruction in Basic Addition Facts," in *Journal for Research in Mathematics Education* 14 (May 1983): 198–203. The authors report a pilot study involving specific addition fact strategies.

Trafton, Paul. "Tests—a Tool for Improving Instruction," in *The Arithmetic Teacher* 35 (December 1987): 17–18. Trafton illustrates how data for specific items can suggest ways to improve instruction.

Travis, Betty. "Computer Diagnosis of Algorithmic Error," in *Computers in Mathematics Education,* 1984 Yearbook (Reston, VA: National Council of Teachers of Mathematics, 1984): 211–16. The author describes a research study in which diagnostic and remedial problems are addressed through computer technology.

Tucker, Benny F. "Seeing Addition: A Diagnosis-Remediation Case Study" in *The Arithmetic Teacher* 36 (January 1989): 10–11. Tucker provides an illustration of how diagnosis can lead to specific instructional tasks that get results.

Underhill, Robert G., A. Edward Uprichard, and James W. Heddens. *Diagnosing Mathematical Difficulties* (Columbus, OH: Charles E. Merrill Publishing Company, 1980). Models for diagnosis in clinic and classroom are presented and their implications discussed. Considerable attention is also given to diagnostic tests.

VanLehn, Kurt. *Bugs Are Not Enough: Empirical Studies of Bugs, Impasses and Repairs in Procedural Skills* (Palo Alto, CA: Cognitive and Instructional Sciences Group of the Xerox Palo Alto Research Center, March 1981). VanLehn summarizes research with DEBUGGY and describes how Repair Theory has been developed to account for error patterns or "bugs" not diagnosed by DEBUGGY.

Virginia Council of Teachers of Mathematics, *Mathematics Assessment for the Classroom Teacher* (Charlottesville, VA: 1983). (ERIC Document Reproduction Service SE 046 813). The articles include many specific examples of classroom assessment practices.

Wearne-Hiebert, Diana, and James Hiebert. "Junior High School Students' Understanding of Fractions," in *School Science and Mathematics* 83 (February 1983): 96–106. The analysis of errors on specific tasks suggested that student understanding of fractions suffered not so much from being incorrect; rather, understanding was incomplete.

Weaver, J. Fred. "Evaluation and the Classroom Teacher," in Begle, E. G., ed., *Mathematics Education,* 69th Yearbook of the National Society for the Study of Education, Part 1 (Chicago: The University of Chicago Press, 1970): 335–66. A model is described which relates mathematical content, levels of desired behavior, and techniques for observing instructional outcomes.

Williams, Linda V. *Teaching for the Two-Sided Mind: A Guide to Right Brain/ Left Brain Education.* (New York: Simon and Schuster, 1983). Williams describes instructional techniques associated with right hemisphere functioning including evocative language, metaphor, and visual strategies such as mind maps.

Ysseldyke, Salvia. *Assessment in Special and Remedial Education,* 4th edition. (Boston, MA: Houghton Mifflin, 1987). Chapter 18, in particular, is devoted to diagnostic assessment in mathematics.

References Focusing on Instruction in Computation

Allinger, Glenn D. "Mind Sets in Elementary School Mathematics," in *The Arithmetic Teacher* 30 (November 1982): 50–53. The author illustrates how a teacher's thoughtless use of words or examples can lead to students acquiring a "functional fixedness" that makes learning a concept more difficult.

Ando, Masue, and Ikeda Hitoshi. "Learning Multiplication Facts—More Than Drill," in *The Arithmetic Teacher* 18 (October 1971): 366–69. The authors suggest varied activities to help children understand and remember the basic multiplication facts.

Arnold, William R. "Computation Made Interesting," in *The Arithmetic Teacher* 18 (May 1971): 347–50. The author describes several pattern-seeking and pattern-extending activities that can be used for practice with the basic facts of arithmetic in place of worksheets.

Ashlock, Robert B. "Use of Informal Language When Introducing Concepts," in *Focus on Learning Problems in Mathematics* 9 (Summer 1987): 31–36. The author illustrates situations in which more formal language can be introduced in apposition to informal language while teaching concepts.

Ashlock, Robert B. et al. *Guiding Each Child's Learning of Mathematics: A Diagnostic Approach to Instruction* (Columbus, OH: Charles E. Merrill Publishing Company, 1983). In their cognitively oriented methods text, the authors present models for guiding both diagnosis and instruction. Useful response forms are included in the accompanying student handbook.

Ashlock, Robert B., and Carolynn A. Washbon. "Games: Practice Activities for the Basic Facts," in Suydam, Marilyn N., and Robert E. Reys, eds., *Developing Computational Skills.* (Reston, VA: National Council of Teachers of Mathematics, 1978 Yearbook): 39–50. The use of games for practice with basic facts is discussed. Games are described in relation to the guidelines presented.

Baroody, Arthur J. *Children's Mathematical Thinking* (New York, NY: Teachers College Press, 1987). Appealing to cognitive theory, Baroody argues for a meaningful approach to early mathematical instruction, with an emphasis on counting activity.

Beardslee, Edward C., Gerald E. Gau, and Ralph T. Heimer. "Teaching for Generalization: An Array Approach to Equivalent Fractions," in *The Arithmetic Teacher* 20 (November 1973): 591–99. The authors illustrate activity cards that can help children make generalizations about equivalent fractions by observing specially constructed arrays.

Beattie, Ian D. "Modeling Operations and Algorithms," in *The Arithmetic Teacher* 33 (February 1986): 23–28. Beattie presents specific procedures for correlating manipulatives, language, and algorithms—for subtraction and division.

Bolduc, Elroy J., Jr. "The Monsters in Multiplication," in *The Arithmetic Teacher* 28 (November 1980): 24–26. Reston, VA: National Council of Teachers of Mathematics. The author outlines a strategy for memorizing the basic multiplication facts.

Bradford, John W. "Methods and Materials for Learning Subtraction," in *The Arithmetic Teacher* 25 (February 1978): 18–20. The author describes methods and materials he has used with success in correcting errors in subtraction of whole numbers.

Bright, George W., John G. Harvey, and Margariete M. Wheeler. *Learning and Mathematics Games* (Reston, VA: National Council of Teachers of Mathematics, 1985), Monograph 1 of the *Journal for Research in Mathematics Education*. The authors describe research on game-related instruction at both the elementary and secondary levels.

Broadbent, Frank W. " 'Contig': A Game to Practice and Sharpen Skills and Facts in the Four Fundamental Operations," in *The Arithmetic Teacher* 19 (May 1972): 388–90. "Contig" is a board game that can be easily made and varied according to the needs of participants.

Burton, Grace M. "Focus on Affective Issues in Diagnostic and Prescriptive Mathematics," in *Focus on Learning Problems in Mathematics* 10 (Spring 1988): 55–61. Burton discusses the effects of positive and negative teacher expectations, then summarizes research as to what teachers can do to facilitate positive and realistic student self-concepts.

Burton, Grace M. "Teaching the Most Basic Basic," in *Arithmetic Teacher* 32 (September 1984): 20–25. Burton describes how varied aids can be used for teaching numeration.

Cawley, John F., Anne M. Fitzmaurice Hayes, and Robert A. Shaw. *Mathematics for the Mildly Handicapped* (Newton, MA: Allyn and Bacon, 1988). This methods text focuses on diagnostic instruction of disabled learners.

Cohen, Louis S. "The Board Stretcher: A Model to Introduce Factors, Primes, Composites, and Multiplication by a Fraction," in *The Arithmetic Teacher* 20 (December 1973): 649–56. Board stretching and shrinking machines are used for an approach to renaming fractions.

Davis, Edward J. "Suggestions for Teaching the Basic Facts of Arithmetic," in Suydam, Marilyn N., and Robert E. Reys, eds., *Developing Computational Skills.* (Reston, VA: National Council of Teachers of Mathematics, 1978 Yearbook): 51–60. Davis lists guidelines and illustrates how they are applied.

Davison, David M., and Daniel L. Pearce. "Using Writing Activities to Reinforce Mathematics Instruction," in *The Arithmetic Teacher* 35 (April 1988): 42–45. Different categories of writing activities are illustrated, including "linguistic translation," which provides diagnostic feedback for the teacher.

Dessart, Donald, and Marilyn Suydam. *Classroom Ideas from Research on Secondary School Mathematics* (Reston, VA: National Council of Teachers of Mathematics, 1983). The authors review research on teaching algebra and geometry, and highlight ideas for the classroom.

Driscoll, Mark J. *Research Within Reach: Elementary School Mathematics.* (Reston, VA: National Council of Teachers of Mathematics, 1981). The author summarizes research as he answers questions concerning diagnosis, remediation, algorithms, and mastery learning.

Driscoll, Mark J. *Research Within Reach: Secondary School Mathematics* (Reston, VA: National Council of Teachers of Mathematics, 1983). The author interprets research on teaching mathematics for the classroom teacher.

Ellerbruch, Lawrence W., and Joseph N. Payne. "A Teaching Sequence from Initial Fraction Concepts through the Addition of Unlike Fractions," in Suydam, Marilyn N., and Robert E. Reys, eds. *Developing Computational Skills* (Reston, VA: National Council of Teachers of Mathematics, 1978 Yearbook): 129–47. The authors outline a sequence for developmental teaching of fraction concepts and algorithms.

Fishback, Sylvia. "Times Without Tears," in *The Arithmetic Teacher* 21 (March 1974): 200–201. A teacher describes her successful use of a matrix and distributivity for teaching the basic multiplication facts.

Hall, William D. "Division with Base-Ten Blocks," in *The Arithmetic Teacher* 31 (November 1983): 21–23. The author illustrates a partitive division situation with base-ten blocks.

Harrison, Marilyn, and Bruce Harrison. "Developing Numeration Concepts and Skills," in *The Arithmetic Teacher* 33 (February 1986): 18–21, 60. The authors describe game-like activities for developing specific numeration related concepts.

Hazekamp, Donald W. "Teaching Multiplication and Division Algorithms," in Suydam, Marilyn N., and Robert E. Reys, eds., *Developing Computational Skills* (Reston, VA: National Council of Teachers of Mathematics, 1978 Yearbook): 96–128. The author illustrates the steps in developmental instruction for these algorithms.

Heckman, M. Jane. "They All Add Up," in *The Arithmetic Teacher* 21 (April 1974): 287–89. Games for practicing the basic facts of arithmetic are described.

Hope, Jack A., and Douglas T. Owens. "An Analysis of the Difficulty of Learning Fractions," in *Focus on Learning Problems in Mathematics* 9 (Fall 1987): 25–40. Different physical and symbolic settings facilitate different meanings for fractions, learning fractions is more difficult than it is often recognized.

Hutchings, Barton. "Low-Stress Algorithms," in Nelson, Doyal, and Robert E. Reys, eds., *Measurement in School Mathematics* (Reston, VA: National Council of Teachers of Mathematics, 1976 Yearbook); 218–39. The author describes procedures for whole-number computation, algorithms that children experiencing difficulty with standard procedures have found especially useful.

Irons, Calvin J. "The Division Algorithm: Using An Alternative Approach," in *The Arithmetic Teacher* 28 (January 1981): 46–48. The author tells how to introduce the algorithm using partitive division.

Jencks, Stanley M., Donald M. Peck, and Louis J. Chatterley. "Why Blame the Kids? We Teach Mistakes," in *The Arithmetic Teacher* 28 (Octover 1980): 38–40. The authors illustrate the need to emphasize appropriate concrete referents for symbols and operations.

Klauer, Elizabeth and Ann Rule. *Teaching Strategies in Algebra: The Effectiveness of Relating and Sequencing Algebraic Concepts,* (ERIC Document Reproduction Service, 1985, ED 266 007).

Kulm, Gerald. "Multiplication and Division Algorithms in German Schools," in *The Arithmetic Teacher* 27 (May 1980): 26–27. Algorithms taught in German elementary schools are adapted to a low-stress format in which practice with one operation reinforces skill in the other.

Laing, Robert A., and Ruth A. Meyer. "Transitional Division Algorithms," in *The Arithmetic Teacher* 29 (May 1982): 10–12. The authors argue for introducing the standard algorithm without the use of transitional algorithms.

Lazerick, Beth E. "Mastering Basic Facts of Addition: An Alternate Strategy," in *The Arithmetic Teacher* 28 (March 1981): 20–24. Lazerick describes seven ordered clusters of basic facts that can facilitate memorization.

Litwiller, Bonnie H., and David R. Duncan. *Activities for the Maintenance of Computational Skills* (Reston, VA: National Council of Teachers of Mathematics, 1980). The authors present a variety of activities for practice, with emphasis on the discovery of patterns.

Manning, Brenda H. "A Self-Communication Structure for Learning Mathematics," in *School Science and Mathematics* 84 (January 1984): 43–51. Manning defends and describes teaching students concepts of self-communication; that is, talking to themselves.

McKillip, William D. "Computational Skill in Division: Results and Implications from National Assessment," in *The Arithmetic Teacher* 28 (March 1981): 34–37. The author focuses on the sources of error and recommends three things for improving division computation.

Metzner, Seymour, and Richard M. Sharp. "Cardematics I—Using Playing Cards As Reinforcers and Motivators in Basic Operations," in *The Arithmetic Teacher* 21 (May 1974): 419–21. The authors describe several games for practicing the basic facts of arithmetic, games using regular playing cards.

Myers, Ann C., and Carol A. Thornton. "The Learning Disabled Child—Learning the Basic Facts," in *The Arithmetic Teacher* 25 (December 1977): 46–50. The authors emphasize that learning disabled children need to learn strategies for using what they know to figure out other facts.

Quast, W. G. "On Computation and Drill," in *The Arithmetic Teacher* 16 (December 1969): 627–30. Quast illustrates the dangers to be avoided when working with children on computation.

Rathmell, Edward C. "Concepts of the Fundamental Operations: Results and Implications from National Assessment," in *The Arithmetic Teacher* 28 (November 1980): 34–37. Rathmell focuses on the unrealized potential of the number line for representing operations.

Rathmell, Edward C. "Using Thinking Strategies to Teach the Basic Facts," in Suydam, Marilyn N., and Robert E. Reys, eds., *Developing Computational Skills* (Reston, VA: National Council of Teachers of Mathematics, 1978 Yearbook): 13–38. Thinking strategies are described for use when organizing instruction in the basic facts for addition and multiplication.

Schroeder, Thomas L. "Capture: A Game of Practice, a Game of Strategy," in *The Arithmetic Teacher* 31 (December 1983): 30–31. The author describes an interesting strategy game involving basic operations. It is useful with grades 3 and up.

Shaughnessy, Mina P. *Errors and Expectations* (New York: Oxford University Press, 1977). This book focuses on instruction in written language, but contains thought-provoking ideas that parallel instruction in mathematics; comments about coding, syntax, and teacher responses to student errors are examples.

Silvia, Evelyn M. "A Look at Division with Fractions," in *The Arithmetic Teacher* 30 (January 1983): 38–41. Silvia describes how division with fractions can be introduced with graph paper.

Smith, C. Winston, Jr. "The Witch's Best Game," in *The Arithmetic Teacher* 13 (December 1966): 683–84. The author describes a game in which children focus on renaming the minuend in subtraction involving regrouping.

Suydam, Marilyn N. "Improving Multiplication Skills," in *The Arithmetic Teacher* 32 (March 1985): 52. Suydam summarizes research on teaching multiplication—research which supports a meaningful approach.

Suydam, Marilyn N., and Donald J. Dessart. *Classroom Ideas from Research on Computational Skills* (Reston, VA: National Council of Teachers of Mathematics, 1976). The authors summarize findings from research with reference to introducing, reinforcing, maintaining, transfering and applying computational skills with whole numbers and fractions.

Suydam, Marilyn N., and Robert E. Reys, eds. *Developing Computational Skills* (Reston, VA: National Council of Teachers of Mathematics, 1978 Yearbook). The basic facts and computation procedures for whole numbers and fractions are all considered in this very helpful reference.

Sweetland, Robert D. "Understanding Multiplication of Fractions," in *The Arithmetic Teacher* 32 (September 1984): 48–52. The author describes how cuisenaire rods can be used to make sense out of multiplying fractions.

Thompson, Charles S., and John Van de Walle. "Transition Boards: Moving from Materials to Symbols in Addition," in *The Arithmetic Teacher* 28 (December 1980): 4–8; and "Transition Boards: Moving from Materials to Symbols in Subtraction," in *The Arithmetic Teacher* 28 (January 1981): 4–9. The authors describe a phased transition from the use of symbols alone.

Thornton, Carol A. "Emphasizing Thinking Strategies in Basic Fact Instruction," in *Journal for Research in Mathematics Education* 9 (May 1978): 214–27. The effect of teaching thinking strategies for basic facts in grades two and four is explored and data are reported to support use of the specific strategies presented.

Thornton, Carol A., and Paula J. Smith. "Strategies for Learning Subtraction Facts," in *The Arithmetic Teacher* 35 (April 1988): 8–12. The authors describe how specific activity-based subtraction fact strategies were taught as part of a teaching experiment.

Thornton, Carol A., and Barbara Wilmot. "Special Learners," in *The Arithmetic Teacher* 33 (February 1986): 38–41. Thornton describes specific procedures for teaching computation to learning handicapped students.

Tierney, Cornelia C. "Patterns in the Multiplication Table," in *The Arithmetic Teacher* 32 (March 1985): 36–40. The author describes activities which may help students who are learning the basic multiplication facts.

Trafton, Paul R., and Judith S. Zawojewski. "Teaching Rational Number Division: A Special Problem," in *The Arithmetic Teacher* 31 (February 1984): 20–22. Division with both fractions and decimals is addressed.

Tucker, Benny F. "The Division Algorithm," in *The Arithmetic Teacher* 20 (December 1973): 639–46. Tucker describes how the division algorithm can be introduced using the partitive model and a variety of exemplars.

Uprichard, A. Edward, and Carolyn Collura. "The Effect of Emphasizing Mathematical Structure in the Acquisition of Whole Number Computation Skills (Addition and Subtraction) by Seven-and-Eight-Year-Olds: A Clinical Investigation," in *School Science and Mathematics* 77 (February 1977): 97–104. Instruction on basic facts with sums 11–18 was more effective when emphasizing structures such as place value rather than just games for drill.

Usnick, Virginia, and Jon M. Engelhardt. "Basic Facts, Numeration Concepts, and the Learning of the Standard Multidigit Addition Algorithm," in *Focus on Learning Problems in Mathematics* 10 (Spring 1988): 1–14. From the authors' study it is not clear that actual mastery of basic facts and relevant numeration concepts is necessary before introducing the addition algorithm.

Van de Walle, John, and Charles S. Thompson. "Fractions with Fraction Strips," in *The Arithmetic Teacher* 32 (December 1984): 4–9. Specific guidance is given for using colored strips to develop fraction concepts and relate them to numerals.

Vest, Floyd. "Model Switching Found in Lessons in Subtraction in the Elementary Grades," in *School Science and Mathematics* 70 (May 1970): 407–10. Vest cautions against the practice of confusing children by unnecessarily switching models in the midst of an instructional sequence.

References Available From RCDPM

The following references published by the Research Council for Diagnostic and Prescriptive Mathematics are available through ERIC.

Beattie, Ian D., and others. *Research Reports from the Seventh National Conference on Diagnostic and Prescriptive Mathematics. 1981 Research Monograph* (Kent, OH: Research Council for Diagnostic and Prescriptive Mathematics, 1982). (ED 243 709).

Denmark, Tom, ed. *Issues for Consideration by Mathematics Educators: Selected Papers* (Kent, OH: Research Council for Diagnostic and Prescriptive Mathematics, 1978). (ED 243 693).

Glennon, Vincent, J. *Neuropsychology and the Instructional Psychology of Mathematics.* (Kent, OH: Research Council for Diagnostic and Prescriptive Mathematics, 1981). (ED 243 697).

Hynes, Mary Ellen, ed. *Topics Related to Diagnosis in Mathematics for Classroom Teachers.* (Kent, OH: Research Council for Diagnostic and Prescriptive Mathematics, 1978). (ED 243 694).

Hynes, Michael, C., ed. *An Annotated Bibliography of Periodical Articles Relating to the Diagnostic and Prescriptive Instruction of Mathematics* (Kent, OH: Research Council for Diagnostic and Prescriptive Mathematics, 1979). (ED 243 695).

Romberg, Thomas A. *Research Reports from the Fourth and Fifth National Conferences on Diagnostic and Prescriptive Mathematics. 1980 Research Monograph.* Revised Third Ed. (Kent, OH: Research Council for Diagnostic and Prescriptive Mathematics, 1981). (ED 243 708).

Sadowski, Barbara, ed. *An Annotated Bibliography Relating to the Diagnostic and Prescriptive Instruction of Mathematics,* Volume 2. (Kent, OH: Research Council for Diagnostic and Prescriptive Mathematics, 1982). (ED 243 696).

Speer, William R. *A Bibliography Related to the Nature of Diagnosis and Re-mediation in Mathematics* (Kent, OH: Research Council for Diagnostic and Prescriptive Mathematics, 1981). (ED 243 701).

Speer, William R. *Clinical Investigations in Mathematics Education. Thematic Address from the Fourth Annual Conference on Diagnostic and Prescriptive Mathematics* (Kent, OH: Research Council for Diagnostic and Prescriptive Mathematics, 1978). (ED 243 702).

Additional Children's Papers and Key to Error Patterns

On the following pages are brief excerpts from the written work of children using erroneous computational procedures. Practice the skill of identifying error patterns by finding the erroneous procedure in each of these papers. Briefly describe each error pattern, then check the key on page 197 if you wish.

Paper 1

$$
\begin{array}{r} 35 \\ +28 \\ \hline 18 \end{array}
\qquad
\begin{array}{r} 24 \\ +17 \\ \hline 14 \end{array}
\qquad
\begin{array}{r} 43 \\ +26 \\ \hline 15 \end{array}
$$

Description of Pattern _____

_____

Paper 2

$$
\begin{array}{r} 40 \\ +26 \\ \hline 60 \end{array}
\qquad
\begin{array}{r} 31 \\ +18 \\ \hline 38 \end{array}
\qquad
\begin{array}{r} 70 \\ +15 \\ \hline 70 \end{array}
$$

Description of Pattern _____

_____

Paper 3

```
   1            1 1          1 1
  28           248          457
  29            68          368
+ 34         + 165        + 192
────         ─────        ─────
  82           472          927
```

Description of Pattern _____

_____

Paper 4

```
  645          482          576
+237         + 363        + 189
────         ─────        ─────
  871          715          611
```

Description of Pattern _____

_____

Paper 5

```
   2            7            9
   6            5            8
+  3         +  6         +  7
────         ────         ─────
  29           81          105
```

Description of Pattern _____

_____

Paper 6

```
   1            1            1
  15           84           76
+ 67         + 56         + 87
────         ────         ────
  82           10           13
```

Description of Pattern _____

_____

Paper 7

$$\begin{array}{r} 165 \\ +33 \\ \hline 498 \end{array}$$

$$\begin{array}{r} 369 \\ +56 \\ \hline 8115 \end{array}$$

$$\begin{array}{r} 4543 \\ +69 \\ \hline 10111012 \end{array}$$

Description of Pattern _____

_____

Paper 8

$$\begin{array}{r} {}^{\prime\prime\prime} \\ 864 \\ +589 \\ \hline 3343 \end{array}$$

$$\begin{array}{r} {}^{\prime\prime} \\ 478 \\ +295 \\ \hline 2663 \end{array}$$

$$\begin{array}{r} {}^{\prime\prime} \\ 775 \\ +483 \\ \hline 2158 \end{array}$$

Description of Pattern _____

_____

Paper 9

$$\begin{array}{r} 47 \\ -3 \\ \hline 14 \end{array}$$

$$\begin{array}{r} 65 \\ -2 \\ \hline 43 \end{array}$$

$$\begin{array}{r} 78 \\ -4 \\ \hline 34 \end{array}$$

Description of Pattern _____

_____

Paper 10

$$\begin{array}{r} 62 \\ -5 \\ \hline 75 \end{array}$$

$$\begin{array}{r} 84 \\ -8 \\ \hline 67 \end{array}$$

$$\begin{array}{r} 51 \\ -3 \\ \hline 84 \end{array}$$

Description of Pattern _____

_____

Paper 11

$$\begin{array}{r} 65 \\ -29 \\ \hline 46 \end{array} \qquad \begin{array}{r} 437 \\ -84 \\ \hline 453 \end{array} \qquad \begin{array}{r} 226 \\ -173 \\ \hline 153 \end{array}$$

Description of Pattern _____

_____

Paper 12

$$\begin{array}{r} 248 \\ -75 \\ \hline 73 \end{array} \qquad \begin{array}{r} 734 \\ -69 \\ \hline 65 \end{array} \qquad \begin{array}{r} 565 \\ -98 \\ \hline 67 \end{array}$$

Description of Pattern _____

_____

Paper 13

$$\begin{array}{r} 52 \\ -27 \\ \hline 30 \end{array} \qquad \begin{array}{r} 615 \\ -142 \\ \hline 503 \end{array} \qquad \begin{array}{r} 322 \\ -156 \\ \hline 200 \end{array}$$

Description of Pattern _____

_____

Paper 14

$$31-7=22 \qquad 23-4=\underline{13}$$
$$42-5=\underline{33} \qquad 51-3=\underline{46}$$

Description of Pattern _____

_____

Paper 15

```
 539        457        928
- 83       - 65       -34
 206        102        524
 351        211        615
 557        313       1139
```

Description of Pattern _____

_____

Paper 16

```
  705        602        304
- 108      -238       -176
  507        274         38
```

Description of Pattern _____

_____

Paper 17

```
   98         37         56
 x 13        x24        x 32
  294        148        112
   98         74        168
  392        222        280
```

Description of Pattern _____

_____

Paper 18

```
  723        368        475
 x  6        x  6        x  9
 4338       1978        3745
```

Description of Pattern _____

_____

Paper 19

$$
\begin{array}{r}
{}^{1}{}_{3} \\
36 \\
\times\ 25 \\
\hline
180 \\
102 \\
\hline
1200
\end{array}
\qquad
\begin{array}{r}
{}^{3}{}_{2} \\
78 \\
\times\ 43 \\
\hline
234 \\
332 \\
\hline
3554
\end{array}
\qquad
\begin{array}{r}
{}^{1}{}_{3} \\
65 \\
\times\ 37 \\
\hline
455 \\
225 \\
\hline
2705
\end{array}
$$

Description of Pattern _____

_____

Paper 20

$$
\begin{array}{r}
{}^{4} \\
37 \\
\times\ 6 \\
\hline
72
\end{array}
\qquad
\begin{array}{r}
{}^{1} \\
85 \\
\times\ 3 \\
\hline
95
\end{array}
\qquad
\begin{array}{r}
{}^{2} \\
25 \\
\times\ 4 \\
\hline
40
\end{array}
$$

Description of Pattern _____

_____

Paper 21

$$
\begin{array}{r}
436 \\
\times\ 25 \\
\hline
2180 \\
872 \\
\hline
6660
\end{array}
\qquad
\begin{array}{r}
379 \\
\times\ 42 \\
\hline
758 \\
1516 \\
\hline
15618
\end{array}
\qquad
\begin{array}{r}
754 \\
\times 268 \\
\hline
6032 \\
4524 \\
1508 \\
\hline
111612
\end{array}
$$

Description of Pattern _____

_____

Paper 22

$$
\begin{array}{r}
132 \\
\times\ 6 \\
\hline
1512
\end{array}
\qquad
\begin{array}{r}
358 \\
\times\ 4 \\
\hline
1522
\end{array}
\qquad
\begin{array}{r}
492 \\
\times\ 7 \\
\hline
3264
\end{array}
$$

Description of Pattern _____

_____

Paper 23

$$47 \times 36 \over 14$$

$$526 \times 25 \over 543$$

$$837 \times 294 \over 122$$

Description of Pattern _____

_____

Paper 24

$$\overset{4\ 1}{48} \times 63 \over 28944$$

$$\overset{2\ 3}{67} \times 35 \over 20435$$

$$\overset{1\ 7}{92} \times 48 \over 37536$$

Description of Pattern _____

_____

Paper 25

$$5402 \times 6 \over 32502$$

$$603 \times 27 \over \begin{matrix} 4401 \\ 1206 \\ \hline 16461 \end{matrix}$$

$$8704 \times 74 \over \begin{matrix} 34906 \\ 61108 \\ \hline 645986 \end{matrix}$$

Description of Pattern _____

_____

Paper 26

$$72 \times 43 \over \begin{matrix} 216 \\ 2892 \\ \hline 3108 \end{matrix}$$

$$43 \times 23 \over \begin{matrix} 129 \\ 866 \\ \hline 995 \end{matrix}$$

$$52 \times 14 \over \begin{matrix} 208 \\ 524 \\ \hline 732 \end{matrix}$$

Description of Pattern _____

_____

Paper 27

$$4\overline{)129} \;\; \overset{252}{} \text{r.3}$$

$$\begin{array}{r} 252 \text{ r.3} \\ 4\overline{)129} \\ \underline{8} \\ 21 \\ \underline{20} \\ 11 \\ \underline{8} \\ 3 \end{array}$$

$$\begin{array}{r} 357 \\ 4\overline{)1230} \\ \underline{28} \\ 22 \\ \underline{20} \\ 12 \\ \underline{12} \end{array}$$

$$\begin{array}{r} 514 \text{ r.3} \\ 6\overline{)3924} \\ \underline{24} \\ 9 \\ \underline{6} \\ 33 \\ \underline{30} \\ 3 \end{array}$$

Description of Pattern _____

_____

Paper 28

$$\frac{20}{4} = 5 \qquad\qquad \frac{4}{12} = 3 \qquad\qquad \frac{7}{30} = 4\frac{2}{7}$$

Description of Pattern _____

_____

Paper 29

$$\frac{2}{3} + \frac{1}{4} = 37 \qquad \frac{5}{6} + \frac{1}{2} = 68 \qquad \frac{1}{5} + \frac{3}{4} = 49$$

Description of Pattern _____

_____

Paper 30

$$\frac{1}{3} + \frac{2}{9} = \frac{3}{9} \qquad \frac{3}{4} + \frac{3}{2} = \frac{6}{4} \qquad \frac{5}{6} + \frac{1}{2} = \frac{6}{6}$$

Description of Pattern _____

_____

Paper 31

$$\frac{3}{4} + \frac{1}{2} = 55 \qquad \frac{2}{3} + \frac{2}{5} = 75 \qquad \frac{5}{6} + \frac{1}{3} = 87$$

Description of Pattern _____

_____

Paper 32

$$\frac{1}{6} + \frac{2}{3} = 12 \qquad \frac{3}{4} + \frac{1}{5} = 13 \qquad \frac{7}{8} + \frac{2}{6} = 23$$

Description of Pattern _____

_____

Paper 33

$$
\begin{array}{r}
3\frac{5}{12} \\
-1\frac{5}{12} \\
\hline
20
\end{array}
\qquad
\begin{array}{r}
5\frac{2}{3} \\
-2\frac{1}{3} \\
\hline
3\frac{1}{3}
\end{array}
\qquad
\begin{array}{r}
9\frac{3}{4} \\
-4\frac{3}{4} \\
\hline
50
\end{array}
$$

Description of Pattern _____

_____

Paper 34

$$\frac{5}{6} - \frac{4}{5} = \frac{1}{30} \qquad \frac{4}{5} - \frac{1}{2} = \frac{3}{10} \qquad \frac{5}{6} - \frac{3}{5} = \frac{2}{30}$$

Description of Pattern _____

_____

Paper 35

$$1\frac{3}{5} = 1\frac{8}{15}$$
$$+2\frac{1}{3} = 2\frac{7}{15}$$
$$\overline{\phantom{+2\frac{1}{3}=}3\frac{15}{15}}$$

$$4\frac{2}{4} = 4\frac{18}{4}$$
$$+1\frac{1}{2} = 1\frac{3}{4}$$
$$\overline{\phantom{+1\frac{1}{2}=}5\frac{21}{4}}$$

$$6\frac{2}{3} = 6\frac{20}{6}$$
$$+3\frac{1}{6} = 3\frac{19}{6}$$
$$\overline{\phantom{+3\frac{1}{6}=}9\frac{39}{6}}$$

Description of Pattern _____

_____

Paper 36

$$7 = 6\frac{7}{7} = 6\frac{28}{28}$$
$$-3\frac{3}{4} = 3\frac{3}{4} = 3\frac{21}{28}$$
$$3\frac{7}{28} = 3\frac{1}{4}$$

$$5 = 4\frac{5}{5} = 4\frac{15}{15}$$
$$-2\frac{1}{3} = 2\frac{1}{3} = 2\frac{5}{15}$$
$$2\frac{10}{15} = 2\frac{2}{3}$$

$$9 = 8\frac{9}{9} = 8\frac{45}{45}$$
$$-1\frac{4}{5} = 1\frac{4}{5} = 1\frac{36}{45}$$
$$7\frac{9}{45} = 7\frac{1}{5}$$

Description of Pattern _____

_____

Paper 37

$$4\frac{2}{3} \times \frac{1}{4} = 4\frac{2}{12}$$
$$6\frac{3}{4} \times \frac{2}{3} = 6\frac{6}{12}$$

$$9\frac{1}{2} \times \frac{3}{4} = 9\frac{3}{8}$$

Description of Pattern _____

_____

Paper 38

$$5\tfrac{1}{3} \times 6\tfrac{3}{4} = 30\tfrac{3}{12}$$

$$7\tfrac{2}{5} \times 2\tfrac{1}{8} = 14\tfrac{2}{40}$$ $$1\tfrac{7}{8} \times 4\tfrac{2}{3} = 4\tfrac{14}{24}$$

Description of Pattern _____

_____

Paper 39

$$2\tfrac{1}{2} \times 1\tfrac{3}{10}$$
$$2\tfrac{5}{10} \times 1\tfrac{13}{10} = 2\tfrac{65}{10}$$

$$1\tfrac{3}{4} \times 3\tfrac{1}{8}$$ $$2\tfrac{2}{3} \times 2\tfrac{1}{6}$$
$$1\tfrac{7}{8} \times 3\tfrac{25}{8} = 3\tfrac{175}{8}$$ $$2\tfrac{8}{6} \times 2\tfrac{13}{6} = 4\tfrac{104}{6}$$

Description of Pattern _____

_____

Paper 40

$$\tfrac{4}{8} \div \tfrac{2}{8} = \tfrac{8}{8}$$

$$\tfrac{5}{10} \div \tfrac{3}{10} = \tfrac{15}{10}$$ $$\tfrac{3}{4} \div \tfrac{1}{2} = \tfrac{3}{4} \div \tfrac{2}{4} = \tfrac{6}{4}$$

Description of Pattern _____

_____

Paper 41

$$\frac{5}{6} \div \frac{2}{3} = \frac{5}{6} \div \frac{4}{6} = \frac{1}{6}$$

$$\frac{1}{2} \div \frac{3}{4} = \frac{2}{4} \div \frac{3}{4} = \frac{1}{4} \qquad \frac{7}{8} \div \frac{1}{5} = \frac{35}{40} \div \frac{8}{40} = \frac{4}{40}$$

Description of Pattern _____

_____

Paper 42

$$.4 + .3 = \underline{.07}$$

$$\begin{array}{r} 1.32 \\ + 3.46 \\ \hline .0478 \end{array}$$

$$\begin{array}{r} 27.5 \\ + 8.9 \\ \hline 3.64 \end{array}$$

Description of Pattern _____

_____

(This pattern is commonly seen in seventh grade classrooms.)

Paper 43

7.7 + 13.2 = ?   2.5 + 4.32 = ?   15.4 + 8.69 = ?

$$\begin{array}{r} 7.7 \\ + 13.2 \\ \hline 20.9 \end{array} \qquad \begin{array}{r} 2.5 \\ + 4.32 \\ \hline 6.37 \end{array} \qquad \begin{array}{r} 15.4 \\ + 8.69 \\ \hline 23.73 \end{array}$$

Description of Pattern _____

_____

Paper 44

$$.7 = \frac{7}{10} \qquad .25 = \frac{7}{100} \qquad .302 = \frac{5}{1000}$$

Description of Pattern _____

_____

Key to Error Patterns in Additional Children's Papers

1. The sum of all digits is determined, regardless of place value.

2. The child is applying to addition the properties of zero and one for multiplication.

3. The child writes the largest digit and "carries" the smallest digit to the next column.

4. When the sum is ten or more, the child writes the tens digit and ignores the units digit.

5. The top two numbers are perceived as a two-digit number, and the third number added or counted on (e.g., 2 + 6 + 3 is 26 + 3).

6. When a sum in the tens column has two digits, write only the "tens" digit (actually, the digit is the number of hundreds). "There is no room for the other number."

7. Sums are written fully (place values are ignored) and the left digit in the shorter numeral is added repeatedly.

8. All ones which result from regrouping are collected above the left-hand column. The number of ones is then written in the thousands place.

9. The minuend is subtracted from both the ones and the tens.

10. The child counts backwards to determine the missing addend but reverses the digits when recording the number.

11. The child is not remembering to subtract one ten (or one hundred) when he regroups.

12. Though regrouping correctly, the child does not subtract hundreds if there are no hundreds in the subtrahend.

13. The child thinks, "seven from two is nothing;" or he just writes zero when he "can't subtract."

14. The minuend is rounded down to the nearest decade, then the known addend is subtracted. Finally, the number of units in the minuend is subtracted.

15. Using the computational sequence associated with multiplication, the child is comparing digits and recording each difference (S-W-1). As is true for multiplication, addition precedes the final answer.

16. The child regroups directly from hundreds to ones.

17. The second partial product is placed incorrectly.

18. In regrouping, one is always added regardless of the number required.

19. When multiplying by the tens digit, both crutch figures are used.

20. For the tens, the child just adds without multiplying first.

21. The partial products are "subtracted" by finding differences.

22. After adding the number of tens to be remembered, the *tens* digit is recorded (in the tens place!) and the units digit is "carried."

23. Basically, an addition procedure is used with multiplication facts (M-W-4), but when the product for a fact has two digits the tens figure is recorded.

24. Multiplication facts are recalled in the correct sequence, but crutches are recorded at the left, then the right, and then at the left again. Place values are ignored in the product.

25. When there is a zero in the minuend, the child inserts a zero before regrouping.

26. The tens digit is used to multiply the other three digits, proceeding counterclockwise. Also, the second partial product is placed incorrectly.

27. Division proceeds from right to left. As one child using this procedure

said, "We always start with the ones." Place values are necessarily confused.

28. The larger number (numerator *or* denominator) is divided by the smaller.

29. The numerators are added and recorded (as tens), then the denominators are added and recorded to the right (as ones).

30. The numerators are added and recorded as the new numerator. The larger denominator is used as the new denominator because the smaller denominator "will go into" the larger denominator.

31. The first denominator and second numerator are added and written as the number of units; then the first numerator and second denominator are added for the tens digit.

32. All numerators and denominators are added together as if they were whole numbers, though the explanation may sound something like: "2 over 3 is 5, 1 over 6 is 7, and 5 plus 7 is 12."

33. When the difference between the fractions is zero, the zero is recorded as a whole number in what becomes the one's place—effectively multiplying the answer by ten.

34. The numerators are subtracted and the denominators are multiplied. Why does this work for two of the three examples? For help see Mona S. Haddad, "An Error Pattern Leads to a Discovery Lesson," *The Mathematics Teacher* 73, no. 3 (March 1980): 197.

35. After the least common denominator is determined, the child computes each numerator by multiplying the original denominator times the whole number and then adding the original numerator.

36. The whole number is always used for the numerator and denominator when creating n/n, even though this unnecessarily complicates the procedure with unlike denominators. You may want to call this an inefficient algorithm rather than an error pattern, for it *does* produce the correct answer.

37. The common fractions are multiplied, with the result affixed to the whole number.

38. The whole numbers and common fractions are multiplied independently.

39. After a common denominator is determined, a new numerator is computed by multiplying the original denominator times the whole number and then adding the original numerator. The whole numbers are multplied; only the numerators are multiplied in the common fractions. This is an example of how an error pattern adopted for one operation (see Paper 35 above) is used to create other erroneous procedures.

40. Common denominators, if needed, are provided first; then the numerators are multiplied to determine the resulting numerator.

41. After common denominators are determined, one numerator is divided by the other (with remainder ignored) to determine the resulting numerator.

42. The rule for placing the decimal point in a product is applied to a sum.

43. The student is careful to do two things he has been taught: line up the digits on the right, and line up the decimal points.

44. The denominator is determined by the number of places in the decimal; digits are added to find the numerator. This misunderstanding is sometimes prompted by the explanation: $.25 = \dfrac{2}{10} + \dfrac{5}{100}$

Error Patterns in Other Areas of Mathematics

The phenomenon of students adopting erroneous procedures is not limited to the simpler computations of arithmetic, as is clearly illustrated in the examples which follow. Look carefully at each student's paper. Can you determine the error pattern? Why might a student learn such procedures? Are there things you can do as you teach mathematics which will make it less likely that students adopt erroneous patterns?

Paper A

1. 57 = __5__ tens + __7__ ones

2. 483 = __4__ ones + __8__ hundreds + __3__ tens

3. 270 = __2__ hundreds + __7__ ones + __0__ tens

Paper B

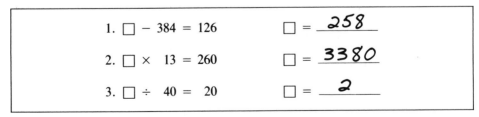

1. ☐ − 384 = 126   ☐ = __258__

2. ☐ × 13 = 260   ☐ = __3380__

3. ☐ ÷ 40 = 20   ☐ = __2__

Paper C

1. $65 \div 13 = \square$	$\square = \underline{5}$
2. $\square \div 12 = 36$	$\square = \underline{432}$
3. $17 \times \square = 68$	$\square = \underline{4}$
4. $60 \div \square = 30$	$\square = \underline{1800}$
5. $24 \times 8 = \square$	$\square = \underline{192}$
6. $90 \div \square = 15$	$\square = \underline{1350}$

Although the unknown was correctly identified in four of the six examples, the same error pattern was applied to all six. For an interesting discussion of this pattern, see Barbara R. Sadowski and Delayne H. McIlveen, "Diagnosis and Remediation of Sentence-solving Error Patterns," *The Arithmetic Teacher* 31, no. 5 (January 1984): 42–45.

Paper D

1. John spent $4.50 at the fair. Now he has $2.75 remaining. How much money did he have before the fair?

$$\$1.75$$

2. The store had a sale of red and blue shirts. There were 46 red shirts left after the sale, and 28 blue shirts were left. How many shirts were left after the sale?

$$\underline{18}$$

Are "key words" effective in problem solving?

Paper E

> 1. If a 9-pound ham costs $17.01, what is the cost of a 12-pound ham?
>
> $$^\$22.68$$
>
> 2. Mrs. Jones gave $10 to Mark and asked him to put 5 gallons of gasoline in her car. Gasoline sells for $1.23 a gallon. What is her change?
>
> $$\$48.77$$

The order in which operations are presented is not always the order in which they are computed. Reordering data is particularly difficult for the child who tends to use each number in the sequence presented.

Paper F

> 1. $^-8 + 6 = \underline{-2}$ 3. $7 + ^-2 = \underline{5}$
>
> 2. $5 + ^-9 = \underline{4}$ 4. $^-4 + 10 = \underline{-6}$

This child probably made his rule while working with examples like 1 and 3 in which the sign of the first addend is also the sign of the sum.

Paper G

> 1. $3 - (^-4) = \underline{7}$ 3. $7 + ^-2 = \underline{5}$
>
> 2. $^-6 - 2 = \underline{8}$ 4. $^-5 - 4 = \underline{9}$

Do two negatives make a positive?

Paper H

> 1. $\dfrac{3\cancel{4}^{/3}}{4^5} = 7^8$ 2. $\dfrac{7\cancel{8}^{/2}}{8^3} = 15^9$ 3. $\dfrac{2\cancel{3}^{/3}}{3^6} = 5^7$

Paper I

1. $3(x + 2) =$ $3x + 2$

*2. $a(b + c) =$ $ab + c$

Does "multiply" mean "remove the brackets"? (* One reviewer said with reference to this one: "I see it in calculus all of the time.")

Paper J

1. $6 (1 + 4x) + 2 =$ $6(5x) + 2$

$= 30x + 2$

2. $7 + 5 (2 + 3x) =$ $7 + 5(5x)$

$= 7 + 25x$

Paper K

Add:

1. $\dfrac{1}{3b} + \dfrac{5a}{6c} = \dfrac{6a}{9bc}$

2. $\dfrac{3x}{2y} + \dfrac{4}{5z} = \dfrac{7x}{7yz}$

Paper L

1. $3x + 2x = 60$ $x = 5$

$\begin{array}{r} 35 \\ + 25 \\ \hline 60 \end{array}$

2. $5x + 3y = 81$ $x = 0$ $y = 1$

Paper M

1. $(a^2)^2$ = a^4

2. $(b^2)^3$ = b^5

3. $(a^3b^4)^2$ = a^5b^6

Paper N

1. $\dfrac{x + 3}{4 + x} = \dfrac{3}{4}$

2. $\dfrac{8 + x}{x + 2} = 4$

What does it mean to "cancel like terms"?

Paper O

In each case, complete drawing number 2 so that it is the *same shape* as drawing number 1, only larger. What will be the measure of *A'B'*?

1.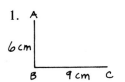

2.

B'   *12 cm*   C'

The measure of *A'B'* will be

<u>9 cm</u>

1.

2.

B'   6cm   C'

The measure of *A'B'* will be

<u>8 cm</u>

Paper P

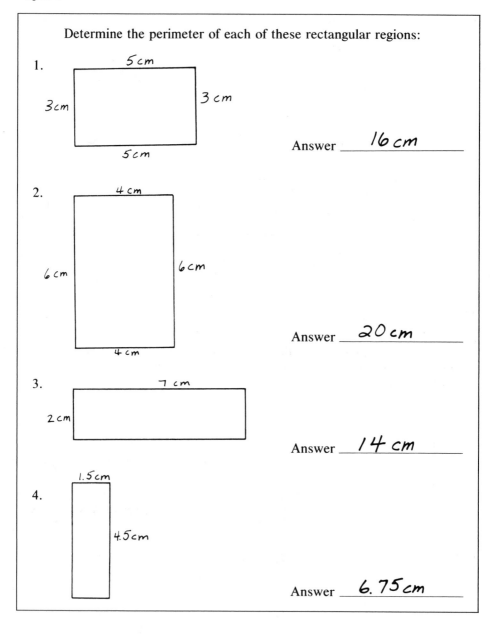

Determine the perimeter of each of these rectangular regions:

1.

5 cm

3cm   3 cm

5 cm

Answer _____16 cm_____

2.

4 cm

6 cm   6 cm

4 cm

Answer _____20 cm_____

3.

7 cm

2 cm

Answer _____14 cm_____

4.

1.5 cm

4.5 cm

Answer _____6. 75 cm_____

The Nature of Wrong Answers

Whole Numbers

There were 2173 possible answers to the thirteen exercises with whole numbers by the 176 pupils interviewed. . . . Of these possible answers 1658 (76%) were right; 449 (21%) were wrong; and 66 (3%) were omitted. . . .

Addition

1. Many combinations were recalled incorrectly in addition, as in "9 + 8 = 18, + 1 = 19 and 8 is 27," or "7 × 8 = 63," or "8 × 5 = 35," or "7 × 8 = 48." The same was true in each of the operations.

2. When counting was used pupils often lost count of the counting as in counting 9 on to 17 in 17 + 9 and getting 25, or in "7 × 8 = 57 (7 × 5 = 35; 7 × 6 = 42; 7 × 7 = 49; 50, 51, 52, 53, 54, 55, 56, 57)."

3. Many pupils failed to add the carried digit even when it was written above the top digit in the column to the left.

4. Sometimes the wrong digit was carried from the sum of one column to the next as in "2 + 3 = 5, + 9 = 14, + 7 = 21, put down the 2 and carry 1."

5. Intending to add, a pupil may have, in fact, multiplied as in "7 + 2 is 14, + 5 is 19, + 2 is 21, + 4 is 25."

Subtraction

6. Some pupils intended to subtract but in fact divided as in 93 − 32, "2 from 3 is 1; 3 from 9 is 3."

From Francis G. Lankford, Jr., *Some Computational Strategies of Seventh Grade Pupils*, U.S. Department of Health, Education, and Welfare, Office of Education, National Center for Educational Research and Development (Regional Research Program) and The Center for Advanced Study, The University of Virginia, October 1972 (Project number 2-C-013, Grant number OEG-3-72-0035), pp. 27–33.

7. A wrong order was often used in subtraction as in 86 − 49, a pupil would say "9 minus 6 is 3; 8 − 4 is 4" or "9 from 6 leaves 3 and 4 from 8 leaves 4" or in 708 − 329 a pupil said "9 from 8 is 1; 2 from 0 is 0; 7 from 3 is 4."

8. A pupil would think to borrow to increase a digit but not reduce the digit from which borrowed, as in 86 − 49 "16 − 9 = 7 [counting]; 8 − 4 = 4."

9. When borrowing, as in 708 − 329, a pupil might borrow twice, once to make 0 a 10, and again to make 8 an 18, leaving the 7 as 5.

10. Some pupils borrowed from the tens column only, when they should have borrowed from both tens and hundreds columns, as in 708 − 329, rewrote 708 as 7-9-18, then "18 from 9 is 9; 9 from 2 is 7; 7 from 4 is 3."

11. Other pupils borrowed from the hundreds column only and rewrote the tens digit incorrectly. As in 708 − 329; rewritten as 6-10-18. Then 18 − 9 = 9; 10 − 2 = 8; 6 − 3 = 3.

12. The minuend was rewritten simply by affixing ones where needed, as in 708 − 329 which became 7-10-18 for 708 and the answer was 18 − 9 = 9; 10 − 2 = 8; 7 − 3 = 4.

Multiplication

13. The ones digit was multiplied by the ones digit and the tens digit by the tens digit only, as in 19 × 20 = _____, rewritten as 19, then "0 × 9 = 0 and 2 ×
$$\begin{array}{r} 19 \\ \times 20 \\ \hline \end{array}$$
1 = 2" answer 20; or 58 "5 × 8 = 40; 7 × 5 = 35, + 4 = 39. Written as a
$$\begin{array}{r} 58 \\ \times 75 \\ \hline \end{array}$$
single product 390.

14. The carried number was not included in the partial product, as in 19 × 20 = _____, rewritten as 19, then "0 × 9 = 0; 0 × 1 = 0; 2 × 9 = 18; 2 × 1 = 2."
$$\begin{array}{r} 19 \\ \times 20 \\ \hline \end{array}$$
Throughout the remaining pages of this report a hyphen or hyphens after a numeral indicate an indentation in the arrangement of a partial product. For example, partial products 1824, 000, and 1520- were arranged by the pupil this way

$$\begin{array}{r} 1824 \\ 000 \\ 1520 \\ \hline 17024 \end{array}$$

or partial products 1824, 000-, 1520-- were arranged this way

$$\begin{array}{r} 1824 \\ 000 \\ 1520 \\ \hline 153824 \end{array}$$

15. Place value of partial products was confused as in 19 "0 × 9 = 0; 0 × 1 = 0; 2
$$\begin{array}{r} \times 20 \\ \hline 3800 \end{array}$$

$\times 9 = 18; 2 \times 1 = 2, + 1 = 3.$" Or in 304 "$6 \times 304 = 1824; 0 \times 304 = 000;$
$$\times 506$$
$5 \times 304 = 1520\text{-}$ for sum 17024.

16. The wrong product was written when one factor was 0, as in $19 \times 20 = $ _____;
"$0 \times 9 = 9; 0 \times 1 = 1; 2 \times 9 = 18; 2 + 1 = 2, + 1 = 3.$" Pupil wrote 38-
under 19 for sum of 399.

17. A multiplication fact was recalled incorrectly as $7 \times 8 = 54$, in 58×75 "$8 \times$
$5 = 40; 5 \times 5 = 25, + 4 = 29; 7 \times 8 = 54; 7 \times 5 = 35, + 4 = 40.$" Then 290
$+ 404\text{-} = 4330.$

18. One of the digits in the multiplier was not used in finding the product, as in 304
$$\times 506$$
only two partial products $6 \times 304 = 1824; 5 \times 304 = 1520\text{-}$. Sum 17024.

19. Partial products were found correctly but errors were made in adding them, as
in 58 $5 \times 58 = 290; 7 \times 58 = 406\text{-}$ for sum 4360, said "$9 + 6 = 16$" in adding
$\times 75$
partial products.

Division
20. A remainder was interpreted wrong as in $27\overline{)81}$ $81 \div 27 = 3; 3 \times 27 = 81; 81$
$- 81 = 0$; "27 won't go into 0, so answer is 30"; or in $48\overline{)93}$ "48 goes into 93
one time; $1 \times 48 = 48; 93 - 48 = 45$; 48 can't go into 45; put 0 up; $45 - 0 =$
45" for answer 10 R45.

21. Long division was confused with short division as in $27\overline{)81}$ "2 goes into 8 four
times; $2 \times 4 = 8$. Then $81 - 8\text{-} = 01; 2$ won't go into 1" so answer is 4 R1. Or
in $48\overline{)93}$ "4 goes into 9 two times; $4 \times 2 = 8; 9 - 8 = 1$; bring down 3; 8 goes
into 13 one time; $8 \times 1 = 8; 13 - 8 = 5$" answer 21 R5.

22. Quotient digit was multiplied by the divisor incorrectly, as in $74\overline{)6484}$ "8×74
$= 572$" ($8 \times 4 = 32; 8 \times 7 = 54, + 3 = 57$).

23. Errors were made in repeated multiplications to find quotient digit, as in
$74\overline{)6484}$ decided 74 goes into 648 seven times, then $7 \times 74 = 658$ (thought
$7 \times 4 = 28$ and $7 \times 7 = 56, + 7 = 63$).

24. Derived an answer before operation was complete, as in $74\overline{)6484}$ "74 goes into
684, eight times; $648 - 592 = 56$," so answer is 8 R56.

25. By repeated multiplication tried incorrectly to derive entire quotient instead
of one digit at a time as in $74\overline{)6484}$; multiplied 74 by 12, by 24, by 52 and by 61.
Chose 52 for quotient "because 3848 is closest to 6484"; then $6484 - 3848 =$
2636. Placed 2734 (incorrect product of 74×61) under 2636. Then $2636 -$
$2734 = 102$. Answer 5261 R102.

26. Place value was handled incorrectly in the quotient, as in $15\overline{)7590}$ "15 goes
into 75 five times $75 - 75 = 0$; bring down your 9; 15 won't go into 9 so bring
down 0; $6 \times 15 = 90$" so answer is 56. Or 15 into 75 five times; $75 - 75 = 0$

"15 won't go into 0 so bring down 9; 15 won't go into 9 so bring down 0; 15 into 90 goes 6 times; 90 − 90 = 0; 15 into 0 zero times" so answer is 560.

Fractions

There were 2640 possible answers to the sixteen exercises in computation with fractions by the 176 pupils interviewed. . . . Of these possible answers, 924 (35%) were right; 865 (33%) were wrong; and 851 (32%) were omitted. . . .

Addition

1. A prevalent practice was to add numerators and place the sum over one of the denominators or over a common denominator, as in $\frac{3}{4} + \frac{1}{2} = \frac{8}{4}$ "5 + 3 = 8. You don't add the bottom numbers because 2 will go into 4."

2. The most prevalent practice in adding fractions was to add numerators for the numerator of the sum and the same for the denominators, as in $\frac{3}{4} + \frac{1}{2} = \frac{8}{6}$ or $\frac{3}{8} + \frac{7}{8} = \frac{10}{16}$.

3. Many errors were made as pupils undertook to write equivalent fractions with common denominators, as in $\frac{3}{4} + \frac{1}{2} = $ _____; chose 4 as C.D. Then, for $\frac{3}{4}$, "4 times 1 equals 4 and 1 + 3 is 4," so $\frac{4}{4}$; for $\frac{1}{2}$ "2 × 2 = 4 and 4 × 5 = 20," so $\frac{20}{4}$; or $\frac{8}{8}$ for $\frac{7}{8}$ ("8 into 8 one time and 1 + 7 = 8"). The same thing was done in the other operations.

4. Several relatively large whole number answers were a surprise, as in $\frac{3}{4} + \frac{1}{2} = 86$ (5 + 3 = 8; 4 + 2 = 6) or $\frac{3}{4} + \frac{1}{2} = 59$ ("4 and 5 is 9; 3 and 2 is 5"), or $\frac{3}{8} + \frac{7}{8} = 26$ ("7 over 8 is 15; 3 over 8 is 11; 15 + 11 = 26").

5. The numerator and denominator of one fraction were added for the numerator of the sum, and the same with the second fraction for the denominator of the sum, as in $\frac{3}{8} + \frac{7}{8} = \frac{11}{15}$ ("8 and 3 is 11; 7 and 8 is 15"), or $\frac{3}{4} + \frac{1}{2} = \frac{7}{7}$ ("3 + 4 = 7; 2 + 5 = 7"), or $\frac{2}{3} + \frac{1}{2} = \frac{5}{3}$ ("2 + 3 = 5; 2 + 1 = 3").

Subtraction

6. As in addition, a very prevalent practice was to subtract numerators for the numerator of the difference and the same with denominators; as in $\frac{3}{4} - \frac{1}{2} = \frac{2}{2}$ (3 − 1 = 2; 4 − 2 = 2); or $8\frac{2}{5} - 4\frac{3}{10} = 4\frac{1}{5}$ (8 − 4 = 4; 3 − 2 = 1; 5 from 10 is 5), or $7\frac{1}{2} - 4\frac{1}{4} = 3\frac{2}{2}$ (7 − 4 = 3; 1 − 1 = 0; 2 from 4 = 2), or $\frac{5}{8} - \frac{1}{3} = \frac{4}{5}$ (1 from 5 is 4; 3 from 8 is 5).

7. In writing equivalent fractions, some pupils divided a denominator into the C.D. and added this quotient to the numerator of the original fraction for the numerator of the equivalent fraction, as in $\frac{3}{4} = \frac{4}{4}$ (4 goes into 4 one time; 3 + 1 = 4). Others subtracted for the new numerator, as in $\frac{5}{8} = \frac{2}{24}$ ("8 goes into 24, three times, 3 take away 5 is 2").

8. As in addition, some surprising whole numbers were derived for answers, as in $\frac{3}{4} - \frac{1}{2} = 22$ ("2 take away 4 is 2; 1 take away 3 is 2"), or $8\frac{2}{5} - 4\frac{3}{10} = 394$ ("2 over 5 would leave 3; 3 over 10 would leave 9; 4 from 8 would leave 4"),

or $7\frac{1}{2} - 4\frac{1}{4} = 133$ ("1 over 2 leave 1; 1 over 4 would be 3; 7 from 4 would leave 3").

9. There were cases of the wrong use of borrowing, as in $8\frac{2}{5} - 4\frac{3}{10} = 3\frac{2}{5}$ (borrowed 1 from 8; made it a 7; changed 2 of $\frac{2}{5}$ into 12; then $7\frac{12}{5} - 4\frac{3}{10} = 3\frac{2}{5}$), or $8\frac{2}{5} - 4\frac{3}{10} = 3\frac{1}{10}$ (wrote $\frac{4}{10}$ for $\frac{2}{5}$ and $\frac{4}{10}$ for $\frac{3}{10}$; "you can't subtract 4 from 4, so you borrow 1 from 4 [remainder from $8 - 4$] make it a 3." Made first $\frac{4}{10}$ into $\frac{5}{10}$, then $\frac{5}{10} - \frac{4}{10} = \frac{1}{10}$).

10. A frequent error in writing equivalent fractions was to choose a C.D.; use it for the denominator of the new fraction but retain the numerator of the old fraction; as in $\frac{5}{8} = \frac{5}{24}$ and $\frac{1}{3} = \frac{1}{24}$.

11. The borrowed number was used incorrectly as in $9\frac{2}{3} - 5\frac{7}{8}$ rewritten as $9\frac{16}{24} - 5\frac{21}{24}$. Then $8\frac{26}{24} - 5\frac{21}{24}$.

Multiplication
12. Many pupils first wrote equivalent fractions, unnecessarily, and then incorrectly multiplied numerators and placed the product over the C.D., as in $\frac{2}{3} \times \frac{3}{5} = \frac{10}{15} \times \frac{9}{15} = \frac{90}{15}$, or $\frac{2}{3} = \frac{7}{15}$ ("3 goes into 15 five times; $5 + 2 = 7$") and $\frac{3}{5} = \frac{6}{15}$ ("5 goes into 15 three times; $3 + 3 = 6$"). Then $\frac{7}{15} \times \frac{6}{15} = \frac{46}{15}$ because $6 \times 7 = 46$, or $2\frac{1}{2} \times 6 = \frac{5}{2} \times \frac{12}{2} = \frac{60}{2}$.

13. Here, as in addition and subtraction, surprisingly large whole numbers were derived as products, as in $\frac{2}{3} \times \frac{3}{5} = 100$ ("$2 \times 5 = 10$, put down 0 and carry 1; $3 \times 3 = 9, + 1 = 10$. Answer 100"), or $2\frac{1}{2} \times 6 = 120$ (wrote vertically with 6 below $2\frac{1}{2}$. Then "0 times $\frac{1}{2} = 0$; there is nothing under $\frac{1}{2}$ so multiply by 0; $6 \times 2 = 12$, answer 120"), or $\frac{2}{3} \times \frac{3}{5} = 615$ ("$2 \times 3 = 6; 3 \times 5 = 15$").

14. In all the operations there were examples of correctly derived answers with errors introduced with conversions to simpler form, as in $2\frac{1}{2} \times 6 = \frac{5}{2} \times \frac{6}{1} = \frac{30}{2} = 15\frac{1}{2}$ ("2 goes into 30 fifteen times, and the denominator is 2"), or $\frac{2}{3} \times \frac{3}{5} = \frac{2}{3}$ ("$\frac{2}{3} \times \frac{3}{5} = \frac{6}{15}$, to reduce divide by $\frac{3}{3}$; 6 goes into 3 two times; 15 goes into 3 three times, so that'll be $\frac{2}{3}$").

15. Some pupils wrote the reciprocal of the second factor before multiplying, as in $\frac{2}{3} \times \frac{3}{5} = \frac{2}{3} \times \frac{5}{3} = \frac{10}{9}$, or $2\frac{1}{2} \times 6 = \frac{5}{2} \times \frac{1}{6} = \frac{5}{12}$.

16. In a mixed number times a fraction the fractions would be multiplied and the whole number affixed, as in $5\frac{1}{2} \times \frac{3}{4} = 5\frac{3}{8}$ ("$1 \times 3 = 3; 2 \times 4 = 8$; bring over 5"), or in $5\frac{1}{2} \times \frac{3}{4} = 5\frac{3}{2}$ ("$5\frac{1}{2} = 5\frac{2}{4}$ and $5\frac{2}{4} \times \frac{3}{4} = 5\frac{6}{4} = 5\frac{3}{2}$").

17. In a mixed number times a whole number the whole numbers would be multiplied and the fraction affixed, as in $2\frac{1}{2} \times 6 = 12\frac{1}{2}$ ("$6 \times 2 = 12$, bring over $\frac{1}{2}$").

Division
18. As in multiplication a widely used practice was to divide numerators and place the produce over the C.D., as in $\frac{9}{10} \div \frac{3}{10} = \frac{3}{10}$, or even in $\frac{7}{8} \div \frac{2}{3} = \frac{3}{2}$ ("2 goes into 7 three times; 3 goes into 8 two times"), or $15\frac{3}{4} \div \frac{3}{4} = \frac{63}{4} \div \frac{3}{4} = \frac{21}{4}$.

19. After writing equivalent fractions errors were made in dividing numerators, as in $\frac{7}{8} \div \frac{2}{3} = \frac{21}{24} \div \frac{16}{24} = 1\frac{5}{24}$, or $\frac{21}{24} \div \frac{16}{24} = 1$ R5.

20. In dividing a mixed number by a whole number the whole number was divided by the whole number and the fraction was affixed, as in $6\frac{9}{10} \div 3 = 2\frac{9}{10}$.

21. In dividing a mixed number by a fraction, the fractions were divided and the whole number affixed, as in $15\frac{3}{4} \div \frac{3}{4} = 15\frac{1}{4}$ ("$3 \div 3 = 1$, bring over 15, the answer is $15\frac{1}{4}$"), or $15\frac{3}{4} \div \frac{3}{4} = 16$ ("$\frac{3}{4} \div \frac{3}{4} = 1$, bring over 15 and $15 + 1 = 16$").

22. Numerators of like fractions were multiplied instead of divided, as in $\frac{9}{10} \div \frac{3}{10} = \frac{27}{10}$ ("the denominator would be 10; $3 \times 9 = 27$, and 27 would be numerator"), or in $15\frac{3}{4} \div \frac{3}{4} = 15\frac{9}{4}$ ("bring over 15; $3 \times 3 = 9$; bring over 4").

23. Numerators and denominators were multiplied without writing a reciprocal of the divisor, as in $6\frac{9}{10} \div 3 = \frac{69}{10} \times \frac{3}{1} = \frac{207}{10}$.

Sample Learning Hierarchy for Addition of Unlike Fractions

The hierarchy on the following page identifies specific skills which should be learned before other skills; simpler skills are at the bottom, with more complex tasks toward the top. When two or three skills are shown as immediately subordinate there is no specific order for teaching the subordinate skills, but *all* of the subordinate skills should be learned before the next higher skill. Note that multiplication of fractions precedes addition of unlike fractions.

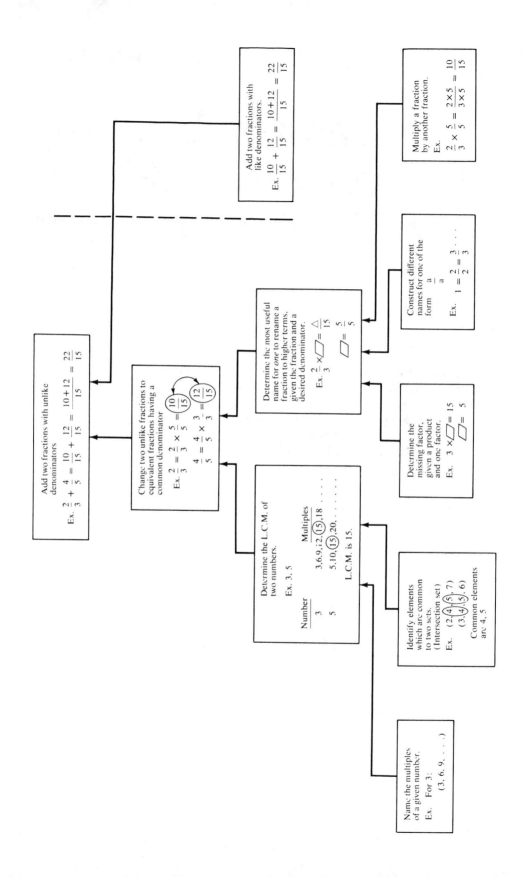

Appendix E

Selected Materials

Descriptions of Materials

Arithmablocks
>   This is a set of blocks or rods primarily used in teaching addition and subtraction concepts. The materials are especially useful for helping children learn addend pairs for a given sum.

Base-Ten Blocks
>   These blocks include a small cubic unit, long blocks that are ten units long, flat square blocks that are the equivalent of ten of the ten-unit blocks, and large cubes that are the equivalent of 1000 units.

Chip-Trading Activities
>   This program is a sequence of games, problems, and other activities involving the trading of colored chips. The activities emphasize concepts of place value, patterns in numeration, decimal notation, regrouping in addition and subtraction, the multiplication and division processes, and numeration systems other than base ten.

Cuisenaire Rods
>   These colored rods can be used to help children understand number relations, basic operations on whole numbers, and much about fractions.

Fraction Bars
>   The generic term *fraction bars* is frequently applied to rectangular unit regions that are partitioned and used to represent fractions. However, there is a useful instructional program entitled Fraction Bars, a program involving games, manipulative materials, workbooks, tests, and other activities. The fraction bar model is central to the program.

Fraction Blocks or Rods

These vary in size according to specific ratios and can represent fractional parts of any block or rod defined as the unit. Many kindergarten building blocks meet this criterion, as do Cuisenaire Rods. The Comparative Fraction Blocks (from Educational Teaching Aids) are similar, but have numerals.

Fractional Parts of Unit Regions

These are usually circular or rectangular regions separated into parts of equal area. They may be "pies" or "cakes," felt pieces, or pieces of poster board.

Math Balance

This is a highly motivating aid for teaching the fundamental operations of arithmetic. It can be used for exploring open-ended problems or for solving specific equations. The fact that it provides immediate confirmation makes it particularly effective.

Modern Computing Abacus

This device is an abacus with at least 18 discs on each rod. Children can show *both* addends before combining and trading. Some form of clothespin-like device is often used to separate sets of discs (the addends).

Multibase Arithmetic Blocks

These include base-ten blocks, but similarly structured blocks are also available for other number bases.

Place-Value Chart

This is a chart, or series of charts, in which positions are labeled as ones, tens, etc., and cards or tickets placed within each position are assumed to have the value assigned to that position.

TUF

This is an example of games that are often used in remedial instruction. TUF is actually a series of games that use cubes to form equations as children practice operations with numbers. Timers are included for the games, which vary from simple to complex.

Unfix Materials

These colored plastic cubes, boards, trays and tracks can help children understand number relationships and the meaning of operations on whole numbers.

WE VALUE YOUR OPINION—PLEASE SHARE IT WITH US

Merrill Publishing and our authors are most interested in your reactions to this textbook. Did it serve you well in the course? If it did, what aspects of the text were most helpful? If not, what didn't you like about it? Your comments will help us to write and develop better textbooks. We value your opinions and thank you for your help.

Text Title _____ Edition _____

Author(s) _____

Your Name (optional) _____

Address _____

City _____ State _____ Zip _____

School _____

Course Title _____

Instructor's Name _____

Your Major _____

Your Class Rank _____ Freshman _____ Sophomore _____Junior _____ Senior

_____ Graduate Student

Were you required to take this course? _____ Required _____Elective

Length of Course? _____ Quarter _____ Semester

1. Overall, how does this text compare to other texts you've used?

_____ Superior _____Better Than Most _____ Average _____Poor

2. Please rate the text in the following areas:

	Superior	Better Than Most	Average	Poor
Author's Writing Style	_____	_____	_____	_____
Readability	_____	_____	_____	_____
Organization	_____	_____	_____	_____
Accuracy	_____	_____	_____	_____
Layout and Design	_____	_____	_____	_____
Illustrations/Photos/Tables	_____	_____	_____	_____
Examples	_____	_____	_____	_____
Problems/Exercises	_____	_____	_____	_____
Topic Selection	_____	_____	_____	_____
Currentness of Coverage	_____	_____	_____	_____
Explanation of Difficult Concepts	_____	_____	_____	_____
Match-up with Course Coverage	_____	_____	_____	_____
Applications to Real Life	_____	_____	_____	_____

3. Circle those chapters you especially liked:
   1 2 3 4 5 6 7 8 9 10 11 12 13 14 15 16 17 18 19 20
   What was your favorite chapter? _____
   Comments:

4. Circle those chapters you liked least:
   1 2 3 4 5 6 7 8 9 10 11 12 13 14 15 16 17 18 19 20
   What was your least favorite chapter? _____
   Comments:

5. List any chapters your instructor did not assign. _____

6. What topics did your instructor discuss that were not covered in the text?_____

   _____

7. Were you required to buy this book? _____ Yes _____ No

   Did you buy this book new or used? _____ New _____ Used

   If used, how much did you pay? _____

   Do you plan to keep or sell this book? _____ Keep _____ Sell

   If you plan to sell the book, how much do you expect to receive? _____

   Should the instructor continue to assign this book? _____ Yes _____ No

8. Please list any other learning materials you purchased to help you in this course (e.g., study guide, lab manual).

   _____

9. What did you like most about this text? _____

   _____

10. What did you like least about this text? _____

   _____

11. General comments:

   May we quote you in our advertising? _____ Yes _____ No

   Please mail to: Boyd Lane
                    College Division, Research Department
                    Box 508
                    1300 Alum Creek Drive
                    Columbus, Ohio 43216

   Thank you!